Crossing into America

Crossing

into America

★ ★ ★ ★ ★ ★ ★

The New Literature of Immigration

Edited by
Louis Mendoza and S. Shankar

The New Press
New York

Published in the United States by The New Press, New York, 2003
Distributed by W. W. Norton & Company, Inc., New York

Pages 361–365 constitute an extension of this copyright page.

LIBRARY OF CONGRESS CATALOGING-IN-PUBLICATION DATA

Crossing into America : the new literature of immigration / edited by Louis
Mendoza and S. Shankar.
    p. cm.
    Includes bibliographical references.
    ISBN 1-56584-720-2 (hc.)
    1. Immigrants' writings, American.   2. Immigrants' writings, American—
History and criticism.   3. Emigration and immigration—Literary collections.
4. Children of immigrants—Literary collections.   5. American literature—
Minority authors.   6. Ethnic groups—Literary collections.   7. American
literature—20th century.   8. Immigrants—Literary collections.   I. Mendoza,
Louis Gerard, 1960-   II. Shankar, Subramanian, 1962-

PS508.I45 C76 2003
810.8'0920691—dc21

                                                            2002041055

The New Press was established in 1990 as a not-for-profit alternative to the large,
commercial publishing houses currently dominating the book publishing industry.
The New Press operates in the public interest rather than for private gain, and is
committed to publishing, in innovative ways, works of educational, cultural, and
community value that are often deemed insufficiently profitable.

The New Press, 450 West 41st Street, 6th floor, New York, NY 10036
www.thenewpress.com

Printed in the United States of America

Book design by Lovedog Studio

2   4   6   8   10   9   7   5   3   1

Contents

Part I: Crossing . . .

Part II: . . . into America

Part III: Debates and Contexts

Acknowledgments

At The New Press: Many thanks to Andy Hsiao, who was enthusiastic and insightful about this project from the beginning, and to Steve Theodore and Isa Quintana.

At University of Texas at San Antonio: Thanks to James Codd, Angela Fondren, Marcos Marquez, Diana Moreno, and Magdalena Martínez of the Hispanic Research Center. They helped make portions of this work possible through their technical expertise and organizational skills. Marianne Bueno deserves special thanks for her support and assistance with permissions.

Thanks also to the following academic units at UTSA for their co-sponsorship of the roundtable on immigration ("Between Necessity and Freedom") that appears in this anthology: the College of Liberal and Fine Arts; the College of Public Policy; the Department of English, Classics, and Philosophy; the Department of Political Science and Geography; the Department of Sociology; and the Division of Bicultural-Bilingual Studies.

Thanks to the following individuals, who were helpful with suggestions about who and what should be included in the anthology: Cynthia Franklin and Ruth Hsu.

List of Illustrations

Introduction

The New Literature
of Immigration

We are living through a period when the United States is being changed by new immigration. Millions of immigrants have been added to the population of the United States since the 1965 Hart-Celler Immigration Act, which radically revised the immigration laws at a time of burgeoning progressive social movements. Though this most recent wave of immigration in the centuries-long history of North American settlement might be said to have passed in the mid 1990s, when restrictive federal legislation and ballot initiatives (such as California's Proposition 187) signaled a changing mood with regard to immigration, the effects are still being felt—indeed, they are likely to continue to be felt in American society for many years to come.

The immigrants who have entered since 1968—when the 1965 legislative reforms went into effect—are beginning to visibly transform a society that has long prided itself on being a nation of immigrants. As is to be expected, this transformation has been the subject of voluminous writing. Dinesh D'Souza, Juan Gonzalez, Thomas Sowell, Ronald Takaki, and Pat Buchanan are only a few of the authors who have been weighing in on the policy debates around immigration from a variety of perspectives ranging from the multiculturalist Left to the isolationist Right. Surprisingly, what seems to have gone mostly unnoticed is that this outpouring of opinion and study by policy makers, social scientists, and journalists has been more than matched by novelists, poets, and essayists. This is the lacuna that this anthology aspires to fill. An increasing number of literary figures from immigrant communities have explored the new immigration in their writing, and the bulk of this anthology is a selection of their works.

No doubt it is not always evident whether a writer (for example, Richard Rodriguez) belongs in the first category—policy maker or journalist—or the second. Nevertheless, it seems to us that the contribution of a novelist or a poet or an essayist is to represent the experience of immigration in ways that are markedly different from a journalist or a policy maker. Sometimes a poet from an immigrant community (Li-Young Lee) himself lyrically expresses the wonder and the challenge experienced in coming face-to-face with a new immigrant; or a fiction writer (Sandra Cisneros) composes a profoundly evocative story presenting the tragic outcome of immigrating to a hostile society; or an essayist (Julia Alvarez) offers her subtle and personal rumination on the refuge offered by America. In myriad ways, the new literature of immigration presents the subjective experiences of the new immigrants in ways difficult, if not impossible, in other kinds of writing.

One of the main objectives of this anthology, then, is to present selections from the literature of immigration emerging after 1965 in order to make what may be termed a literary intervention into debates and discussions of this new immigration. The public discourse on the new immigration has thus far largely been framed in narrow policy terms. But what is the emotional terrain of this immigration? What are the subjective experiences of the immigrants and their children? What psychological motivations and consequences accompany the experience of immigration? Such are the questions explored in a rich, lively, and sometimes contradictory manner in the literary selections of this anthology. They are the principal concern of a distinct body of work we are calling *the new literature of immigration.*

Which brings us to the second objective of this anthology. It is to direct attention to the very existence of this corpus of literature—to make the reading public aware that there is such a thing as the new literature of immigration, to show that there are a variety of works regarded as having significant literary value that, despite their many differences, may in this one respect be seen to belong to the same body of works. Some members of the reading public may be surprised at the kinds of work that rub shoulders within these pages, but the variety only goes to show how diverse the immigrants are, how diverse their experiences of immigration are, and how diverse their methods of literary expression can be. This second objective then is not so much to make a literary intervention into public discourse but to make a public intervention into literary discourse.

From another perspective the main purpose of this anthology might be said to be descriptive rather than prescriptive. As editors, we have set out to capture as best as such an anthology can the broad contours (generic, political, ethnic, aesthetic) of the new literature of immigration. We have been guided in what to include more by this principle of representational fidelity than our own aesthetic or political predilections. This is not to say that we are entirely innocent of standards; however, we have tried to keep in mind the specific requirements of an anthology such as this and be inclusive as well as self-reflexive in the exercise of these standards.

The New Immigration

The first difficulty in attending to the "new immigration" is in deciding what we mean by immigration. Typically, the history of immigration into the United States is divided—as detailed below—into three major phases beginning with the early nineteenth century. This traditional paradigm ignores the first great wave of nonindigenous peoples that came before the United States was established as a nation-state. For the first three centuries after European settlement and colonization of the Americas the principal source of new entrants to the Americas and the Caribbean was Africa not Europe. It was the early nineteenth century before the accumulated total of European settlers in the Americas surpassed the almost 10 million Africans who were carried across the Atlantic after 1492. No doubt there are important reasons to distinguish both (European) settler and (African) slave from immigrant; but the three do share at the very least the experience of transportation to a new land and a new life, as well as of rupture with an established way of life, whether by force or by choice. It is of course also *necessary* to remember in any discussion of immigration and settlement—of any period whatsoever—the violence done in their name to the indigenous people already living on the land before Columbus. There are any number of careful distinctions to be made here, and an introduction such as this can only gesture toward them.

The difficulty with definitions of immigration, however, recedes somewhat after 1776, when the more conventional understanding of immigration—as a journeying to a new life in a new country with new laws by individuals with varying degrees of ability to choose to make the journey—becomes more clearly paradigmatic. The first major period of immigration in this conventional sense after 1776 began in the late 1840s and came to a climax in the 1880s. During the decade of the 1880s the number of immigrants was more than 5 million. The majority of these immigrants, leaving because of famines and social upheavals, came for the most part from the United Kingdom, Ireland, Germany, and Scandinavia.

But it is the first quarter of the twentieth century that constitutes the most intense period of immigration into the United States. About 17 million people—about half the total number who had entered the country since 1820—came to the United States during this period. These immigrants were the first "new" immigrants. Mostly Italians, Poles, and Jews from central and eastern Europe, they were distinct from the "old" immigrants who had come from northern and western Europe. This intense period of immigration, which continued to be marked by bias against immigrants from non-European parts of the world, came to an end in the 1920s with new legislative restrictions aimed at stemming the flow of immigrants.

A more expansive attitude to immigration does not return to official policy until after World War II, and the 1965 legislation is a key—albeit contradictory—step in this process of liberalization. In the three-and-a-half decades since 1965, more than 20 million immigrants have entered the United States. The peak was during the 1980s, when almost 10 million new immigrants arrived. Most of these new immigrants have come from Asia and Latin America. From 1980–1993 European immigrants were only 13 percent of the total, whereas those from Asia were 39 percent, and those from Latin America (including the Caribbean) were 43 percent. More than half of these new "new" immigrants have come from the following seven countries: Mexico, the Philippines, China, Vietnam, Korea, India, and the Dominican Republic. According to a report by the Urban Institute on this new immigration, the "absolute number of immigrants who enter each year and stay—currently about 1.1 million (legal and illegal)—matches the previous historical peak." Yet the *proportion* of this immigration in relation to the current population of the United States is better captured by another figure. According to the U.S. Census Bureau, foreign-born people represented 8.7 percent of the American population in 1994. This is just a bit more than half the proportion that they made up in the census of 1910. Arguably, then, despite the alarmist rhetoric in some quarters about the impact of the new immigration taking place after 1965, the intensity of immigration was much greater during 1900–1925 than during 1965–1995—though surely it is beyond dispute that the last thirty years constitute a significant period of immigration in ways both historically unprecedented and similar to earlier periods in U.S. history.

The contemporary politics of immigration are as complicated as ever. On the one hand, recent immigration has generally been opposed by conservative movements desirous of preserving a "traditional," if mythical, view of the United States as an Anglo-European nation. On the other hand, there has also been antipathy to immigration from some elements in the African American and indigenous communities who might otherwise be opposed to conservative policies. For many African Americans, immigrants appear as rivals for economic and social opportunities. For many members of indigenous communities, immigrants, no matter what their ethnicity, are only the latest manifestation of waves of settlers who have dispossessed them of their land.

A number of inclusions in Part III of this anthology—Leti Volpp's review of the legal background to and ramifications of the 1965 legislation, the roundtable discussion on immigration moderated by Anannya Bhattacharjee, a selection of newspaper articles and editorials from the thirty-year period—show just how complex both the impact of the 1965 legislation and response to it have been. Together these contributions offer valuable context for the new literature of immigration gathered in Parts I and II of the anthology.

The New Literature of Immigration

We define *the new literature of immigration* as that literature emerging out of communities formed or re-formed (after all, such communities as the Mexican, the Chinese, and the Irish predate the new immigration in significant numbers) by post-1965 immigrations. Sometimes immigrants write the works themselves. Sometimes the children or grandchildren of immigrants write them. However, for us, one of the defining characteristics of the new literature of immigration is that the works of this literature are written by those living and writing in close proximity to the experience of immigration either because they are immigrants themselves or because they are members of communities in which the experience of immigration is ongoing and foundational. In other words, what is gathered in this anthology is not a volume of literature *about* the new immigration (a rubric that might include many writers not represented here). Without discounting the value of a volume of literature about the new immigrants, we believe that there are important reasons to direct special attention to writers who are working within what we are calling immigrant communities (of course we do not mean by this that each and every member of that community is an immigrant, values the experience of immigration, or identifies with the way we are defining an immigrant community). Such a focus allows the unique literary voices of the new immigrant communities to be appreciated on their own.

A second important criterion that we have used in making selections for this anthology—and therefore in proposing a preliminary sketch of a new literature of immigration—is to foreground literary rather than biographical chronology. That is to say, we focus on literary career rather than on other details of biography. Thus the dates of Frank McCourt's literary career fall within the post-1965 framework of this anthology, although the experience he narrates in the excerpt from *Angela's Ashes* included here predates the 1965 legislative revisions. His work is published and circulates within a society transformed by those revisions. As a narrative about immigration it cannot but be received differently because of this new context, which affected the Irish immigrant community to which he belongs as much as others. For us the excerpt from McCourt's work also testifies to the continuities between older waves of immigration and the new immigration after 1965. As noted above, immigration from Europe, though dramatically reduced, still constituted 13 percent of the total between 1980 and 1993. The McCourt excerpt, and also the poem by Andrei Codrescu included here, alerts us to this dimension of the new immigration, which might otherwise be read exclusively in non-European terms. In a variety of ways, then, a work such as *Angela's Ashes,* especially when read alongside other more typical works as an example of the new literature of immigration, provides a bridge between this new literature and older literary depictions of immigration.

The most important of these earlier depictions come from the early twentieth century. For a number of decades writers from immigrant communities consistently turned their attention to the immigrant experience that either they or their family members had undergone. Examples of such work are O. E. Rolvag's *Giants in the Earth* (1927), Vilhelm Moberg's *The Emigrants* (1951), James Farrell's Studs Lonigan trilogy (1932–1935), Carlos Bulosan's *America Is in the Heart* (1943), Conrado Espinosa's *The Texas Sun* (1926), Michael Gold's *Jews without Money* (1930), Mary Antin's *The Promised Land* (1912), and Abraham Cahan's *The Rise of David Levinsky* (1917). In *The Immigrant Experience in American Literature*, Edward Abramson suggests that by and large this older literature of immigration—it is a problem that he ignores narratives by non-European immigrants such as Bulosan—can be divided into an immigrant Scandinavian prairie literature of pioneering (*Giants in the Earth*, written in Norwegian, and *The Emigrants*) and an urban Jewish literature (*Jews without Money, The Promised Land,* and *The Rise of David Levinsky*). This body of work from before World War II, composed during a period of immigration to the United States that was arguably the most intense, sketches out many of the paradigmatic themes of immigrant literature—themes that Katherine Payant usefully summarizes, in her introduction to a collection of essays entitled *The Immigrant Experience in North American Literature: Carving Out a Niche,* as "issues of identity formation, cultural and generational conflict, assimilation and guilt, and alienation, sometimes from the old-world traditions and sometimes from American culture."

In the decades following World War II, however, this tradition of writing died out. As more than one critic (for example, Thomas Ferraro in *Ethnic Passages* or Edward Abramson in *The Immigrant Experience in American Literature*) has pointed out, during this period the notion of an "immigrant literature" gave way to "ethnic literature." The reasons for this change are not hard to discern. Immigration began to be restricted in the 1920s and in the decades following the effects of the previous flow of immigrants gradually dissipated. Accordingly, the tradition of writing so dependent on the particular experience of immigration also declined. Fewer and fewer writers wanted to or were able to depict the immigrant experience from within the immigrant communities. "Ethnicity," it would seem, now did some of the work of "immigration" in representing an evolving America to itself.

It is not until well after 1965 that the experience of immigration becomes once again the subject of intense and varied literary expression. The issues of identity, cultural and generational conflict, and assimilation have remained dominant concerns in the new literature of immigration. In other important respects, however, this new literature of immigration reveals new concerns.

One such new concern is the preoccupation with race and the limitations imposed by it in America. The writers of the older literature of immigration were for the most part from Europe or of European descent. American history no doubt shows that the racial category of "white" is contingent and evolving, so that at various points in American history the whiteness of the Irish or the Jew was a matter of some contestation; nevertheless, it is safe to say that race is an altogether more complicated and important an issue in the new literature of immigration, which overwhelmingly deals with the experiences of people who are not from Europe or not of European descent. (Of course certain individual works of the old literature of immigration such as Bulosan's *America Is in the Heart* can be similar to the new literature of immigration in their engagement with racial concerns.)

Perhaps it is this potency and this tragedy of America's investment in race that is behind the difference in mood that some critics have noticed in the new literature of immigration. Once again, Payant expresses the point well when she writes, "One salient difference between older and

more recent immigrant writing is the tendency of newer writers to critique American culture and find it wanting." In *New Strangers in Paradise*,
Gilbert Muller makes the same point when he writes of "the shifting,
dualistic, increasingly oppositional behavior to American culture that becomes the hallmark of the immigrant experience in [contemporary]
American fiction." Perhaps also contributing to this mood is the fact
that the vast majority of the new immigrants come from countries with
long experiences of colonialism and neocolonialism (sometimes indeed
at the hands of Americans). A critical knowledge of racial prejudice is
almost second nature to them. Assimilation remains an option—and
even a recommendation—in the new literature of immigration (an example is Richard Rodriguez's work included here). But in some of the
works—for example the piece by Benjamin Sáenz—there is a deep and
thoroughgoing rejection of the option of assimilating to America.

In other works of the new literature of immigration there is an attempt
to step around the issue of assimilation without thereby being led to a
rejection of America—rather than about *becoming* American, these works
are about *being* American. Thus Chang-rae Lee, the author of the novel
Native Speaker excerpted here, is quoted in an article in the *New York
Times* on the new literature of immigration as saying, "The old immigrant
would say, 'I'm becoming an American. . . .' The new person is now
starting out saying, 'I *am* American.'" Though this is something of a
generalization (and not it seems to us applicable to Lee's own *Native
Speaker,* though he intends it to be), there certainly are some immigrants
for whom this kind of easy claim to America seems possible. Their
experience too adds a distinctive element to the new literature of immigration.

Of course, the experience of immigration has itself changed enor-
mously since the days of the old literature of immigration. Now, in the
era of email and inexpensive international calls, most immigrants can
expect to stay in close contact with their countries of origin, even if they
are not able to travel back on a regular basis. It would seem then that

the experience of immigration has become less wrenching. Leaving home is not what it used to be. This has led some critics of the new literature of immigration to wonder whether the very notion of a literature of immigration is not approaching an end. Can the immigrant experience—and therefore a literature of immigration—survive the inexorable shrinking of the globe by the technologies of communication? The question is broached in Alpana Sharma Knippling's introduction to *New Immigrant Literatures in the United States* where, after reviewing the ways in which transnational processes have changed the world, she suggests that "the figure of the new immigrant" points to a transcending of "national concerns." National boundaries and national identities no longer have the power that they once had to control the movements, communications, and allegiances of immigrants.

But have the links between the experience of international relocation (immigration) and "national concerns" really been weakened so far as to threaten the very notion of immigration? Knippling herself later demurs from the implications of her conclusion when she notes that the notion of a "post-immigration" historical context is not very meaningful, that new immigration laws are likely to counter some of the changes that she herself has pointed out. And so it would certainly seem—especially now after the calamities of September 11, which have already had, and are likely to continue to have, enormous impact on immigrants and immigration.

Finally, the experience of immigration is not primarily about ease of travel or communication but about the depth of engagement, willing or involuntary, with the "host" nation into which the immigrant, in whatever spirit, enters. In this respect, the immigrant is different from the traveler, the tourist, or even the exile. The exile may live in the "host" country for as many years as the immigrant but without engaging with it in quite the same manner. The very power of a literature of immigration springs from this engagement that is such an important part of the experience of immigration; this engagement is the source of its profound ability to call forth for scrutiny, validation, and rejection the deepest acknowledged and unacknowledged beliefs of the "host" country. At its best, the new literature of immigration will make audible to the reader both untold aspects of "America," that symbolic space into which every immigrant to the United States journeys, and unheard articulations of the subjective experience of that crossing.

The crossing into America, as the reader will see, is not one thing alone—it is freedom and death, violence and happiness, hate and love. The story of that crossing, too, is not made into literature in one way alone—there are poems and short stories, essays and excerpts from novels, letters and excerpts from memoirs. There are easily recognized names and others most readers will be encountering for the first time. There is humor and sadness, anger and sympathy. In all this variety, these works are united and made into what we call a new literature of immigration by the following: an engagement in however explicit or subtle a manner with the idea of "America"; and an experience of a crossing, of a journeying, across a legally and otherwise policed line to that fateful encounter with America. Our sense of the new literature of immigration as a literature of this crossing *into* America is reflected in the way the readings are organized in Parts I and II of the anthology. Part I begins with preparations for the crossing and leads up to various versions of the crossing. In Part II, the pieces begin with reflections on the crossing that has already happened and progressively shade into reflections on the place of arrival—"America"—from within the immigrant experience. Part II ends with two pieces in which the separating line between immigrant and citizen is blurred.

Part III provides context and background for the new literature of immigration. Reference has already been made to some of the material providing information and discussion on the new immigration. These pieces are joined by two critical essays (by B. V. Olguín and by Seung Hye Suh and Robert Ji-Song Ku) on some of the literature of immigration—on the Latina/o and Asian American examples of this work. These essays provide background, demonstrate how the works they cover may be read as a literature of immigration, and also show how *else* they may be read, that is, how the categorization of these works as examples of a literature of immigration can prove inadequate. Readers interested in understanding the new literature of immigration within a critical context can begin here and then turn to the work that is only now beginning to emerge—Gilbert Muller's *New Strangers in Paradise: The Immigrant Experience and Contemporary American Fiction,* Alpana Sharma Knippling's edited volume *New Immigrant Literatures in the United States: A Sourcebook to Our Multicultural Heritage,* and Katherine Payant's and Toby Rose's edited volume *The Immigrant Experience in North American Literature: Carving Out a Niche.* Few works—edited or otherwise—as of yet bring sustained attention to the new literature of immigration.

We are aware of course of the limitations of this anthology. It confines itself for the most part to works written in standard English; there is, however, no reason to define the new literature of immigration in such a linguistically narrow manner. There is a long and rich history of other-than-English-language literatures in the United States. The new literature of immigration is certainly being written in pidgin and Spanish (some examples of which *are* included here) and Tamil and Chinese as well. Furthermore, although the reader will find the immigrant experience in amazing variety here, it cannot be said that every important nuance has been covered. Every ethnic group is not represented. Every geographical corner of the United States is not ventured into. The gaps in this anthology can and should be filled through future explorations and expansions of the canon of the new literature of immigration.

Shortly before his death, even as the legislation that was to culminate in the 1965 Hart-Celler Act was being forged, President John F. Kennedy was at work on a revised edition of an earlier book meant to spur reform of the immigration laws. A revised edition of *A Nation of Immigrants* (we have taken the title for a section in this anthology) was published posthumously. In it Kennedy wrote:

There is no part of our nation that has not been touched by our immigrant background. Everywhere immigrants have enriched and strengthened the fabric of American life. As Walt Whitman said,

> These States are the amplest poem,
> Here is not merely a nation but
>   a teeming Nation of nations.

To know America, then, it is necessary to understand this peculiarly American social revolution. It is necessary to know why over 42 million people gave up their settled lives to start anew in a strange land. We must know how they met the new land and how it met them, and, most important, we must know what these things mean for our present and for our future.

It is our hope that this anthology, through the power of literature, will show the ways in which the new immigrants entering after 1965 have met the land and the ways in which the land has met them. And then perhaps we will learn what this means for the present and the future of both citizen and immigrant.

S. SHANKAR AND LOUIS MENDOZA

Crossing into America

Part I

★ ★ ★ ★ ★ ★ ★

Crossing...

Ramón "Tianguis" Pérez

from *Diary of an Undocumented Immigrant*

Headed North

In another half hour of walking, I'll arrive at the highway where I'll catch a bus to take me to Oaxaca City. From there another bus will carry me to Mexico City, then yet another one will take me to Nuevo Laredo, on the border. My plan is to go to the United States as a *mojado,* or wetback.

It didn't take a lot of thinking for me to decide to make this trip. It was a matter of following the tradition of the village. One could even say that we're a village of wetbacks. A lot of people, nearly the majority, have gone, come back, and returned to the country to the north; almost all of them have held in their fingers the famous green bills that have jokingly been called "green cards"—immigrant cards—for generations. For several decades, Macuiltianguis—that's the name of my village—has been an emigrant village, and our people have spread out like the roots of a tree under the earth, looking for sustenance. My people have had to emigrate to survive. First, they went to Oaxaca City, then to Mexico City, and for the past thirty years up to the present, the compass has always pointed towards the United States.

My townsmen have been crossing the border since the forties, when the rumor of the *bracero* program reached our village, about ten years before the highway came through. The news of the *bracero* program was brought to us by our itinerant merchants, men who went from town to town, buying the products of the region: corn, beans, coffee, *achiote, mescal,* eggs, fabric dye, and fountain pen ink. The merchants carried these items on the backs of animals, or sometimes, on their own backs, until they reached the city of Oaxaca, about a three days walk from home. On their return trips, they brought manufactured products, like farm tools, cooking utensils, coarse cotton cloth, ready-made clothing and shoes, candies and so on. They sold their goods from house to house, town to town. One of them came with the news that there were possibilities of work in the United States as a *bracero,* and the news passed from mouth to mouth until everyone had heard it.

To see if the rumor was true, a merchant and two others went to the U.S. embassy in Mexico City. The only document the embassy required them to provide was a copy of their birth certificates, for which they came back to the village. On their return to Mexico City, they were contracted to work in California.

From the day of their departure, the whole town followed the fate of those adventurers with great interest. After a little while, the first letters to their families arrived. The closest kinsmen asked what news the letters contained, and from them the news spread to the rest of the villagers. Afterwards, checks with postal money orders arrived, and their families went to Oaxaca City to cash them. The men's return home, some six months later, was a big event because when they came into town they were seen carrying large boxes of foreign goods, mainly clothing.

Their experience inspired others, but not all of them had the same good fortune. Some were contracted for only short periods, because each time there were more people waiting for the same opportunity at the contractors' offices. That's when some men smelled a good business; the men called *coyotes,* the forerunners of today's alien smugglers. They were men who, for a sum of money, intervened in the Mexican offices where contracts were given to make sure that their clients were included in the list of men chosen.

The contractual system came to an end with the *bracero* program, in the mid-sixties, but ending the program didn't end Mexican desires to cross the border. People had learned that in the United States one could earn a wage much higher than the standard Mexican wage, even if to do it one had to suffer privations, like absence from one's family. So when the *bracero* program ended, the coyotes kept working on their own. They looked for employers in the U.S. and supplied them with workers illegally.

I, too, joined the emigrant stream. For a year I worked in Mexico City as a night watchman in a parking garage. I earned the minimum wage and could barely pay living expenses. A lot of the time I had to resort to severe diets and other limitations, just to pay rent on the apartment where I lived, so that one day I wouldn't come home and find that the owner had put my belongings outside.

After that year, I quit as night watchman and came back home to work at my father's side in the little carpentry shop that supplies the village with simple items of furniture. During the years when I worked at carpentry, I noticed that going to the U.S. was a routine of village people. People went so often that it was like they were visiting a nearby city. I'd seen them leave and come home as changed people. The trips erased for a while the lines that the sun, the wind and the dust put in a peasant's skin. People came home with good haircuts, good clothes, and most of all, they brought dollars in their pockets. In the *cantinas* they paid for beers without worrying much about the tab. When the alcohol rose to their heads, they'd begin saying words in English. It was natural for me to want to try my luck at earning dollars, and maybe earn enough to improve the machinery in our little carpentry shop.

During my infancy, I always heard people say *"Estadu,"* because that's the way that *"Estado,"* or state, is pronounced in Zapotec, our language. Later on, people simply said *"El Norte,"* "The North," when referring to the United States. Today when somebody says "I'm going to *Los,"* everybody understands that he's referring to Los Angeles, California, the most common destination of us villagers.

But I'm not going to Los Angeles, at least not now. This time, I want to try my luck in the state of Texas, specifically, in Houston, where a friend of mine has been living for several years. He's lent me money for the trip.

The Runner

The waiting room at the bus station in Nuevo Laredo is spacious and well-lit. It is full of people walking in different directions with bags in their hands. Some are just coming in, some are leaving. Some are in line to buy tickets, and others are seated in the terminal, nervous or bored. A tattered beggar has laid some cardboard sheets on the floor of one corner and he's sitting there, chewing on a piece of hardened bread, his supper before retiring for the night. The waiting-room clock marks nine P.M. My traveling companions seem content to have arrived, but I notice them yawning from tiredness; the trip took fourteen hours. Some of them try to comb their disheveled hair and others rub their red eyes. On seeing them, I decide that I probably have the same appearance.

Disoriented, I take a seat in the waiting room, hoping to shake off my own sleepiness. I know what I should do next. I should go out onto the street, take a taxi to a hotel, rest a while and then look for a *coyote,* or alien smuggler. Before setting out, I take my belongings and head towards the restroom, thinking that a stream of cold water across my face will help me wake up.

With the first steps I take towards the restroom, a dark-skinned guy comes up alongside me. He's short and thin and he's dressed in a t-shirt and jeans. He greets me familiarly, with a handshake. After looking him up and down, I'm sure that I've never seen him before. I give him a stern look, but he smiles broadly at me anyway.

"Where are you coming from, my friend?" he says.

"From Mexico City," I answer.

"From Mexico City!" he exclaims. "Well, man, we're neighbors! I, too, am from Mexico City."

He reaches out and shakes my hand again.

I already know the type from memory. It's not the first time that a stranger has come up to me, saying almost the same things. I am waiting for him to tell me that he had suffered such and such instances of bad luck and that he had a relative in danger of dying and that he had to go to the relative's bedside and that, though it pained him to be without resources, he at least felt encouraged to have come upon a townsman who could give him a little money. But instead of saying that, the stranger keeps walking at my side.

"Where are you headed?" he asks.

I keep silent and without breaking my pace I give him an inquisitorial look, trying to figure out why in the devil's name he's trying to insert himself into my affairs. Still smiling and talking, he repeats his question, as if I hadn't heard him the first time.

"To Houston, I hope to arrive in Houston, with luck, and I'm going to have to find a *coyote*," I tell him, because, given his insistence, I suspect that he might know something about the border-crossing business.

"Are you looking for a particular *coyote?* Has somebody recommended one?" he asks with growing interest.

"I don't know any and nobody has recommended one, and in just a minute, I've got to begin looking for one."

"Well, you're in luck, friend!" he exclaims, adopting the mien of a happy man, content to have brought good news. "You don't have to keep looking, because I"—he points to his chest with the index finger of his right hand—"work for the best and the heaviest *coyote* in Nuevo

Laredo. . . . The heaviest," he repeats, emphasizing every syllable as if pronouncing the word really was a task of heavy labor.

After entering the restroom, I go up to the urinal, an earthen-colored, tiled wall with a narrow drainage canal at its foot. I start making water and my stranger friend does the same.

"Mexican never pisses alone," he says, recalling an old saying. "Right now we have forty *chivos* ready to leave in the early morning, and they're going precisely to Houston, your same destination, my friend."

I'd later learn that they call us *chivos,* or goats, because of the odor we exude from lack of bathing facilities and clean clothing. I am surprised by the ease with which I've run into at least the assistant of a *coyote,* but I don't show much interest in knowing more about his work. After urinating, I go to a sink, open a faucet, and with cupped hands I wet my face a time or two. My friend follows me to the sink and plants himself nearby, without pausing in his praises of his *coyote* boss.

"How much is it going to cost me?" I ask, without raising my head from the sink.

"Four hundred and fifty dollars, plus four thousand pesos for the boat," he answers.

"Good, if that's all, paying will be no problem."

"Very good!" he exclaims with a triumphant gesture. "Well, my friend, in less than eighteen hours you'll be in Houston."

"That's even better," I say, holding back my happiness. Then my unexpected friend takes a couple of steps and thinking, he says to me, "There's something missing. We've got to be sure that you'll pay that amount or that it will be paid for you."

"That's no problem. You will be paid when I get to Houston."

I'm carrying the money, but my distrust tells me that I shouldn't let the stranger know. The money is a loan of $650. I've got $100 in my billfold. The other $550, in bills of $50 each, is sewn into the lining of my jean jacket.

"Oh," he says, answering himself, "you've got a relative who is going to pay for you in Houston. It's incredible how everybody has relatives in the United States."

Without my asking, he has told me what my answer should be, should anyone else question me about money. I'll say that my friend will pay in Houston. Nobody will know that I'm carrying the money myself.

"It's not really a relative that I've got, it's a friend," I say, to get the story rolling.

"You should give us the phone number of your friend so that we can make sure that he really knows you and will pay for you."

"That's no problem," I tell him, just for the moment. The telephone number could be a problem because my friend has asked me to use his name only if it's urgent. He also asked me not to carry his telephone number and address with me. I have complied with his requests. I memorized his name and address. The only problem I can foresee will be to find a way to tell him that if the *coyotes* call, he should promise to pay for me.

The friendly stranger doesn't stop trying to convince me that his boss is a powerful man. He says that his boss is invulnerable because he has paid-off the police.

"On top of that," the stranger says, "he treats the *chivos* better than anyone else, because he gives them a house to stay in while they're waiting. The other *coyotes* put people out in the brush without jackets and a lot of times, without food. Not to mention the way he treats me," the guy adds. "He doesn't pinch pennies when we're out drinking."

I'm more interested in what he says about payment than in his endless homage to his boss.

"Do I have to pay for the boat every time it crosses the Rio Grande, or only to cross without incident?" I ask him, while I'm drying my face with the sleeve of my jacket.

"Oh, no!" he says, as if scolding himself for having forgotten an important detail. "If *La Migra* catches you ten times, we'll put you across ten times for the same money. And what's more"—his face brightens as if with surprise—"my boss is right here in the station. Come on, I'll introduce you!"

We go walking towards the station's cafeteria, and the stranger who says he's my townsman points towards a group of three men seated at a table, each one in front of a can of beer.

"Do you see that dude who's wearing the cowboy hat? Well, that's Juan Serna, he's my boss," he tells me, with the pride and arrogance of someone who has introduced a Pancho Villa. "All you have to do is say that you're a client of Juan Serna, and the police will leave you alone, because—let me tell you—if you go outside to the street right now and you take a taxi at the next block, or if you catch a city bus, the Judicial Police will grab you—and forget it! They'll let you go on the next comer, with empty pockets. They'll rip-off your change, man. But if you tell them that you're with Juan Serna, they themselves will take you to the house where we keep the *chivos*."

"Wait for me here," he says when we've come within a prudent distance of the table where the three men are chatting. "I'm going to tell the boss that you're going to Houston."

He walks towards the table and speaks to the man named Juan Serna, then looks towards me. With a movement of his hand, he tells me to come nearer.

Juan Serna is dressed in an orange, nylon t-shirt with black lettering on its frontside that says, "Roberto Duran #1." He's dark complexioned with somewhat fine facial features. His eyes seem very deep in their sockets. He's clean-shaven, with a wispy moustache. Beneath his eyes are the wrinkles of a man bordering on fifty. Several tattoos adorn both arms, most prominent among them is the head of Jesus, dripping blood from his crown of thorns. Juan Serna doesn't waste good humor like his assistant. He remains rigid, as if preoccupied with other affairs. He leans forward a little, supporting his body upon the table with his forearms, his hands clasped around a can of beer. He makes no gesture and gives no greeting when his assistant introduces us, only a rapid look, a look as indifferent as if he'd been handed the next can of beer. His two companions are seated in front of him, and they're saying something that I can't hear. My "townsman" stands, waiting expectantly at Juan Serna's side.

"Where are you going?" Serna says to me in a northern accent and in a voice so dry that it sounds like he's formed his question not in his mouth, but in his throat.

"To Houston."

"Do you have someone to pay for you there?"

"My friend who lives in Houston."

"So should I take him?" my townsman says.

Juan Serna gives his consent by nodding at my townsman, but he nods without moving a single muscle of his face. I follow my townsman, with the impression that behind us Juan Serna is still nodding, like the branch of a tree that sways involuntarily after somebody has pulled on it.

Outside the bus station, the townsman leads me to a station wagon. He and I get into its back seat.

"We have to wait until the driver arrives," he says.

From the floor of the vehicle he picks up a six-pack and hands me a can.

"What's your name?" he asks.

"Martín," I say, just to give a name.

"My name is Juan, just like the boss," he says without my having asked him. "And I won't give you my last name because I don't know you, but I'll gladly tell you my nickname. You can call me Xochimilco, just like everybody here does."

While I sip on my beer, Xochimilco drinks one, then another, and a third, chatting all the while.

He says that he was a taco vendor in the Xochimilco district of Mexico City, and that was the reason for his nickname. The taco business had been a good one because his boss had lent him a car to go to places where people amassed, like soccer games. But things went bad when the boss had to sell his car. Xochimilco says that he found himself first without work, and then without money. He found it necessary to ask a friend for a loan of five thousand pesos.

Xochimilco began to worry when his friend put twice the amount he'd asked for into his hands. He accepted only after making long declarations of gratitude. A month later, that same friend came to his house in a luxurious new car. "When from the doors to my house I saw him pull up," Xochimilco says, "I immediately thought about the loan he'd made me, and I was really relieved when he said that I should forget about it, because I still didn't have anything in my pockets."

His friend told him that if he was still in need, he'd help him get past his troubles, on the condition that he cooperate with the friend's plans. When Xochimilco asked in what way he could help, his friend laid a .38 caliber automatic pistol in his hands. Xochimilco didn't know what to say, but he looked with fascination upon the gun given to him.

"At first, it frightened me," Xochimilco tells me, "because I'd never shot a pistol, much less shot at a human being."

"Who said that you're going to kill anybody?" his friend said when Xochimilco expressed reservations. Xochimilco decided to trust his friend in the hopes that he, too, would someday have a car like his. His friend and another guy had planned a hold-up.

"Five hundred thousand pesos for only one simple hold-up!" Xochimilco bragged after a long swig of beer. "Your nerves make you tremble after the first job."

But Xochimilco's money troubles were finished. After the first job came others. The gang's biggest and last hit came after they had gotten to know the son of the owner of a slaughterhouse. The son was firmly resolved to rob his father, who he said was swimming in money but was so cheap that he wouldn't spend a cent, not even on himself. And the son, who knew his father's routine, conspired with Xochimilco and his friends. The four of them went into the father's office just as he was counting bills on his desk with the company safe open. When he realized that he was being robbed, the father reached for a pistol that he kept in his desk, but the bandits all opened fire, even the son. They made off with four million pesos; Xochimilco's cut came to half a million. Time passed and investigations began. When the son was arrested, Xochimilco decided to flee to *El Norte.*

"I had enough money to pay a *coyote,*" Xochimilco says, with a slight and fleeting expression of nostalgia. After two attempts, he managed to reach Houston but he only stayed a month because one night, on leaving a beer joint drunk, the police stopped him and turned him over to agents of *La Migra,* the Immigration and Naturalization Service. A couple of days later, he was taken back to Nuevo Laredo. Now with only ten thousand pesos to his name, he could neither return to Mexico City nor cross the border again. He asked the man who is now his boss to give him a job.

"And here you have me," Xochimilco says. "I'm a runner. They call us that because we're always running behind guys that we suspect are headed to the United States."

I ask him how much he earns. He says that of the four thousand pesos that I'll pay for the boat, two thousand are for him. "I make that much for every *chivo* I take to Juan Serna's house."

"I imagine that you're not exactly poor," I tell him.

"Well, okay," he says, teasing, "I've made enough to have money, but I don't have it saved, because . . . well, what good is money? Huh, my friend?" His eyes open into an interrogatory look as he leans closer to me. "To spend it! If not, what good is it?"

His job, he says, pays him different sums on different days, especially because he isn't the only runner.

"You can ask for 'Shell,' for the 'Mosquito,' or for the 'Dog.' Anybody can tell you about them, they're in the same business as me. Today I can pick up ten clients and tomorrow, none. That's the way this job is."

Xochimilco interrupts his explanations to point out a car that has parked in front of the terminal.

"That car without license plates belongs to the Judicial Police, and I can assure you that it won't be long before Juan Serna comes out to talk to them."

Just as he said, a minute later Juan Serna comes out of the terminal and walks directly up to the car without plates.

"Do you see it! Look at that!" Xochimilco exclaims. "What I tell you is no lie. That son-of-a-bitch is well connected."

A few minutes later, a middle-aged man sits down in front of the steering wheel of the car where Xochimilco and I are waiting. Without saying a word, he starts the motor and we pull off.

"That idiot," Xochimilco says, pointing to the driver, "is the one they call 'Shell'."

The car passes over paved streets, and for a few minutes, bumps down dirt streets full of chugholes. Meanwhile, I'm thinking that my circumstances are like those of a fugitive. To avoid being stopped by the police I have to keep company with thieves and maybe murderers, who, oddly enough, enjoy police protection. If the police stop me, I could argue that I'm a Mexican citizen, with a right to be in any part of the Republic, and I could point out that the police don't have the right to suppress my rights unless I'm committing a crime. To be a wetback, to go into the United States illegally, isn't a crime that's mentioned in our Constitution, but whether or not it is, it's not important. Here, he who's going to be a wetback, if he has money, will have trouble with the police, and if he doesn't have money, he'll have even more trouble. The idea that the police watch over the social order is an old tale that's true only in my village, where we name the policemen from among our own townsmen. If they find you drunk, they're likely to drag you home. If you deserve a punishment, the worst that can happen to you is a night in jail.

Julia Alvarez

Our Papers

We never went on trips abroad when I was a child. In the Dominican Republic no one could travel without papers, and the dictatorship rarely granted anyone this special permission.

There were exceptions—my grandparents went to New York regularly because my grandfather had a post in the United Nations. My godmother, who was described as one of the most beautiful widows in the country, got permission to go on a trip because she was clever. At a state function, she told El Jefe that she knew he was a gentleman, and a gentleman would not refuse a lady a favor. She wanted so much to travel. The next morning a black limousine from the National Palace rolled up to her door to deliver her papers, along with some flowers.

"Where did you want to go?" I asked her, years later.

"*Want* to go?" she looked at me blankly. "I didn't want to go anywhere. I just wanted to get away from the hell we were living in."

Those trips were not vacations—though they did share an aspect of vacations: they were escapes, not from the tedium of daily routines, but from the terror of a police state.

When I was a child, then, vacations meant a vacation from school. That was vacation enough for me! Summer vacations also meant a move. During the long, hot months of July and August, the whole extended family—uncles, aunts, sisters, cousins, grandparents—left the capital to get away from the heat and diseases that supposedly festered in the heat. My grandfather had bought an old house a short walk from the beach in the small fishing village of Boca Chica, close to where the new airport was being built. The house itself was nothing elegant: two stories, wood frame, a wraparound porch on the first floor, a large screened-in porch on the second, a big almond tree that dropped its fruit on the zinc roof. Ping! in the middle of the night. *What was that?*

We slept on cots, all the cousins, in that screened-in porch. Meals were eaten in two shifts on a big picnic table—first, the whole gang of children, our seating arrangement planned to avoid trouble, the rowdy ones next to the well-behaved ones, the babies with bibs in high chairs, looking like the little dignitaries of the gathering. The grown-ups ate after we were sent up to our cots to nap so we could "make our digestions" and be able to go swimming in the late afternoon. Our lives, which were communal during the rest of the year, since we all lived in neighboring houses, grew even more communal when we were all under the same roof. The men stayed on in the capital during the week, working hard, and appeared on Friday afternoons to a near-stampede of children running up from the beach to see what our papis had brought us from the city. During the rest of the week, it was just the cousins and our mothers and grandmother and aunts and nursemaids, and the great big sea that splashed in our dreams all night long.

It seemed then that we were not living in a dictatorship but in a fairyland of sand and sun and girlish mothers who shared in our fun. The perpetual worried look disappeared from my mother's face. She went barefoot on the beach, a sea breeze blew her skirt up in the air, she tried to hold it down. We chose the fish for our dinner right off the fishermen's boats. The women gossiped and told stories and painted their fingernails and toenails and then proceeded down the line to do the same for the girl children. They always had some little intrigue going. They especially loved to tease the husbands alone in the capital, making funny phone calls, pretending they were other women ("Don't you remember me, *Edy querido*?!") or pretending they were salesladies calling to say that their wives' order of a hundred dollars' worth of Revlon cosmetics had just arrived. Could payment be sent immediately?

Ha, ha, ha! The women held their sides and laughed wildly at the men's embarrassment. It was fun to see them having such a good time for a change.

And then, suddenly, in 1960, summers at the beach stopped altogether. We stayed home in the capital. The women were too worried to leave the men by themselves. Nightly, a black Volkswagen came up our driveway and sat there, blocking our way out. We were under virtual house arrest by the SIM. The men talked in low, worried voices behind closed doors. The shadows under my mother's eyes grew darker. When we begged and pleaded to go to Boca Chica for the summer, she blurted out, "*¡Absolutamente no!*" before she was hushed by a more circumspect aunt.

That's when talk of a vacation began in my family—vacation as in the American understanding of vacation, a trip far away, for fun.

"Wouldn't you love to go to the United States and see the snow?" one aunt asked my sisters and me one day out of the blue.

"That would be so much fun!" another aunt chimed in.

We sisters looked from one to the other aunt, unsure. Something about the conversation seemed rehearsed. Some adult intrigue was afoot. This one would not involve giggles on the phone and howls of laughter over how gullible the men were. This one would be serious, but just how serious I did not understand until years later.

My father's activities in the underground were suspected, and it would be only a matter of time before he would be hauled away if we stayed. And who knew where else the ax might fall—on his wife and children?

Friends in the States rigged up a fellowship for my father. The pretext was that he would study heart surgery there since there wasn't a heart surgeon in the Dominican Republic. What if our dictator should develop heart trouble? Papi was petitioning for a two-year visa for himself and his family. No, he told the authorities, he would not go without us. That would be a hardship.

"You bet," my mother tells me now. "We would have been held hostage!"

"Why didn't you tell us any of this back then?" I ask her. All we ever heard about was that we were taking a vacation to the United States. "Why didn't you just say, we're leaving forever?"

"Ay sí, and get ourselves killed! You had the biggest mouth back then—" She shakes her head, and I know what is coming, "and you still do, writing, writing, writing."

She is right, too—about the big mouth. I remember my three sisters and I were coached not to mention that we were going to the United States of America—at least not till our papers came, if they ever came.

Before the day was over, I had told our secret to the cousins, the maids, the dog, and the corner candy man, who was always willing to exchange candy for my schoolbooks and school supplies. I hadn't meant to disobey, but it was so tempting to brag and get a little extra respect and a free box of cinnamon Chiclets.

"I'm going to see the snow!" I singsang to my boy cousin Ique.

"So?" he shrugged and threw me a shadow punch. Needless to say, we were two of the rowdy ones.

Toys made a better argument. I was going to the land where our toys came from.

He raised his chin, struggling with the envy he did not want to admit to feeling. "Bring me back something?" he finally pleaded.

"Okay," I said, disarmed. No one had mentioned our return until this very moment. Surely, vacations were something you came back from?

When our papers finally arrived one morning in early August, Papi booked us on the next flight off the Island. The vacation was on. We could tell anybody we wanted. Now, I was the one who grew silent.

"Hello, very pleased to make your acquaintance," one uncle joked in English, holding out his hand to me. He had come by to say good bye, for we were leaving that very night. Meanwhile, we girls better practice our English! We would get so tall and pale and pretty in the United States, and smart! Maybe we would marry Americans and have little blue-eyed babies that didn't know how to speak Spanish!

That gripped my braggart's heart. We were going to be gone *that* long?

As the hours ticked by and more and more visitors and relatives snuck in the back way to say good-bye, my sisters and I grew pale with fear. We didn't really want to go to a place where buildings scraped the sky and everyone spoke English all the time, not just at school in English class. We didn't want to go someplace if all the cousins and aunts couldn't come along.

The uncles mocked us, lifting their eyebrows in shock. "How crazy! Do you know how many children would give their right arms to go to the United States of America?" Their argument, a variation on the starving Chinese children who would give their right arms to eat our vegetables, did not convince us. Our protests increased as the hour drew near.

I don't know which aunt it was, or perhaps it was our own distraught mother, who decided to trick us to calm us down. Never mind the United States, we were really going to Boca Chica! The story wasn't a total untruth. The new airport was on the way to the fishing village.

We were suspicious. Why were we dressed in party dresses if we were going to the beach? Why did we have suitcases like foreign people, instead of the big hampers of clothes and provisions we took with us when we left for the summer for the beach house?

"That's enough, girls!" Mami snapped. "One more word from you and you can all stay here by yourselves!"

Now there was a threat worth its weight in silence. Abandonment was far worse than a long, maybe permanent vacation somewhere weird. By the time we boarded the plane, long past midnight, none of us had raised any further objections. Besides by now, it had been drummed into us how lucky we were to have our papers, to be free to go on this long vacation.

Soon after the roar of take off, we fell asleep, so we did not see the little lights flickering in some of the houses as we flew over Boca Chica. Hours before dawn, the fishermen would already be casting their nets out in the ocean. By mid morning, when we would be gaping at the buildings in New York City, the fish would be laid out on a big board across the rowboats' length, their pink and silver scales iridescent with the water scooped over them to make them look fresher.

For weeks that soon became months and years, I would think in this way. What was going on right this moment back home? As the leaves fell and the air turned gray and the cold set in, I would remember the big house in Boca Chica, the waves telling me their secrets, the cousins sleeping side by side in their cots, and I would wonder if those papers had set us free from everything we loved.

S. Shankar

from *A Map of Where I Live*

I, Valur Vishveswaran, in the fortieth year of my life, having ascertained after great research the exact location of Lilliput, traveled thence for a journey of discovery. The wonderful events of that journey, what I saw, heard, recorded, what all of these events portend for the community of man, for the community of *bandur,* which is the name in high and Northern Lilliputian for us and means "giant ones," shall form the text of these my memoirs.

Skepticism I expect. I expect *bandur* to say, "What! An undiscovered land of tiny dwarfs?! There can be no such thing. This land of Lilliput is but the invention of an Irishman. It is nothing more." Not so, say I. Much is invented in Jonathan Swift's tale of Gulliver's journey to Lilliput. I will not deny this. Swift took the few real details of Mr. Lemuel Gulliver's travels to Lilliput that he knew and surrounded them with the inventions of his own overworked imagination. So successful was this misuse of the imagination, this creation of a monstrous fairy tale, that Swift proceeded to invent three more "journeys" for Gulliver.

The fictions of Swift I will not bother to defend, but that a Lemuel

Gulliver traveled to Lilliput is certain. Gulliver's voyage there has been the subject of considerable inquiry among the Lilliputians, and the details of the great journey have been established by their historians beyond all doubt. I have, in fact, a copy of the authoritative version of these historical events written by Skkrrk Skkrrl. Unfortunately, this great classic I have not yet been able to translate. I hope to undertake that task at some future date and attach the translation as an appendix to these memoirs.

But to return to my own journey to Lilliput, I propose here to begin by setting out, with the skeptics especially in mind, how it is that I ascertained the exact location of Lilliput and managed to journey there. All this I accomplished despite being the subject of contempt and ridicule from the outset of my project. Alone I was in this wide, wide world. So complete was the disbelief in what I was attempting that after the first few rebuffs I spoke no more to any of my work. From then till now, I have lived in anonymity and obscurity. A lesser heart would have broken, but my faith in the importance of my work kept me going.

It is not my intention to settle scores here, but I must note that the Indian government, three universities here in India and elsewhere, and one important international society dedicated to exploration, all declined to participate in my project. All of them ignored my proposal for a team of explorers completely. The last attempt for help in my project I made personally and not through the mail. I cannot let pass without comment the behavior of this eminent explorer who had connections with a wealthy international society for exploration. He fidgeted, he looked at his watch, he strained to hide his disbelief. When I persisted in making my case, he got up abruptly from his chair and said, "Mr. Vishveswaran, we do not have money for crazy schemes with no substance in them."

Crazy schemes! Well, I wish to name no names here, but when finally relations are established between us and the great civilization of Southern Lilliput (as indeed they will be when the Southern Lilliputians are good and ready) the world will know whom to credit for making the first overtures to the Southern Lilliputians. What about Gulliver? some of you may say. Well, what about him? He made no conscious attempt to establish relations with the Lilliputians of the South. Indeed, the few scraps of notes he has left of his trip to Lilliput are singularly critical of them. I dismiss him. He deserves no credit. It is I who first consciously, deliberately, made an advance to them. The significance of this will not be, cannot be, forgotten.

But I must record how Gulliver's few notes on the Lilliputians fell into my hands. About five years ago, Mr. Norman Morrison, who comes of an old Anglo-Indian family, decided to emigrate to Australia to be with his daughter. I bought his house in Ooty from him. When I took possession of the house, I found in one room an old steel trunk with this note taped to it: "Mr. Vishveswaran, you tell me you are a historian associated with Madras University. Here are some things you may find interesting. These papers have been in my family for many, many decades. If you find them of no value, you may dispose of them as you wish. The scrap-paper man I'm sure will be glad to have them! Norman Morrison." And there in that trunk, between the pages of the diary of someone called Mrs. Valerie Morrison dating from the nineteenth century, I found four yellowing sheets of paper covered with very close handwriting. These were Lemuel Gulliver's notes on his accidental journey to Lilliput.

On reading these notes, I knew at once that I had made a discovery of immense importance. There was no doubt whatsoever in my mind that I was looking at a genuine manuscript—of someone who had really traveled to Lilliput. The quality and present condition of the paper, the nature of the script, the language of the narrative, all convinced me of the genuineness of what I was looking at. I should also mention here that I have considerable expertise with ancient manuscripts.

I remembered Swift's book too, of course, and went and consulted it. There were indeed similarities between the manuscript and the book. Swift's account of how Gulliver found himself tied down by the

Lilliputians when he first regained consciousness in Lilliput is taken almost verbatim from Gulliver's manuscript. Some of Swift's descriptions of the physical characteristics of the tiny Lilliputians and their civilization at the time is also real. But that is as far as similarities go. Gulliver never befriended the Lilliputians, which is the term for all these tiny people rather than just those of one kingdom, as Swift would have us believe. The relationship between the Lilliputians and Gulliver was purely hostile. Both Gulliver's own notes and the Lilliputians' account of the incidents are very clear on this point. Gulliver remained for ten days (the chronology of the manuscript is confused, but Skkrrk Skkrrl's work is very detailed in dates) in Lilliput, living off the meat and vegetable produce of the land and hiding from the Lilliputians whenever possible. Skkrrk Skkrrl writes of how Gulliver's wanton acts of depredation, inconsiderate behavior, and dietary needs left an entire agricultural district devastated and forced drastic measures to be taken. This area, the Karunar Punuk, is a desert even today. On the tenth day, Gulliver discovered a boat that had washed ashore, probably from his own ill-fated ship, and set out to sea. The matter of the similarities and differences between Swift and Gulliver is something that I plan to examine at greater length in a monograph that I shall prepare soon.

How Gulliver managed to return home to England can only be a matter of conjecture. Perhaps Lemuel Gulliver left more extensive notes on his great excursion into the lands of the Lilliputians some three hundred years ago. If so, I have not been able to find these notes. The manuscript that I do possess seems to indicate through allusions the existence of other material. The quest for the complete notes written by Lemuel Gulliver must surely be the greatest intellectual and scholarly challenge of our times. I hope someone who reads these lines will take up the quest.

Soon after having discovered Gulliver's manuscript in Mr. Norman Morrison's trunk I went to England on a grant for two months, ostensibly to study papers of the East India Company relating to the siege of

Srirangapatnam, but really to see what I could find on Gulliver and his journey to Lilliput. I went to find anything that would help me make the journey to Lilliput that I had already decided to undertake.

I found, as I have already noted, nothing by Gulliver on his journey. I did find some little information on Lemuel Gulliver himself. I discovered that Lemuel Gulliver had indeed studied "physic" at Leyden (as Swift notes that he had). He had set out in 1699 on a journey to the South Sea Islands. This was the journey that led to his adventure in Lilliput. The next mention I found of him was in relation to three journeys made with Captain Charles Whacker to Surat and Fort St. George. The last journey, to Fort St. George (as Madras was then known), was made in 1707. I assume it was during this time that the manuscript relating to his journey to Lilliput was left behind in Madras and somehow, how I have never been able to learn, got into the Morrison family, who took it to Ooty. It is also of course possible that the manuscript was brought to Madras by the Morrison family at a much later date and the matter of Gulliver's last journey being to Madras is simply coincidence. At any rate the only other mention that I found of Gulliver in all my research was that he had settled in Ireland for the last years of his life.

As you can very well imagine, all this took an immense amount of time and digging. When I returned to India I had of course very little to show on the siege of Srirangapatnam. So when I applied for another grant to go to England, it was refused. This did not deter me. Fortunately, I was independently wealthy and did not need grants to continue my important work. I sold the newly acquired house in Ooty and went to England and Ireland on my own. I spent many months looking at every single scrap of paper associated with Jonathan Swift that I could find. I came up with nothing relating to Gulliver. This was heartbreaking. I returned to India disappointed. I tried to get in touch with Mr. Norman Morrison in Australia, but could get no reply from the only address I had of him.

Where was Lilliput? Where exactly was it to be found? I had nothing to tell me except Swift's locating it in or near the Southern Indian Ocean in his book. How true was this? Could I believe it? I spent many months agonizing over these questions.

And then I had the most wonderful good fortune! One day as I was idly looking at Mrs. Valerie Morrison's diary, I found a sheet of paper I had not looked at closely because it was clearly in Mrs. Morrison's handwriting and I therefore had little interest in it. It was mostly a description of an elephant ride that she had had with the Raja of Mysore through the jungles of his kingdom. But on the back, in what could only be Gulliver's cramped handwriting, were these figures and words—"55 degrees 7 South. 100 degrees 9 East." I had found what could only be the location of Lilliput! Forthwith I went to look up the most detailed atlas of the world I could find, and sure enough, all the atlas indicated for that area was the blank ocean. After months of fruitless and expensive search all over the world, I had found the answer to my questions in my own backyard (so to speak)! When all seemed lost, the answer was given to me.

Some may have found a few jotted-down figures insufficient evidence to plan a long journey, but not I. I tried, as I have already described, to get various organizations interested, but lack of intelligence and imagination prevented them from seeing what I had seen—irrefutable evidence for the existence of Lilliput. In a way, I was glad that I was now alone in my project. I felt none could ever match my intense desire to reach Lilliput. What I did next was to sell everything, absolutely everything, that I had—my house in Madras, my stocks, my car—and invest most of the money in training myself as a pilot through the Madras Flying Club. I also learned how to parachute. I kept back only a little money in case I needed it later.

All these preparations were very expensive but easily done because I had enough money to do what I wished and no family to obstruct me. I had never married and both my parents had died some years before.

I was an only child and my other relatives and I did not keep in close touch. After I had begun making my preparations to go to Lilliput, I kept myself at an even greater distance from them.

And so, a little before September 1991, when I knew summer would be approaching in the Southern Hemisphere, I left for Australia. There, in Albany, I acquired a plane (in not strictly legal ways, so I shall leave out details) and set out toward the South Pole. On the third of September 1991, at two in the morning, I strapped on my parachute, made sure my bag of things was with me, and jumped out of my plane over 55 degrees 7 South, 100 degrees 9 East. The night air was chilly. My plane crashed into the sea many miles farther on, the Lilliputians told me later. As I rushed through the night air toward the darkness below, I wondered what I would find there.

Frank McCourt

from
Angela's Ashes

I'm seventeen, eighteen, going on nineteen, working away at Easons, writing threatening letters for Mrs. Finucane, who says she's not long for this world and the more Masses said for her soul the better she'll feel. She puts money in envelopes and sends me to churches around the city to knock on priests' doors, hand in the envelopes with the request for Masses. She wants prayers from all the priests but the Jesuits. She says, They're useless, all head and no heart. That's what they should have over their door in Latin and I won't give them a penny because every penny you give a Jesuit goes to a fancy book or a bottle of wine.

She sends the money, she hopes the Masses are said, but she's never sure and if she's not sure why should I be handing out all that money to priests when I need the money to go to America and if I keep back a few pounds for myself and put it in the post office who will ever know the difference and if I say a prayer for Mrs. Finucane and light candles for her soul when she dies won't God listen even if I'm a sinner long past my last confession.

I'll be nineteen in a month. All I need is a few pounds to make up the fare and a few pounds in my pocket when I land in America.

The Friday night before my nineteenth birthday Mrs. Finucane sends me for the sherry. When I return she is dead in the chair, her eyes wide open, and her purse on the floor wide open. I can't look at her but I help myself to a roll of money. Seventeen pounds. I take the key to the trunk upstairs. I take forty of the hundred pounds in the trunk and the ledger. I'll add this to what I have in the post office and I have enough to go to America. On my way out I take the sherry bottle to save it from being wasted.

I sit by the River Shannon near the dry docks sipping Mrs. Finucane's sherry. Aunt Aggie's name is in the ledger. She owes nine pounds. It might have been the money she spent on my clothes a long time ago but now she'll never have to pay it because I heave the ledger into the river. I'm sorry I'll never be able to tell Aunt Aggie I saved her nine pounds. I'm sorry I wrote threatening letters to the poor people in the lanes of Limerick, my own people, but the ledger is gone, no one will ever know what they owe and they won't have to pay their balances. I wish I could tell them, I'm your Robin Hood.

Another sip of the sherry. I'll spare a pound or two for a Mass for Mrs. Finucane's soul. Her ledger is well on its way down the Shannon and out to the Atlantic and I know I'll follow it someday soon.

The man at O'Riordan's Travel Agency says he can't get me to America by air unless I travel to London first, which would cost a fortune. He can put me on a ship called the Irish Oak, which will be leaving Cork in a few weeks. He says, Nine days at sea, September October, best time of the year, your own cabin, thirteen passengers, best of food, bit of a holiday for yourself and that will cost fifty-five pounds, do you have it?

I do.

———

I tell Mam I'm going in a few weeks and she cries. Michael says, Will we all go some day?

We will.

Alphie says, Will you send me a cowboy hat and a thing you throw that comes back to you?

Michael tells him that's a boomerang and you'd have to go all the way to Australia to get the likes of that, you can't get it in America.

Alphie says you can get it in America yes you can and they argue about America and Australia and boomerangs till Mam says, For the love o'Jesus, yeer brother is leaving us and the two of ye are there squabbling over boomerangs. Will ye give over?

Mam says we'll have to have a bit of party the night before I go. They used to have parties in the old days when anyone would go to America, which was so far away the parties were called American wakes because the family never expected to see the departing one again in this life. She says 'tis a great pity Malachy can't come back from England but we'll be together in America someday with the help of God and His Blessed Mother.

On my days off from work I walk around Limerick and look at all the places we lived, the Windmill Street, Hartstonge Street, Roden Lane, Rosbrien Road, Little Barrington Street, which is really a lane. I stand looking at Theresa Carmody's house till her mother comes out and says, What do you want? I sit at the graves of Oliver and Eugene in the old St. Patrick's Burying Ground and cross the road to St. Lawrence's Cemetery where Theresa is buried. Wherever I go I hear voices of the dead and I wonder if they can follow you across the Atlantic Ocean.

I want to get pictures of Limerick stuck in my head in case I never come back. I sit in St. Joseph's Church and the Redemptorist Church and tell myself take a good look because I might never see this again. I walk down Henry Street to say goodbye to St. Francis though I'm sure I'll be able to talk to him in America.

Now there are days I don't want to go to America. I'd like to go to O'Riordan's Travel Agency and get back my fifty-five pounds. I could wait till I'm twenty-one and Malachy can go with me so that I'll know at least one person in New York. I have strange feelings and sometimes when I'm sitting by the fire with Mam and my brothers I feel tears coming and I'm ashamed of myself for being weak. At first Mam laughs and tells me, Your bladder must be near your eye, but then Michael says, We'll all go to America, Dad will be there, Malachy will be there and we'll all be together, and she gets the tears herself and we sit there, the four of us, like weeping eejits.

Mam says this is the first time we ever had a party and isn't it a sad thing altogether that you have it when your children are slipping away one by one, Malachy to England, Frank to America. She saves a few shillings from her wages taking care of Mr. Sliney to buy bread, ham, brawn, cheese, lemonade and a few bottles of stout. Uncle Pa Keating brings stout, whiskey and a little sherry for Aunt Aggie's delicate stomach and she brings a cake loaded with currants and raisins she baked herself. The Abbot brings six bottles of stout and says, That's all right, Frankie, ye can all drink it as long as I have a bottle or two for meself to help me sing me song.

He sings "The Road to Rasheen." He holds his stout, closes his eyes, and song comes out in a high whine. The words make no sense and everyone wonders why tears are seeping from his shut eyes. Alphie whispers to me, Why is he crying over a song that makes no sense?

I don't know.

The Abbot ends his song, opens his eyes, wipes his cheeks and tells us that was a sad song about an Irish boy that went to America and got shot by gangsters and died before a priest could reach his side and he tells me don't be gettin' shot if you're not near a priest.

Uncle Pa says that's the saddest song he ever heard and is there any chance we could have something lively. He calls on Mam and she says, Ah, no, Pa, sure I don't have the wind.

Come on, Angela, come on. One voice now, one voice and one voice only.

All right. I'll try.

We all join in the chorus of her sad song,

A mother's love is a blessing
No matter where you roam.
Keep her while you have her,
You'll miss her when she's gone.

Uncle Pa says one song is worse than the one before and are we turning this night into a wake altogether, is there any chance someone would sing a song to liven up the proceedings or will he be driven to drink with the sadness.

Oh, God, says Aunt Aggie, I forgot. The moon is having an eclipse abroad this minute.

We stand out in the lane watching the moon disappear behind a round black shadow. Uncle Pa says, That's a very good sign for you going to America, Frankie.

No, says Aunt Aggie, 'tis a bad sign. I read in the paper that the moon is practicing for the end of the world.

Oh, end of the world my arse, says Uncle Pa. 'Tis the beginning for Frankie McCourt. He'll come back in a few years with a new suit and fat on his bones like any Yank and a lovely girl with white teeth hangin' from his arm.

Mam says, Ah, no, Pa, ah, no, and they take her inside and comfort her with a drop of sherry from Spain.

It's late in the day when the *Irish Oak* sails from Cork, past Kinsale and Cape Clear, and dark when lights twinkle on Mizen Head, the last of Ireland I'll see for God knows how long.

Surely I should have stayed, taken the post office examination, climbed in the world. I could have brought in enough money for Michael and Alphie to go to school with proper shoes and bellies well filled. We could have moved from the lane to a street or even an avenue where houses have gardens. I should have taken that examination and Mam would never again have to empty the chamber pots of Mr. Sliney or anyone else.

It's too late now. I'm on the ship and there goes Ireland into the night and it's foolish to be standing on this deck looking back and thinking of my family and Limerick and Malachy and my father in England and even more foolish that songs are going through my head Roddy McCorley goes to die and Mam gasping Oh the days of the Kerry dancing with poor Mr. Clohessy hacking away in the bed and now I want Ireland back at least I had Mam and my brothers and Aunt Aggie bad as she was and Uncle Pa, standing me my first pint, and my bladder is near my eye and here's a priest standing by me on the deck and you can see he's curious.

He's a Limerickman but he has an American accent from his years in Los Angeles. He knows how it is to leave Ireland, did it himself and never got over it. You live in Los Angeles with sun and palm trees day in day out and you ask God if there's any chance He could give you one soft rainy Limerick day.

The priest sits beside me at the table of the First Officer, who tells us ship's orders have been changed and instead of sailing to New York we're bound for Montreal.

Three days out and orders are changed again. We are going to New York after all.

Three American passengers complain, Goddam Irish. Can't they get it straight?

The day before we sail into New York orders are changed again. We are going to a place up the Hudson River called Albany.

The Americans say, Albany? Goddam Albany? Why the hell did we have to sail on a goddam Irish tub? Goddam.

The priest tells me pay no attention. All Americans are not like that.

I'm on deck the dawn we sail into New York. I'm sure I'm in a film, that it will end and lights will come up in the Lyric Cinema. The priest wants to point out things but he doesn't have to. I can pick out the Statue of Liberty, Ellis Island, the Empire State Building, the Chrysler Building, the Brooklyn Bridge. There are thousands of cars speeding along the roads and the sun turns everything to gold. Rich Americans in top hats white ties and tails must be going home to bed with the gorgeous women with white teeth. The rest are going to work in warm comfortable offices and no one has a care in the world.

The Americans are arguing with the captain and a man who climbed aboard from a tugboat. Why can't we get off here? Why do we have to sail all the goddam way to goddam Albany?

The man says, Because you're passengers on the vessel and the captain is the captain and we have no procedures for taking you ashore.

Oh, yeah. Well, this is a free country and we're American citizens.

Is that a fact? Well, you're on an Irish ship with an Irish captain and you'll do what he goddam tells you or swim ashore.

He climbs down the ladder, tugboat chugs away, and we sail up the Hudson past Manhattan, under the George Washington Bridge, past hundreds of Liberty ships that did their bit in the war, moored now and ready to rot.

The captain announces the tide will force us to drop anchor overnight opposite a place called, the priest spells it for me, Poughkeepsie. The priest says that's an Indian name and the Americans say goddam Poughkeepsie.

After dark a small boat put-puts to the ship and an Irish voice calls up, Hello, there. Bejasus, I saw the Irish flag, so I did. Couldn't believe me two eyes. Hello, there.

He invites the First Officer to go ashore for a drink and bring a friend and, You, too, Father. Bring a friend.

The priest invites me and we climb down a ladder to the small boat with the First Officer and the Wireless Officer. The man in the boat says his name is Tim Boyle from Mayo God help us and we docked there at the right time because there's a bit of a party and we're all invited. He takes us to a house with a lawn, a fountain and three pink birds standing on one leg. There are five women in a room called a living room. The women have stiff hair, spotless frocks. They have glasses in their hands and they're friendly and smile with perfect teeth. One says, Come right in. Just in time for the pawty.

Pawty. That's the way they talk and I suppose I'll be talking like that in a few years.

Tim Boyle tells us the girls are having a bit of a time while their husbands are away overnight hunting deer, and one woman, Betty, says, Yeah. Buddies from the war. That war is over nearly five years and they can't get over it so they shoot animals every weekend and drink Rheingold till they can't see. Goddam war, excuse the language, Fawder.

The priest whispers to me, These are bad women. We won't stay here long.

The bad women say, Whatcha like to drink? We got everything. What's your name, honey?

Frank McCourt.

Nice name. So you take a little drink. All the Irish take a little drink, You like a beer?

Yes, please.

Gee, so polite. I like the Irish. My grandmother was half Irish so that makes me half, quarter? I dunno. My name is Frieda. So here's your beer, honey.

The priest sits at the end of a sofa which they call a couch and two women talk to him. Betty asks the First Officer if he'd like to see the house and he says, Oh, I would, because we don't have houses like this in Ireland. Another woman tells the Wireless Officer he should see what they have growing in the garden, you wouldn't believe the flowers. Frieda asks me if I'm okay and I tell her yes but would she mind telling me where the lavatory is.

The what?

Lavatory.

Oh, you mean the bathroom. Right this way, honey, down the hall.

Thanks.

She pushes in the door, turns on the light, kisses my cheek and whispers she'll be right outside if I need anything.

I stand at the toilet bowl firing away and wonder what I'd need at a time like this and if this is a common thing in America, women waiting outside while you take a splash.

I finish, flush and go outside. She takes my hand and leads me into a bedroom, puts down her glass, locks the door, pushes me down on the bed. She's fumbling at my fly. Damn buttons. Don't you have zippers in Ireland? She pulls out my excitement climbs up on me slides up and down up and down Jesus I'm in heaven and there's a knock on the door the priest Frank are you in there Frieda putting her finger to her lips and her eyes rolling to heaven Frank are you in there Father would you ever take a good running Jump for yourself and oh God oh Theresa do you see what's happening to me at long last I don't give a fiddler's fart if the Pope himself knocked on this door and the College of Cardinals gathered gawking at the windows oh God the whole inside of me is gone into her and she collapses on me and tells me I'm wonderful and would I ever consider settling in Poughkeepsie.

Frieda tells the priest I had a bit of a dizziness after going to the bathroom, that's what happens when you travel and you're drinking a strange beer like Rheingold, which she believes they don't have in Ireland. I can see the priest doesn't believe her and I can't stop the way the heat is coming and going in my face. He already wrote down my mother's name and address and now I'm afraid he'll write and say your fine son spent his first night in America in a bedroom in Poughkeepsie romping with a woman whose husband was away shooting deer for a bit of relaxation after doing his bit for America in the war and isn't this a fine way to treat the men who fought for their country.

The First Officer and the Wireless Officer return from their tours of the house and the garden and they don't look at the priest. The women tell us we must be starving and they go into the kitchen. We sit in the living room saying nothing to each other and listening to the women whispering and laughing in the kitchen. The priest whispers to me again, Bad women, bad women, occasion of sin, and I don't know what to say to him.

The bad women bring out sandwiches and pour more beer and when we finish eating they put on Frank Sinatra records and ask if anyone would like to dance. No one says yes because you'd never get up and dance with bad women in the presence of a priest, so the women dance with each other and laugh as if they all had little secrets. Tim Boyle drinks whiskey and falls asleep in a corner till Frieda wakes him and tells him take us back to the ship. When we're leaving Frieda leans toward me as if she might kiss my cheek but the priest says good night in a very sharp way and no one shakes hands. As we walk down the street to the river we hear the women laughing, tinkling and bright in the night air.

We climb the ladder and Tim calls to us from his little boat, Mind yourselves going up that ladder. Oh, boys, oh, boys, wasn't that a grand night? Good night, boys, and good night, Father.

We watch his little boat till it disappears into the dark of the Poughkeepsie riverbank. The priest says good night and goes below and the First Officer follows him.

I stand on the deck with the Wireless Officer looking at the lights of America twinkling. He says, My God, that was a lovely night, Frank. Isn't this a great country altogether?

*   *   *

'T is.

Tara Bahrampour

from *To See and See Again: A Life in Iran and America*

Outside, the freezing desert night.
This other night inside grows warm, kindling.
Let the landscape be covered with thorny
    crust.
We have a soft garden in here.
The continents blasted,
cities and little towns, everything
become a scorched, blackened ball.

The news we bear is full of grief for that
    future,
but the real news inside here
is there's no news at all.

        —Jelaluddin Rumi

The Soft Garden

When Baba was a boy it took all day to drive from one end of his family's property to the other. For errands around the village they went on horseback, but for longer trips he and his father would climb into the back of their big black Dodge and be ceremoniously chauffeured over all the land they owned, sending up clouds of dust from the dirt road which until then only horses and camels had traveled.

"The servants would stand along the running boards and then jump off and wave as we drove away," Baba used to tell us, his eyes glowing. "We would drive past the rivers and farms, and in each village our driver would stop and all the men there would line up to kiss our hands."

As Baba talked, the sunbaked mud walls of the village, the rows of poplar trees, and the distant purple mountains would take shape in my mind. The men in camel-hair hats and woven cloth slippers would stand in the road with one hand on their chests in a gesture of respect as my grandfather Agha Jan emerged from the massive car. A fedora rested on Agha Jan's slicked-back hair, a square mustache punctuated his round Mongolian face, and his bushy eyebrows cut together sharply as he nodded to the men. Baba himself would stand as straight as his father, shoulders back, eyebrows raised, eyes lowered, as the villagers lined up. "Esfandiar-khan," they called him—a lord, although he was only nine—and after they kissed his father's hand they bent to kiss his too. Then they kissed the ends of their own fingers and touched them to their foreheads, chins, and chests, finally looking upward with a sigh as if they'd touched heaven.

The way Baba told it, nothing in the world today could ever be as good as those early days. On summer days he and a couple of cousins would head into the hills to hike, fish, shoot rabbits and swim in the river. Returning through the village, where everyone knew them, they would stop to greet other children, joining a ball game before going home to a leisurely meal with the family. Even breakfast in those days was a magical event. Every morning in the whitewashed mud farmhouse, Baba and his six brothers and sisters would awake to the sounds of roosters and cowbells and workers singing in the darkness on their way to the fields. Inside the house, the tea water simmered in a big brass samovar as the servants moved from room to room, getting the day started. The night before, the maids would have milked the cows, boiled the milk, and set it out in the cold desert air, and when they brought the large copper pans inside, the cream lay fixed in a thick, white layer for the children to fight over. The family sat around a big cloth on the floor and feasted on hard-boiled eggs, flat bread, honey, walnuts and quince jam, as an oil lamp in the center spread soft light over everything.

*   *   *

My grandfather was born without a last name. Nobody in Iran had one until the 1920s when Reza Shah, the last Shah's father, decreed that everyone must choose a surname. But even after Baba's father picked out a name for our family, people rarely addressed him by it. The family called him Agha Jan, which literally means "Beloved Sir." Other people called him Haji-khan, because he had journeyed to Mecca as a young man. That was long before he married Baba's mother, back when making the *Haj* still meant a two-week camel caravan to Abadan and a ten-week boat ride around the triangle of Arabia, during which anyone who got sick was thrown overboard so as not to contaminate the other pilgrims.

Being a *Haji* only added to the respect Agha Jan had already accrued through his wealth and connections. He owned a large number of villages (Baba never knew exactly how many), and received a percentage of all the crops produced by the villagers. In return, he provided them with medicine, schools, and mosques, as well as food and shelter. When merchants from nearby towns went on holy pilgrimages to Qom or Mashhad or Mecca, they brought him their bags of silver coins and he became their bank. If anyone had a problem—a land dispute, a sick child, a neighbor who used too much of the communal water—he became their judge, sipping his tea and frowning and deciding what should be done. Politicians running for local office also came to Agha Jan because if he agreed to support a candidate and told all his villagers to vote for him, that person would win.

To Western eyes, Agha Jan would not have looked particularly rich or powerful. In public he wore rough wool suits; at home he simply wore pajamas. Like everyone else in the village, he owned almost no furniture. The family slept and ate on the floor. He did not force his wives and daughters to stay inside the house and he did not enforce separate men's and women's quarters as many people still did, but male guests were always shown to a specific room where Agha Jan awaited; they were never led through the rooms used by the family.

Agha Jan was deeply religious. He had endured many hardships. He had lost his parents when he was still young, his first three children had died of diseases and then his first wife had become barren, which was why he had taken my grandmother Aziz, a mullah's daughter, as a second wife. His misfortunes had strengthened his faith, and his preferred method for tackling a question or a problem was to open his worn leather Qoran to a random page and follow whatever advice he found there.

My mother likes to say that Baba grew up with four mothers—his own mother, Aziz; Aziz's mother; the woman who was his wet nurse; and Agha Jan's first wife, Wife-of-Agha Jan, who had her own room in the house and was loved and respected by everyone except Aziz, who was jealous and made bitter remarks about her "low, villagey ways."

Baba, the youngest child, was adored and indulged. His sparkling black eyes and the quick, engaging smile that teased the dark mole above his lip made even strange women stop in the street to hug and kiss him. Surrounded by so much affection, he never felt unloved by his gruff father, although the old man might yell and chase the children with a stick if their playing interrupted his nap.

Baba did not pay much attention to religion. He played tricks on the little *mullah* with thick glasses whom Agha Jan brought over twice a week to teach the Qoran to the children, and he avoided the mosque as much as he could, especially on mourning days.

"They would tell us to fast and pray, and force us to sit in the mosque for hours," Baba remembered. "Everyone would be crying about the martyrs and gathering like black crows around those dusty graves. I just wanted to go outside and play, so I would climb over all the women to get to the door and they would reach out and pinch me for stepping on them."

For Aziz, going to the mosque was more of a social event than a spiritual one. She would walk over to the mosque, talk a little with the other women, and come home furious about the *mullah's* hour-long discussion about "which hand to eat with and which hand to wipe yourself with." Ranting about how they were making a fool of her, she would swear that she wasn't going back anymore, but she always did.

It fell to Aziz to care for Baba's material needs. "Don't you see anything, old man?" she would say to Agha Jan. "All the other children have bicycles and Essie is sad. You have to buy him one." Aziz also insisted that the family go live in the nearest town during the cold months so Baba and his brothers and sisters could be close to school.

Aziz was more modern than her husband. She had been a young wife when Reza Shah had established a new law banning chadors; upon hearing the news, she had thrown hers off, put on a European dress and hat, and hurried out for a walk. She was a firm believer in a secular, preferably foreign, education for her sons (at age fifty she would teach herself to read and write in order to send them letters when they went abroad). But she also relied upon ancient traditions to help run her household. If someone fell ill she drew symbols and letters on an egg, blew on it, and then tapped it on the patient's forehead to break the evil spell of sickness. If that didn't work, she made cuts in the back of the sick person's neck to let the bad blood drain away. Certain problems required experts. When someone lost a key, Aziz called for the key finder, a woman who came to the house and chanted something against the jinns who had hidden the key. Or, if a strange thump was heard from an unused storage room, Aziz called a jinn catcher, who went alone into the room—no one dared follow—and came out a little later to announce that all the jinns had been banished.

But Aziz's remedies had no effect when her sixteen-year-old son Khosrow began to feel tired and sick all the time. So she put her faith in modern medicine and convinced Agha Jan to buy a house in Tehran, where the best doctors were. She also brought along her crazy uncle Dai-Hossein, who had tried to kill himself three times already—in the hopes that the Tehran doctors could do something for him.

The new house in the city was three stories high, with the bottom floor reserved for servants brought in from the village. There were nine servants in all, plus a tenth man whose job was to watch over Dai-Hossein and chain him to a radiator every night so he wouldn't kill himself or anyone else. There was the driver, the cook, the gardener and his wife (although the city garden was barely as big as the village chicken yard), two young maids, handpicked by Aziz from among the prettiest girls in the village—"so when my children wake up in the morning they will see beautiful faces"—and two retired old servant women, brought along for sentimental reasons, who spent the days begging family members for cigarettes. Finally, there was the old poet who taught everyone the Qoran and who specialized in making up poems about how wonderful Baba and his sisters and brothers were.

The neighbors laughed. It showed what villagers they were, with all these people lining up to see them off in the morning and greeting them when they came home.

Later, when the family moved to a bigger, newer house off Amirabad Avenue, they decided that the first house had been a bad-luck house. First it had caught fire and burned out an entire side of one floor. Then Dai-Hossein had escaped and run to the outskirts of town, where his body was found the next day floating in a well. Worst of all, in that house Khosrow only grew sicker, despite the family's best efforts. They made Parviz, the third son, get rid of his beloved pet pigeons because an old lady had said that playing with pigeons caused people to die. They forbade Baba to play in the mud because another old lady said that touching mud made people die. They brought in a turbaned old man who scattered beads on the floor to read Khosrow's fate, and who sat mumbling to himself as the top doctors conducted their examinations and drank tea and whispered together. Khosrow had a fever in his heart, they said, and nothing they knew of could cure it.

After Khosrow died, Aziz cried inconsolably for months and went to the graveyard in South Tehran every day. Agha Jan retreated to the village to be comforted by his first wife. The older children felt guilty, responsible, perhaps, for the various bad-luck omens that might have brought about their brother's death. But Baba and Massi, the sister closest to his age, had passed the months of Khosrow's illness playing outdoors with the gang of cousins and servant children who lived nearby. If anything, they came away with an almost rebellious determination to preserve their happiness through any catastrophe.

When Baba was in high school in Tehran he used to go to the Iran America Cultural Association for American novels and glossy brochures about the United States. Since 1953, when the oil was nationalized and taken away from British control, the American association and its Soviet counterpart had been giving out free literature to any Iranian who walked into their office. The American pictures were bigger and shinier than the Russian ones; and in any case, no picture, however beautiful, could dispel the Iranians' fear of the Soviet Union. Baba remembers *The Siege of Stalingrad* showing at a local theater and the audience hurling ripe tomatoes at the screen. Huge and close, the Soviet Union seemed to lie in wait to take over Iran and make Iranians stand in line for bread like the Russians did.

America was different. In the movies Baba stood in line to watch every Friday, he saw an America full of beautiful women and big cars. America had John Wayne, Gregory Peck, and Gary Cooper, all dubbed into Farsi; and Baba and his friends dreamed of going there. It was not educational or professional opportunity that Baba wanted. Neither he nor his brothers would ever need to worry about job skills; Agha Jan's property could easily support them throughout their lifetimes. America was alluring simply because it was America, the land of cowboys and gangsters and Esther Williams in a silvery bathing suit.

Baba's older brothers Parviz and Jamsheed had already joined the wave of wealthy young Iranians going to college in America, and Baba wanted so badly to follow them that after graduating from high school he refused to take the Tehran University entrance exam. Agha Jan didn't see the point of all his sons spending so much money to attend school in a place so far away from their family, but Aziz understood their desire for adventure. "Open your eyes, old man," she said to Agha Jan. "Can't you see Essie wants to go to America like his brothers? You have to send him." And, as he increasingly did as he got older and Aziz got bolder, Agha Jan threw up his hands, cast his eyes heavenward and gave in.

Baba left Iran in the summer of 1958. He departed like the old-time travelers, with his money sewn into the lining of his coat; just to be safe he wore his coat into the airplane rest room, where after staring for a minute at the mystifying chair, he finally climbed on top of it and squatted over the opening as he always had. In Germany he boarded a propeller plane that crossed the flat ocean and wended slowly down over the mountains and forests of a green land that went on and on without stopping.

To Baba, everything in America was magical. In the Washington, D.C., airport, he walked by a door that opened on its own, and he jumped back in terror before being rescued by his brothers. At the supermarket he marveled at the coldness of the milk and at the butter that came whipped in a jar or wrapped in paper in neat yellow bricks. But most amazing were the girls. They walked down the street in shorts. They smiled at Baba for no reason. In Iran, he had once asked a girl he saw every day on the bus to meet him after school; she had agreed, and then at the appointed time, she had sent her brothers instead. They had surrounded Baba and punched and kicked him until a policeman rescued him, rode him home on the front of his bicycle, and demanded ten *toumans* not to tell Baba's parents.

But in America, when Baba said hello to a beautiful blonde, she said hi back. "Let us go to a movie," he said haltingly, and after she heard his broken English she was even nicer to him. They kissed in the dark theater, oblivious to the movie, until the girl glanced back and said, "Oh, my brother's here." Baba jumped up. Then his eyes fell upon a young boy sitting a few rows back, smiling and licking an ice-cream cone. This was the brother. America was even better than Baba had dreamed.

Baba was accepted into an agriculture program at Cornell University, but when he found out it required him to work on a farm for a year, he told his brother Jamsheed that he had come to America to get away from raising goats, and the two of them boarded a Greyhound bus for California. They enrolled in school at Berkeley, where Jamsheed decided to study economics and Baba chose medicine—until an Iranian friend explained, "To be a doctor takes eleven years of school, Essie-jan. You're good at drawing. Why don't you study architecture?"

The brothers moved into an apartment above LaVal's Pizza. Baba took up ceramics and photography, and he and tall, wavy-haired Jamsheed found girlfriends among each fall's new crop of freshmen. During college, Baba did not pay much attention to events taking place back in Iran, and he was unaware of the turmoil erupting in his own parents' house. In his junior year of school, the Shah signed a land reform bill that wiped out Iran's feudal system and dissolved Agha Jan's empire.

The Shah was photographed handing rolled-up land deeds to the villagers, and the large areas that had been tilled under Agha Jan became small
patches owned by individuals. In America, Baba felt only mild ripples
of this upheaval. His family stopped sending money, but by then he was
almost done with his studies. He earned the rest of his tuition by waiting
tables at the Faculty Club, and after graduation he got a drafting job at
a small architecture firm in Oakland.

People sometimes ask in an awestruck voice how my parents "ever got
together," as if some mysterious factor must have been responsible for
a boy from Iran marrying a girl from Los Angeles in 1965. But it was
not so strange. By the time my parents met, Baba had decided against
the Iranian way of marriage. On his one college visit back to Iran the
women in his family had plied him with hints and suggestions. *You know,
you're handsome and American-educated; you could marry anyone. Dai Mohsen-
khan's youngest daughter is a very good girl; you should take her as your wife. Go
to their house next week and see her; they'll be expecting you.* But it never occurred to Baba to let his family select his wife, although that is how all
his brothers and sisters except for Massi eventually married. After seven
years in America, where his relationships were "full of tears and crying
and declarations of love," he could not imagine getting married any
other way.

Whenever I asked either of my parents how they got together, they
always mentioned Mama's jeans. Mama's roommate had considered Baba
her own discovery, and had invited him to drop by one afternoon. The
roommate offhandedly introduced him to Mama, who was stretched out
on the couch in a pair of tight new blue jeans. Her red hair was pulled
back, setting off her deep brown eyes, pretty mouth, and pale, freckled
skin. As soon as the roommate left the room for a minute, Baba made
his move.

"You want to go to Carmel with me on Sunday?" he asked.

"Sure," Mama said.

"I'll pick you up at five in the morning."

Back in the days when Baba was sitting in Tehran movie theaters and dreaming about the land of cowboys and gangsters, Mama was growing up in a split-level house in the soft glow of Hollywood's periphery. Her father had a psychoanalytic practice in Beverly Hills, and although the location gave her childhood a tinge of glamour, Mama describes it as "a regular old fifties growing up. Dad worked, Mom stayed at home. There was Christmas; there was golf; there was going to the beach; there were the parties where Dad served the drinks and Mom played the piano." Mama spent her days going to ballet classes, camp and cotillion, hiking in the nearby canyons and eating hot dog dinners in front of the TV with her younger brother.

It was not until high school that she began to sense that something was missing. Part of this started at home, where, as perfect as they might have seemed from the outside, her parents were slowly discovering how mismatched they were. They had married young—he was a thin, shy premed student at Stanford and she was a vivacious Berkeley freshman with long dark hair, a dazzling smile, and a determined-looking jaw that masked her under-confidence. She had grown up without much money in a wealthy town in Northern California, and later she always talked about how she had envied the girls who came to school in the luxurious cashmere sweaters she could not afford. Marrying a doctor from a prosperous family made Grandma feel included in a world she had always longed to be part of, and in the early years of the marriage she was full of exuberance. But gradually it faded. Grandma began to complain that Grandpa was "more comfortable with psychoanalytic interpretation than with simple emotional expression." Mama remembers Grandma slowly retreating into the only role she felt suited for—wife and mother—while Grandpa sat at the head of the table, thoughtfully discussing Freud with his children while testing the dinner plates to see if they had been properly warmed.

By the time Mama was in high school her parents seemed to disagree about everything. Grandma came down with an ulcer and began what would be a thirty-year litany of grievances along the lines of "Well, he's a good provider but he can't understand the most basic things about people." Grandpa, on the other hand, was frustrated by Grandma's "block against exploring mankind's darker sides." During the Cuban missile crisis he developed an intense interest in the apocalypse. To Grandma, all this doom and gloom seemed designed to arrive just as she was about to give birth to their third child. "Why can't we be like other people?" she asked irritably. "No one else I know has to plot the course of radioactive fallout during dinner."

The missile crisis had a different effect on Mama. Sixteen years old and believing that the world could end any day, she conceived an urgent desire to see as much as she could of the world beyond the warm, eucalyptus-scented hills of Los Angeles. Her imagination was fueled by the Italian art films she watched at the theaters on Wilshire Boulevard, and she developed a romantic idea of an outside world of sophisticated women living exciting, passionate lives. The missile crisis only heightened her impatience to see this world. Walking dreamily out of an Antonioni movie one day, Mama made a pledge to herself that for the rest of her life she would say yes to everything that came her way.

She and a school friend decided that after graduation they would go to Italy. They saved up money from part-time jobs and had just bought their tickets when, without warning, her friend's parents whisked their daughter off to Australia to evade the imminent nuclear disaster. So Mama went on her own. She lived in an Italian *pensione,* accompanied a group of student Communists to Hungary, and sailed to a Greek island with a boy she had met on the ship from New York. After six months she returned to attend college at Berkeley, where she dated a civil rights activist and a series of boys much like the ones she had known in high school—until the day her roommate brought over the boy from Iran.

It was not by mistake that Mama was perched on the couch in her new stretch jeans that afternoon when Baba walked in. She had seen him driving around town with no shirt on and the windows rolled down and she had thought he was cute. When he asked her to go to Carmel with him at five in the morning, the fact that she had a date planned for the night before did not daunt her. She said yes right away.

Whenever Mama talked about that first date, her eyes would soften and a little smile would play on her lips. Baba's black-and-white Nash Rambler glided up the dim street, he opened the door for her, and by the time the sun spilled over the eastern mountain ridge they were coasting through the velvety yellow hills of the Almaden Valley. There remains just one photograph from that day, copied and enlarged, so it has a bright but misty quality, like the sun breaking through fog. Mama is sitting in front of the Mission Carmel in a straight skirt and sandals, her loose red hair framed by a powder-blue scarf. Her eyes are tired but she is smiling, and something about her expression makes it easy to understand what Baba liked in her—a kind of openness, as if she were ready for anything that might happen.

Later she joked that that first date should have warned her about what she was getting into; this was an excursion to the most distant place they could go to in one day. But that kind of adventure was precisely what she was looking for, and in this foreign architect whose warm eyes and slightly asymmetrical nose gave his handsome face an easy informality, she saw a spontaneous energy that promised to take her beyond the world she had grown up in.

After three more dates he showed up at her door one night and said, "How would you like to live with me?"

Mama said yes immediately. It was 1964, and they knew of no other un-married couple who lived together, although a year or two later most of their friends would start doing it. Mama says she and Baba were not trying to set a trend; they were simply blind to everything but each other. They found a little cottage in Oakland shrouded by trees, although Mama con-tinued to pay her thirty-five dollar rent at Peggy's and kept a few dresses in the closet for when her grandparents visited from down the street.

Back in L.A., her parents complained that she was never home when they called. Her father awkwardly warned her about the reputation of a girl who has lived with a man who doesn't end up marrying her; she shrugged it off. Her father had always encouraged her to trust her im-pulses, and in any case she was prepared for either outcome. She would marry Baba or move on to something else—either way, she would be experiencing the world.

She bought a Persian cookbook and skipped classes to prepare elab-orate meals. They drank wine and read poetry late into the night. One evening, a few months into it, he said, "I'd marry you in a second if I thought you could live in Iran."

She did not stop to think about whether or not it would work. They drove down to Los Angeles to tell her parents, whose only request was that they be allowed to throw a big wedding. Only a few of their Berkeley friends attended. The guest list was mostly comprised of her parents' friends, who drank champagne and whispered about how attractive the couple was, and how young, and how, after all, Mama could always get a divorce and come back home.

My parents ended up going to Iran by mistake. They had planned only to go to Europe, to attend Baba's family's first—and only—vacation abroad. It was summer, and Jamsheed had driven Aziz, Agha Jan, and his sisters Massi and Homa from Tehran to Geneva, where Parviz joined them from Washington and Baba and Mama flew in from California.

———

Massi, a tall, striking woman with flashing dark eyes, spotted Mama in the bathroom of the Geneva train station and guessed who she was. After triumphantly hurrying her out to the snack bar to meet the rest of the family Massi took her new sister-in-law aside. "You baby?" she said, pointing at Mama's stomach, rounding her hands out in front of her own stomach and raising her eyebrows in a question.

"Not yet," Mama said.

Massi made a circle with her thumb and index finger and poked her other index finger in and out of it. "You—Essie—kaput?"

Thinking "kaput" meant finished, Mama smiled and shook her head. "No, no. No kaput."

"No kaput?" said Massi. She looked at her sister and mother and repeated it to them. "Essie and Karen, no kaput!"

Later, Mama found out "kaput" meant condom. The Iranian women she met were preoccupied with babies—either with having them or with not having them—and one of the objectives of the European trip for Massi and Homa was to get birth-control pills, which were not yet available in Iran.

Their other objective was shopping. In each country, my aunts and grandmother spent large segments of the day at department stores. Mama had imagined her in-laws to be a more cosmopolitan version of her own parents, whose luxurious European vacations revolved around sightseeing and fine dining. But except for shopping excursions, Baba's family rarely went out. They did not visit tourist sites, and most of their meals consisted of bread, butter and jam on the hotel room floor—as much a factor of habit as of frugality. Mama and Baba followed them from shop to shop, but after a couple of weeks, desperate to be alone together, they decided to spend a few days in Venice and meet the family in Istanbul. They left most of their money and belongings with the family for safekeeping and enjoyed Venice so much that they stayed an extra day. When they arrived at the Istanbul hotel the proprietor handed them a note.

Sorry, we couldn't wait. We went back to Iran.

—Jamsheed

The family had left an hour earlier.

Although they had only a couple of dollars between them, they decided not to telegram Mama's parents for money. It would have been embarrassing; moreover, they could not even afford a hotel for the days it would take for money to arrive. So they went to the Iranian Consulate.

"Here is enough money for food and a train to Erzerum," said the consul general, a sympathetic young Iranian Turk. "From Erzerum you can catch a bus into Iran. You can send the money back to me once you get there."

The family's house in Tehran was not as Baba had left it. Most of the servants had returned to the village. Wife-of-Agha Jan, Baba's beloved stepmother, had died several months earlier, although in Europe no one had mentioned it to Baba for fear of upsetting him. But the family was as hospitable as ever, and when it became clear that Baba was going to be stuck in Iran for a few months while he waited to see if he would be drafted, he and Mama moved into an apartment at the top of the family home.

Soon after they arrived, Baba's sisters and female cousins pulled Mama into a bedroom to compare breasts. "Who has the best ones?" they asked eagerly, turning it into a contest. Mama spoke no Farsi, and, not wanting to offend, she undid her shirt along with everyone else. They all looked around for a minute and then buttoned their shirts back up. The reason, Mama guessed later, had to do with an old tradition. In the old days, when a man could not see his wife before the wedding, his female relatives had only to go to the bathhouse to see everything about her. If her looks pleased them, they could take their investigation further: greeting her with kisses on the mouth to see if her breath was sweet, stroking her head affectionately to make sure her hair was really her own. But

Essie had married without any advice or approval, even after Jamsheed had written a letter warning him not to, because "surely Karen has dated before." Later Massi reported to Baba that Mama's were among the two sets of breasts voted as the best. The other set belonged to the cousin the family had hoped he would marry when he came back from America—in other words, he'd made a wise choice on his own but the choice they had made had been good too.

The household settled into a comfortable routine around Agha Jan, who, too old to dominate the family as he once had, sat on the floor puffing on his water pipe and drinking tea. Mama sat with him and read poetry books in English; he smiled at her through the haze of smoke and paid her small compliments through intermediaries. It was hard for the rest of Baba's family to find much wrong with Mama. She was good-humored and polite and clearly in love with their son. Unable to communicate with her beyond single words and pantomimes, they treated her with a bemused mix of condescension and respect ("See, she knows how to sew!" Massi gushed. "Exactly like an Iranian woman!") injected with an occasional tinge of disapproval ("Just look at how much she likes Essie," Aziz's sister whispered in a scandalized voice, as if there was something commendable but also something incautious about a woman who liked her husband so much). In any case, Baba made it clear from the beginning that he would not tolerate any of the heckling so often leveled at daughters-in-law, and that if they attempted even so much as a criticism of the way Mama peeled oranges he would refuse to listen.

In general, though, they were less concerned with her flaws than with her virtues. Being foreign, she was considered an expert on anything Western. She was the one who deciphered the instructions on the Valium and birth-control pills from Europe; and if someone was sick she was often called upon to give a diagnosis, which everyone would listen to with respectful nods.

She was also the expert on chic. Had an Iranian woman tried to go around in the miniskirts and sleeveless blouses Mama had bought for the trip to Europe, her father and brothers would most likely have locked her up in her room. But the fact that Mama's wardrobe raised no objections from Baba, coupled with Agha Jan's obvious affection for her, resulted in a kind of amnesty for everyone. Her in-laws initially explained her outfits to outsiders as "the way American women dress," but soon the younger women in the family were taking Mama's clothes to the tailor and asking for exact copies. As for Agha Jan, he hardly noticed the sartorial changes in his household, which in any event coincided with the advent of miniskirts in Tehran later that year. The only comment he made was to Baba, one night when his bachelor cousins had invited him out for the evening. "Never be like the men who go out at night," he said. "Karen is too good a girl to leave alone at home."

In the meantime, even as the women consulted Mama about birth control, they could not refrain from asking her every few days if she was pregnant. As the months passed, their questions intensified. My parents had already decided to go to New York so Baba could get a master's degree and Mama could finish her bachelor's degree; but for now they were stuck where they were. Baba couldn't go to school or even work in Iran until he found out about the draft. In the meantime, having nothing much to do, the two of them decided that having a baby might not be such a bad idea, and soon Mama was able to give the women the answer they wanted.

Sandra Cisneros

Geraldo
No Last Name

She met him at a dance. Pretty too, and young. Said he worked in a restaurant, but she can't remember which one. Geraldo. That's all. Green pants and Saturday shirt. Geraldo. That's what he told her.

And how was she to know she'd be the last one to see him alive. An accident, don't you know. Hit and run. Marin, she goes to all those dances. Uptown. Logan. Embassy. Palmer. Aragon. Fontana. The Manor. She likes to dance. She knows how to do cumbias and salsas and rancheras even. And he was just someone she danced with. Somebody she met that night. That's right.

That's the story. That's what she said again and again.

Once to the hospital people and twice to the police. No address. No name. Nothing in his pockets. Ain't it a shame.

Only Marin can't explain why it mattered, the hours and hours, for somebody she didn't even know. The hospital emergency room. Nobody but an intern working all alone. And maybe if the surgeon would've come, maybe if he hadn't lost so much blood, if the surgeon had only come, they would know who to notify and where.

But what difference does it make? He wasn't anything to her. He wasn't her boyfriend or anything like that. Just another *brazer* who didn't speak English. Just another wetback. You know the kind. The ones who always look ashamed. And what was she doing out at three A.M. anyway? Marin who was sent home with her coat and some aspirin. How does she explain?

She met him at a dance. Geraldo, in his shiny shirt and green pants. Geraldo going to a dance.

What does it matter?

They never saw the kitchenettes. They never knew about the two-room flats and sleeping rooms he rented, the weekly money orders sent home, the currency exchange. How could they?

His name was Geraldo. And his home is in another country. The ones he left behind are far away, will wonder, shrug, remember. Geraldo—he went north . . . we never heard from him again.

Jessica Hagedorn

from
The Gangster of Love

Purple Haze

Jimi Hendrix died the year the ship that brought us from Manila docked in San Francisco. My brother, Voltaire, and I wept when we read about it in the papers, but it was Voltaire who was truly devastated. Hendrix had been his idol. In homage to Jimi, Voltaire had learned how to play electric guitar, although he'd be the first to admit he wasn't musically gifted. "It's okay for me to dream, isn't it?" He'd laugh. Voltaire grew his bushy hair out and teased it into what he called a "Filipino Afro." Voltaire caused a sensation whenever he appeared in his royal purple bell-bottoms and gauzy shirts from India. My parents were appalled, especially when Voltaire took the next logical step and adopted an "indigenous Filipino" hippie look. The crushed velvet was replaced by batik fabric; the corny peace medallions replaced by carabao horn, scapulars, and amulets he purchased from bemused market vendors in front of Baclaran Church.

My father once threatened to have Voltaire arrested by the Marcos secret police for looking like an effeminate *bakla*. Then there was the incident of Voltaire's guitar, which he set fire to in a very public ritual in Luneta Park. According to my father, Voltaire was on the military's growing shitlist of subversives and hippie dissidents. Nothing much came of my father's threats, except after one of their more physical confrontations when Voltaire disappeared for weeks. My mother was sure he was dead. "He's probably holed up in some Ermita drug den," my father scoffed, though he was plainly worried. Voltaire eventually showed up without explaining himself, but by then no one cared: my mother's announcement that she was finally leaving my father overshadowed everything.

Voltaire and I convinced ourselves that our parents' breakup was temporary, that the journey we were taking with our mother was some sort of weird vacation. Our lives as the children of Milagros Rivera had often consisted of startling events and irreversible showdowns. We were relieved to be away from the Philippines after the bang-bang, shoot-'em-up elections. Who gave a damn about voting anyway? Even my father was forced to admit that the elections were a joke. Everyone knew Crocodile had fixed it to win. That's what Voltaire called Marcos now—Crocodile. Imelda was Mrs. Croc, or Croc of Shit, as Voltaire sometimes said when he was in a truly bitchy mood. Voltaire blamed Marcos, the CIA, and the Catholic Church for everything that was wrong with our country. He once said the CIA had contaminated the Pasig River with LSD as part of their ongoing chemical warfare experiments against the Vietcong. He also claimed that we were the original gooks. He and our sister, Luz, the eldest, used to argue about politics all the time. "Didn't you know the term gook originated in the Philippine-American war?" he once yelled at her. "Enough!" Luz yelled back at Voltaire.

Excited and distracted by our sudden trip to America, we didn't dare ask too many questions—even when Luz stubbornly refused to leave Manila and my father.

Voltaire croons softly to himself as he leans over the deck railing and studies the faces of the motley crowd waiting on the pier. " 'Purple Haze was in my brain, lately things don't seem the same...' There she is!" He waves to a tiny woman bundled up like an Eskimo in a hooded down parka and pants. Voltaire must've recognized Auntie Fely from those Kodak cards she sends every Christmas with photos of her with her stepchildren and husband stiffly posed under a lavishly decorated artificial tree and "Merry Xmas & a Happy New Year to You & Yours from the Cruz Family" embossed in gold.

According to my brother, I was three when Auntie Fely left to find work in America. A few years older than my mother, Auntie Fely was unmarried then, and she doted on all of us. She stopped by our house on her way to the airport for one last teary goodbye, though family and friends had already bid their farewells at numerous ceremonial breakfasts, lunches, *meriendas,* and dinners held a month before my aunt's scheduled departure. Luz was the first to receive kisses and hugs, then Voltaire. My aunt gave each of them envelopes stuffed with peso bills. "Don't spend it all on sweets." Because I'm the baby of the family, Auntie Fely saved me for last. She scooped me up with her strong arms and peered into my face as if to memorize it. The intensity of her gaze, magnified through Coke-bottle eyeglasses, frightened me.

Auntie Fely was a nurse, and since I'd been diagnosed as borderline anemic by our family physician, Dr. Katigbak, she had the dubious honor of administering my dreaded vitamin B shot every Tuesday. I would run and hide whenever I saw my aunt approaching in her starched cap and uniform—Auntie Fely took her profession very seriously—carrying that ominous black medical kit packed with glass vials and a sinister array of gleaming silver needles. She'd huff and puff up the winding, graveled pathway, drenched in sweat by the time she reached the front door.

"Where's my little patient?" I'd hear her call out in a sweet, singsong voice, as she and my *yaya* Emy hunted for me in every shadowy nook of our rambling ruin of a house.

"Your Auntie Fely's going to miss her little patient so much." She kissed me noisily several times on both cheeks and wept. "Don't ever forget your Auntie Fely."

My right arm still throbbing from yesterday's injection, I howled in terror for my mother, my *yaya* Emy—anyone who could rescue me from my aunt's smothering embrace.

Shortly after she found a job in a public hospital in San Francisco, Auntie Fely was set up by her supervisor, another Filipino nurse named Mrs. Garcia, with a flashy widower from Stockton named Basilio Cruz. Basilio's wife, Dolly, had recently died in the ICU after a mysterious ailment. There were rumors of foul play—worrisome *tsismis* my mother heard all the way back in Manila—but only rumors. Dolly Cruz had worked as a managing housekeeper at the Hilton Hotel, leaving behind a bubblegum pink, two-bedroom tract home in Daly City, quite a bit of insurance money, and no debts. There were three grown children. The eldest was a postal worker named Boni—short for Bonifacio—who moved back to Stockton after his father remarried and never spoke to him again. The twins, Peachy and Nene, seemed more adaptable and took to calling our aunt Mama Fely. They were unbelievable academic achievers, graduating from high school with honors, then majoring in medicine at the University of San Francisco on scholarships. "USF is the best," Auntie Fely had written my mother proudly in her last Christmas card. "A strict Catholic school."

"Look! We're approaching the Golden Gate." My mother points at the shadowy outline of the bridge through the thick morning fog.

"But it's not gold," I say, disappointed.

On the windy pier, a burnished man in a dapper felt hat and fur-trimmed overcoat makes face talk, eyebrows going up and down in furious Filipino sign language: *Welcome! Hurry up! What are you waiting for? Everything okay,* ba?

My mother can't help scowling. "That must be the famous Bas." Then she forgets herself, blowing kisses and making twisted crazy faces of her own. Another passenger hands her confetti and streamers, which she flings at the people huddled and waiting below. "Fely! Fely!" Her eyes are moist and I could swear she is sniffling. Is it possible? I nudge Voltaire with my elbow. My mother has always been too tough to let anyone see her cry. "Fely!" She is jumping up and down in her four-inch heels. Voltaire and I exchange amused glances as the other passengers on deck turn to gawk at her.

Our passports are stamped, our suitcases inspected. "My sister is a citizen," my mother informs the warehouse crowded with immigration officials and customs agents. Voltaire's long hair, beads, and fringed buckskin jacket (bought off an enterprising Australian hippie in Manila) inspire hostile stares as we exit the customs area into the biting wind. "Thinks he's Tonto," I hear one of the officials saying. Someone laughs.

Auntie Fely is weeping and smiling. Her exclamations and questions overlap, uttered with that same lilting, singsong cadence. "Raquel! Dios *ko!* Remember me? My little patient! *Naku!* How old are you now! Not even a teenager yet! Ay! *Talaga! So* big!" She means mature when she says big. Even after all her years in America, Auntie Fely still says "Open the light . . . close the light" when she orders someone to turn a light switch on or off and "for a while" when she has to put a phone call on hold.

My mother is holding back tears. "Fely, we finally made it."

In my childhood, my mother was a volatile presence, vampy, haughty, impulsive. "Who the fuck do you think you are?" my father used to yell at her. He was a mystery to me, aloof and distracted, anxious about money. I was never sure what he did for a living, except that he employed eleven people. The sign at the entrance to his cramped office read RIVERA TRADING CO.

Whenever she fought with my father, my mother would hop on the next plane bound for Hong Kong or Tokyo. Glamorous cities, distant and exotic enough to provide a distraction, yet only a few hours away from Manila. We were her reluctant, loyal, sullen companions, tagging along on our mother's spur-of-the-moment adventures. That time in Hong Kong, for example. Luz, Voltaire, and I were the only children present in Patsy Lozano's presidential suite at the Peninsula Hotel, brought along by my mother for who knows what reason. Patsy and my mother were both pretty drunk, having a grand time with a rather decadent crew. The men all vaguely resembled my father, with feline Chinese Portuguese nymphets clinging to their sharkskin suits.

The radio was on loud, blaring Perez Prado's heated music. My mother danced with a fat, graceful man, and they showed off some breathtaking mambo moves. Suddenly she pulled away from her sweaty partner and climbed up on the coffee table. Lost in her own world, lithe and exuberant in her green mermaid dress, she shook her bare perfumed shoulders and tossed her head back with abandon. I was enthralled and ashamed of my mother's torrid performance. The music ended, and the fat man helped my mother down as Patsy Lozano applauded. More drinks were consumed, and everyone forgot about us. The fat man whispered in my mother's ear.

Luz locked herself in the bathroom to sulk. Voltaire snuck out and was later found by hotel security, aimlessly going up and down the elevators. No one even noticed he was missing. I stayed, sure I was going to die from having to sit there and watch my mother make a spectacle of herself. An eternity later, back in the safety of our much humbler hotel, Luz, Voltaire, and I got in my mother's king-size bed and watched unfunny British comedies on the king-size television. Our mother went nightclubbing with Patsy and the fat man. To spite them all, we ran up a huge bill ordering junk food from room service—making ourselves sick on soda pop, banana splits with chocolate syrup, hot dogs and club sandwiches doused in ketchup and mayonnaise. I threw up all night long, alternating between chills, diarrhea, and a burning fever.

"There, there," Voltaire murmured, helping me wash up for the hundredth time. We ran out of clean towels.

"Are you playacting?" Luz asked me snidely, suspicious as always.

Then there was Tokyo. Voltaire wasn't with us, so there was no one to mediate between my mother and Luz. Now a tall, sour adolescent, Luz shadowed my mother relentlessly like a stern, disapproving chaperone. "Why don't you go sightseeing and let me breathe?" My mother wailed in desperation.

The day we arrived, we ran into a smooth businessman from Manila named Alfonso Something-or-Other. Alfonso's last name was too baroque, too Spanish, and too long to take seriously. We were in the midst of checking in, exhausted and surrounded by luggage, most of it my mother's. "You remember Mr. Something-or-Other, don't you?" My mother gave us one of her warning glances. "He plays golf with your father."

"Ah," Luz said.

"I don't," I chimed in.

We were in no mood for being nice to yet another one of my mother's insincere and fawning admirers. Plus, I never forgot what Sister Immaculada at Our Lady of Perpetual Sorrow had drummed into us in daily catechism class: sex in any form was a mortal sin, and the sin of adultery the absolute worst. Sister Immaculada was the oldest living nun at my school, with bushy gray eyebrows that curled over her eyes. "Not only will you end up in hell forever," Sister Immaculada droned in a raspy voice, "but Lucifer himself will make a special point of torturing you personally. He'll carve out your private parts, barbecue while you watch, then make you eat yourself slowly, morsel by morsel."

"Call me Tito Alfonso," the man said in Spanish to Luz and me. He smelled of leather and expensive soap.

I spoke to him in English. "You're not my uncle."

Luz pinched me, but said nothing.

Alfonso invited us to eat with him in the hotel dining room that evening, and we were annoyed with our mother for accepting his invitation. Luz and I were determined not to leave her alone with him, however, so we tagged along. We made Alfonso suffer by pretending not to hear every time he spoke to us, or else by responding with a terse yes or no. Luz made things worse by speaking to me only in Tagalog.

I drank iced Coca-Cola in a very tall glass, aware of the flirtation going on between my mother and Alfonso. She kept laughing at every other thing he said and leaning closer and closer to him. They had both simply decided to ignore Luz and me. I felt impotent and wished Voltaire was with us, sure that Alfonso wouldn't take as many liberties in his presence. Suddenly I bit down hard on the rim of my glass. The sliver felt cold and dangerous on my tongue. Luz squealed like a pig. "She's going to die! Mama, Raquel ate glass and she's going to die!"

Alfonso and my mother stared at the cracked glass I held in my hand. It took a moment for what I'd done to register in their minds. "Open your mouth," my mother commanded, a strange look on her face. I froze, afraid of what she might do. "Open your mouth," she repeated, glaring at me. The diners from nearby tables looked in our direction.

"Are you all right, *hija?*" Alfonso asked solicitously. He put a hand on my mother's braceleted arm, as if to restrain her from attacking me. The sliver of sharp glass prevented me from speaking.

"She's *insane,*" Luz said, to no one in particular. I had gone too far and upset them all, including my sister. The waiter hurried over just as the band onstage began playing "Begin the Beguine." "Filipino," I managed to croak to Luz, pointing at the band. I attempted a smile.

"You're *insane,*" Luz repeated.

"*Eb-ri-ting* okay?" our Japanese waiter asked.

"Spit," my mother growled, holding out her napkin. I did as I was told. She wrapped the shard of glass in the napkin, handed it to the startled waiter, then casually ordered another Coke for me.

Our deluded, beautiful mother thought that by running away and spending money my father didn't really have, she could force him to mend his ways. She was a romantic, defiant, and proud woman who sometimes got what she wanted. My father would actually show up and surprise her with presents and flowers, making promises he couldn't or wouldn't keep. He'd take us children on fatherly outings, making a supreme effort not to look bored. We all fell for his charm. When my father didn't feel up to the chase, he would simply wait for my mother to run out of money and return to Manila. He punished her by flaunting his mistress in public. We all knew about his *querida,* a long-legged beauty queen named Evelyn "Baby" Guzman. Another Baby in a long line of Babys. To this day, my mother can't bring herself to speak Baby's name. "That woman" is about all she can manage.

I have made it a point to try and remember everything. I remember that Baby wasn't much older than my sister, Luz, and therefore more threatening to my youth-obsessed mother than any of my father's other women. I always thought it quite fitting and funny that my mother refused to grant my father, Francisco Rivera, a proper divorce. Two years after we moved to America, he chose to bribe Judge Ramos and marry Baby Guzman in an illegal civil ceremony on September 21, 1972, the day Ferdinand Marcos declared martial law in the Philippines.

Rob Nixon

from *Dreambirds: The Strange History of the Ostrich in Fashion, Food, and Fortune*

In 1980, at the age of twenty-five, I emigrated to America. My grand-parents had left Scotland and Ireland early this century, arriving in South Africa at the height of the feather boom. Now, two generations later, the grandchildren of those immigrants had scattered across four conti-nents: two of us settling in Africa, one each in Europe, Australia and North America.

Politics played a hand in my departure, as it did for so many departing South Africans of my generation. I left clandestinely in response to an apartheid army call-up. I entered an exile of sorts, though I had always felt, from early childhood, that my destiny lay overseas, that emotionally I would have to leave.

Like everyone who travels towards a new life in a land they've never seen, I wondered how much of me would survive the crossing, how translatable I would be. No migrant ever knows how much they're going to need or want their past. A few things, though, I recognized as excess baggage, things that would surely prove worthless in America. Some-where mid-Atlantic I mentally dumped my expertise in African birds and my degree in African languages and watched them hit the ocean far below. For the rest, I guessed, I'd have to wait and see.

I had already done a lot of dumping, starting years before. The novelist Nadine Gordimer has spoken of the moment in early adulthood when she went "falling, falling through the South African way of life." I experienced that trapdoor sensation at college, as I discovered the full enormities of apartheid and felt assumptions of normality slide from beneath my feet. A world that had seemed to possess an ordinary stability became foundationless.

The Karoo scrub desert had always held for me the emotional density of a child's first landscape. All childhoods are provincial: they start from me, from us, from here. In the absence of a social analysis, where we are becomes the centre of everything. My boyhood and adolescent passions had flowed straight from that centre: my desert rovings and the unwavering knowledge that I possessed a calling—ornithology.

But after my fall into politics, the landscape around me seemed illusory, distorted by an unethical geography. I lost all interest in Oudtshoorn, the ostrich world and birds. The Karoo became code for a long hallucination, a mirage-thin dream—like the shimmery haze above a tarmac that skews your vision, rippling through everything. Emotionally, that world, that time of life, sank from sight. For many years before leaving South Africa, I avoided travelling through the sparse interior. Driving between Port Elizabeth and Cape Town as I often did, I always opted for the coastal route.

So before migrating to America, I'd already folded childhood and adolescence carefully away. I'd placed them in a box, tied the string and dropped them down a chute marked Forgotten Things. I found myself living almost beyond reach of memory.

Every migration is an opportunity and a kind of death. The new world may be rich and strange, but you're somehow weightless in it. I moved through my first two American years—spent in Iowa—with a certain spectral insubstantiality. I had such a shallow purchase on the place and the place on me; every day, I felt the force of my absence from its past. In Iowa I lived as an extraterrestrial, an "immigrant alien" in the full sense of the phrase. I probably won't ever feel so otherworldly again, this side of the grave.

There's a burial ritual in certain West African cultures that has long haunted me. It's called the crossing fee. The mourners place a sacrificial bird on the dead person's grave. Like the obolus left for Charon, the bird guarantees that the boatman who links past and future, this world and the next, will ferry the departed spirit across the waters to the other side. The bird must die: no journey is made for free.

But it's not just our final passage that demands a crossing fee. Every migrant knows the sensation of arriving in some kind of afterlife. It's a disembodied feeling: your solid self lies buried in the place that you've abandoned, that gave you the ballast of a past.

After crossing the Atlantic, it took me two years to find my way to New York City. I became a convert, an instant cosmopolitan. I loved the company I found: crowds of weightless people who'd made the journey from some other side. The freedom to be weightless here gave us all, I felt, en masse, a paradoxical solidity. I hung out with former misfits— foreigners and Americans—who'd grown up at an angle to places that had made them strange. Struggling people, many of them, yet at liberty to forget the places, the people they needed to forget. Here, for the first time in America, I didn't lack a history because almost everyone I knew lived past-free.

I was still uncomfortable with the idea of a permanent address. I wasn't ready to belong, I just wanted a place to be. Unlike towns, pro- vincial cities, suburbs and nation-states, New York didn't demand that you jump through hoops of conformity. Not insisting that you belong was the city's way of ensuring that people like me did. A stray spirit among stray spirits, I'd arrived in a place where restlessness could be a home. Maeve Brennan—that Irish immigrant to New York (and *New Yorker* writer)—described this sensation perfectly. Hers was a city, she once remarked, peopled by "travellers in residence."

So New York became a counterweight to my Iowa immateriality. But it also served as a perfect antidote to all the one-mistake towns I'd ever known in South Africa. Places where eccentricity, flair, experiment—any defections from the norm—were punishable offences. Here, at last, I felt free to live in a community where defections were the norm.

I acquired a doctorate in literature and watched myself, with a certain immigrant irony, metamorphose into a professor. South Africa still haunted me as a shadowland, but as a place composed purely of politics. For twelve years, the antiapartheid cause became my passion, my revenge against an injustice and an illusion. This obsession stood at the heart of it all: my teaching, my journalism, my scholarship, my political and private life.

My appreciation of the bird world had long since been bankrupted by politics. Nature shrank: it seemed unnatural. At college in South Africa, I'd whittled it down to a line from a Bertolt Brecht poem that I'd hung above my bed: "To speak of trees is treason." Brecht's six words were a note to myself and to my father behind me, still writing his gardening column and putting me through college on the proceeds of "Growing Things." Now in New York, I shared the sentiments of that ur-New Yorker, Woody Allen: "Nature and I are two." I never went anywhere where I risked getting sand inside my shoes.

So I settled happily among people for whom ostriches roamed only on the Discovery Channel or in the menagerie of the mind. I had made a double crossing—first into politics and, later, into America. On the far side of both those journeys, I never thought I'd hear from ostriches again.

Andrei Codrescu

Bi-lingual

I speak two languages. I've learnt one of them in a trance, for no reason at all, in a very short time, on horseback, in glimpses, between silent revolts. One is the language of my birth, a speech which, more or less, contains my rational mind because it is in this tongue that I find myself counting change in the supermarket and filing away my published poems. In a sense, these two languages are my private day and night because what one knows without having learned is the day, full of light and indelicate assumptions. The language of the night is fragile, it depends for most part on memory and memory is a vast white sheet on which the most preposterous things are written. The acquired language is permanently under the watch of my native tongue like a prisoner in a cage. Lately, this new language has planned an escape to which I fully subscribe. It plans to get away in the middle of the night with most of my mind and never return. This piece of writing in the acquired language is part of the plan: while the native tongue is (right now!) beginning to translate it, a big chunk of my mind has already detached itself and is floating in space entirely free . . .

Teresa Palomo Acosta

Crossing
"a piece of earth"

At the border the gatekeepers sit with loaded guns.
Just this side of it I look at the brand newest official government
   map
For directions to a US/Mexico round trip.
Though I know that the map cannot measure precisely
The lay of the land.
Now changed by the brand newest migra laws.
They have altered our conscious excursions to each side
And our ownership or land/rights.

At the border
Where the guards with guns are stationed
I begin to reconsider
The rules I have relied upon
To cross the borders
That divide earth from earth
On the same terrain.

How can I redefine one slice of the land
Turned into a flat treadmill
Of personal causes that stretch over its bridges:
Day labor, drug dealers, simple family outings/
Trading one form of persecution for another?

At the border
Where the gatekeepers eye me
I dream up a way to set my own eyes
On other markings in the desert nearby
—The sagüaros—
As a means to know the land
And our history as a fluid movement in time
Underground.
One that curves into the spaces
Left over in the sagüaro's squarish corners.
It leaps through aqueducts and under the bridges
And into paradise.
It makes its own lay of the land
And tells me that I know the time has come
To stop waiting for a ruling
Promoting the just use of land/rights
On either side of the border I cross.

For the men who keep the rules
Reorder the time and space and lay of the land.
They make our part
Their natural inheritance
And insure that we are soaked inward,
Made invisible and inaudible.

Still, I know that at the border
The places for me to discard my map and wade into the water
And assuredly swim across
Stretch farther
Than either
We
Or laws
Have eyes to see.

Since, well, the truth
About borders is desperate enough
To force upon us many versions
Of the facts
With guns for re-enforcement
If facts alone will not do.

The gatekeepers want so to stop
The flow of history slipping from them
As it undulates underground.
They collar us into migra vans
For the trip back
And we
Plan another crossing to
Another piece
Of the simple earth
In union with our version
Of the Mexico/US map.

This cycle becomes permanently fixed.

Salvador Mendoza

from
Between the Lines

Sonsonate, El Salvador
May 6, 1988

Rafael Mazariego
Los Angeles, CA

Sr. Rafael, dear son,
... Rafael it makes me happy that you have written soon, but also I ask
you to forgive me for not having answered right away, you already know
that I can't write, I'm going to try to do what you ask me, to take the
children to mass, I already talk with them, they understand little, they're
small, but have patience, little by little they're going to recognize, in time.
The children ask me about you, and I tell them you're going to return
soon, that you're working far away, that's why you can't come, I speak
with Dolores, today she recognizes that she misses you and she regrets
having bothered you so much, she says if she hadn't bothered you you
wouldn't have gone, and what use is it to her to have everything if she

doesn't have you, I tell her that it's late to repent, and that she must resign herself to the fact that you are helping her, not to worry about you, that by the grace of God you are well and have work.

Rosita is doing so-so in her studies, the children aren't sick, I'm well, Chela and Carmen are well, all by the grace of God, but one always feels the emptiness, although we didn't see you very often still we miss you, but I'd rather hope that you make progress quickly. About what you tell me of the strangeness up there, I understand you because it's a very big place and here it is small, the customs are different, it has to be that way since it's another state, but you have to get used to it, it's always that way when it's the first time one visits that place, meeting so many new characters and different things like the foods, and the places which are very beautiful, I pray to God many prayers that he take care of you and help you in everything. . . .

I'm very happy because the Good Lord helped you in everything like I asked him and I go on asking him day and night. I don't worry much because I know you are very methodical in everything, but don't be thinking from this that I'm telling you it doesn't worry me that you are far away, how could I not, but not so much. Oscar says he forgives you and he completely agrees with you and he's going to do whatever is possible to carry out what you ask, that he behave himself, and he says that though you never showed him love nor interest he always felt your warmth and love, don't worry about me, I am well.

Your father who loves you and always adores you and goes on adoring you bids you good-bye, in no moment does he forget to ask God on your behalf that He take care of you. . . . All your friends say they feel very pleased and happy to know you find yourself well and you had no problems in arriving and finding work and they always remember you and are never going to forget you because you were very good and never gave them bad examples.

I forgot to tell you, but I'm telling you in advance don't worry much because she's well recovered now. My sister Anita had an accident, two thieves assaulted her there by El Congo canyon, up towards the line, and they were going to strangle her, she was confined in the Santa Ana hospital but now she's well recovered, I tell you because if I didn't you might get angry later for not having told you.

Your father, who loves you so much

Forgive the handwriting, but I wrote the letter in a hurry for Papa.
Carmen

Salvador Mendoza
Sonsonate, El Salvador
May 11, 1988

Rafael Mazariego
Los Angeles, CA

Esteemed friend,
... Rafael, before anything else I want you to forgive me for having hidden the day you came to say good-bye but I hope you understand that for me good-byes are very sad and I don't like saying good-bye to anyone, even more so to a great friend like you. Tell me how it's gone for you in this short time since you left for the U.S.A.

Whether the way was easy or difficult, I'd like to know so that I know what awaits me, because by Almighty God perhaps I'll succeed in reaching there this year or next. Mazariego I couldn't believe you would get there so soon but when Hugo told me that you had arrived I felt such joy, well I felt like it was I who had arrived there, and I congratulate you sincerely for your effort in doing what you had promised, since here one half-eats. Hugo told me your problem and one truly can't deny anything to a friend like you, although Hugo told me that no one should know, as for me, I'll do even the impossible to obtain anything you need since I look upon you as a brother.

Get this, today we are in the most critical phase of the negotiations, since the health management wants to measure its strength against the union's and they put in a clause they invented, and we crossed it out and had to suspend negotiations for that day, and we had thought of moving them to San Salvador but they gave up and we went on negotiating at the office, Mazariego forgive me for telling you all this but since I know that everything that's happening to us interests you, even though you are far away you don't stop being our work companion, much less my friend who some day by the grace of Almighty God I'll get to see again.

I'm surprised you haven't gotten in touch with Moris, my sister knows where he lives or maybe you haven't been able to talk with her, but I'd like you to do me a great favor, if you could try to get in touch with him, since I want you to tell him that his mama is really sad and that she just spends her time crying because she says he already forgot all of us, forgive me for taking advantage, but I know you are a great friend and that you'll be able to do it, I'm sending the telephone number here. . . .

Rafael I want you to realize how things are here since the arrival of the Guat technician, everything is really out of control, Julio missed making boss of the mechanic shop, a thing they denied him because he didn't have the engineer's title.

I again ask you to forgive my conduct but I hope you understand that it is really difficult to see a friend like you leave.

Anyway Rafael I wish you luck and I hope you write me soon and often.

Your friend ("The Russian")
Salvador Mendoza

. . . If Moris asks about David tell him that he doesn't have work and that he wants to go there.

Part II

★ ★ ★ ★ ★ ★ ★

. . . into America

Sylvia Martinez

from *Between the Lines*

Sylvia Martinez
Los Angeles, CA
March, 1989

The Martinez Family
Oaxaca, Mexico

My very dear family,
I hope that on receiving this letter you find yourselves in good health
and in God's good graces.

Mama, Lety and Nancy, I'll tell you all that things here are not as one
imagines, I'll recount them to you point by point.

1. On arriving in Los Angeles as usual I found the arrival very easy
because we ran through it with a person who spoke Spanish who took
us and directed us to Rosa's doors where I called Gaby, and when she
learned of my arrival her first words were why did you come, you're
going to see how things here aren't like you imagine them, her words at

bottom were from anger, to the point that at that moment I got angry, I took her words as though she wasn't going to offer me help, but it was the opposite, later she took us to her apartment which they share with another couple that's from Tlacolula and another who is a sister of the couple.

2. 1 went to visit grandma, where she'd become like a puppet, that is to say really skinny and sick, my aunt was very angry because I didn't have the delicacy to write her that I wasn't going to need the help they offered me, I told her the circumstances didn't present themselves, grandma complained that my uncle was saying words that were insulting her, and I told grandma that if he said something that what he said wasn't what it seemed, because your brother says jokes very seriously and grandma takes them as they come, that is to say, as if the words were true. Ay, Mama, when you're imagining that things or people are in very good shape what a letdown you can have. Your brother has suffered very much and I believe that same suffering has made him very hard; you'll ask why these words, because I imagined that my uncle was in another position, that is to say materially, I thought he had at least for starters a beautiful house, a beautiful living-room, kitchen, bedroom, etc., there's none of that, your brother isn't working anymore in what his work was in billboards, because there's so much competition, or that is they're giving away his job I don't know if they are Egyptians or Chinese, Hindus, so his work was reduced, he has or had problems both of morale and illness. We'll start with the morale, your niece Soledad left the house to live with her boyfriend and unfortunately your brother hit upon her jumping out the window with everything and a suitcase, your brother as usual let her make her decision and she decided to go live with her boyfriend, so your brother stripped her of all her possessions at once since it was all such depravity, or he saw to it that she'd be married even though he didn't like her boyfriend, and he pronounced the same words as your papa, that for him she had died and was buried, and grandma, I believe she was made to endure such great problems, as

usual she also endured this. Things have now calmed down and Soledad visits them sometimes. The other problem is Socrates, who was affected by the worm that comes in pork or in strawberries which reached his brain where he had convulsions but they immediately looked after him and he has a treatment in which they're killing the worm or animal and at the same time they're producing a little thing so that whether it's dead or alive the animal won't cause any damage in the brain, but I think the medicines are altering his character, and by what I saw I think they didn't tell me everything but I think that at any time he's going to have some reaction because according to their attentions and the instructions they give him and the worry that they have, I think that that says it all, and I think that they're in anguish. Anyway moving on to another point, I'm in touch with grandma often and I believe that is reviving her, and she tells me that she eats now and that she's mending a little more, and that she's still quite lucid.

3. Mother, Lety, Nancy, I'm going to recount another point to you, although in these moments that I'm croaking out these letters I feel so sad, because reflecting on it I'm going to be sincere, one's worthless here without English, you'll ask why do you say that Sylvia, because even though the people who live with Gaby say that they suffered much more, they're given to saying that we were lucky to run into them because like me, in two days I already had work. That begins my big problem, even though I was accompanied by Tomi, both she and I feel so demoralized because if we hadn't asked for help I don't know what would have happened, I think that not being able to get in touch with our people and not having an orientation we would have failed because people here don't have an amiable expression because even though they speak Spanish, if they know English they communicate in that language, this is a very sad city here because, you see, the buses here don't even fill up halfway and it's pure blacks driving them and everyone speaks English, you can't even ask them anything, and even if they want to they don't understand us, nor to communicate by telephone either because here

you have to know how to use the phone because here in Los Angeles it's divided into three areas, 818, 714, 213, and if you want to communicate with 818, you should dial a 1 first because now it's long distance and vice versa. And so until I knew, that's why the phone didn't work for us for the places we wanted to communicate with, and even though we asked nobody understood us and I asked someone who spoke Spanish and it's not like Mexico where they give you the information, they make like they don't notice you and like you didn't say anything to them, and I asked another person how much the phone cost, he would have said a dime or ten cents, none of that, nor do they offer you the dime like in Mexico nor a way to change the bill, another woman who saw us was observing us and she offered to change the bill, though somewhat suspicious I gave her a dollar, which they changed into 4 of 25 cents which they don't call by what they are here but by the name "coras." Here in this city by what we've seen they aren't a united people; here the good gambler wins. . . .

Another point. Mother this is from the 1st of April. Lety, mainly you, if you only knew, the 4 days that I was with Gaby were the ones when I talked with everyone, here until this letter reaches you I haven't pronounced anything in Spanish or in English either, it's as if I were mute. This drives you to despair, Lety. In the house where I'm working here like it or not I've got rules, at 8 everyone's sleeping already, so since I sleep with one of the girls the woman tells me to go into the room, I have to do many humiliating things here that I don't think you could put up with for anything. Lety I'll give you some advice, it would be better to get ahead in Mexico, in whatever part of Mexico but in our Mexico. . . . If you only knew, sincerely, what many people who have come to the United States have suffered, you'd be surprised the enormous things that have happened to them.

Warmly,
Sylvia Martinez

＊   ＊   ＊

Los Angeles, CA
July 2, 1989

The Martinez Family
Oaxaca, Mexico

My dear Mama,
. . . You ask me to do my bit from here until December, get this Mom,
when I talked to you I had lost hope from not getting work and afterwards I got myself in as a seamstress without even knowing how to run
a machine, and the first week I got 20 dollars, you'll say that just went
for the bus alone without any extra, then the next week 50, but then
they laid me off because production stopped and then I got in at another
place where I again got 50 dollars a week, and even though I try hard
to be quick I can't get more pieces out because for doing the hems they
pay me from 5 to 8 cents, but rather than being in Gaby's house and
not making anything I'm resigned to it for now, but it's making me
despair because I have to pay 100 dollars in rent, food. For nearly a
month Gaby gave me or is giving me meals, and not Everardo, because
Gaby works and it's her money that she helps me with. I'll see how it
goes for me later but if it's not possible, instead of earning and staying
here owing money it would be better for me to go back because if I
don't I'd stay here in debt to my sister and my debts would never end,
and if I managed to finish off one debt there, now I'm indebted to her.
Anyway I'm going to do everything possible to mend my situation.

You tell me that Victor came and that you gave him the phone number but he never got in touch, that'll be because I didn't write him and
I believe he'd say there isn't that intimacy anymore. Anyway I'll write to
him so that in his own hand he can tell me how he is because they told
me he's there now.

Anyway, I'll think about what you ask me in your letter, that I talk to my uncle.

I received the photo and when I'm alone I'll get to look at it; Mama, since you mention it, I'll write to my uncle but will tell him nothing about the situation here; I'll talk about something else instead.

Anyway about the thing that was sold or that my uncle sold, well I'm sorry because unintentionally the nucleus of the family is being lost.

Well I'll tell you about the quake we went through here, since I went to work downtown, 8th and Broadway, it's the nucleus of Los Angeles, in a 10-story building or it could be more stories but I was on the 6th floor, and it felt horrible, at that moment I thought about you all and that I was very far away from you; the buildings look horrible when they move and one feels a movement that I couldn't explain to you, that second I got very nervous and my hands got really cold and I just commended myself to God because I found myself alone in that building. Anyway thanks to Him all that is now passed.

Warmly,
Sylvia Martinez

Jamaica Kincaid

from *Lucy*

Poor Visitor

It was my first day. I had come the night before, a gray-black and cold night before—as it was expected to be in the middle of January, though I didn't know that at the time—and I could not see anything clearly on the way in from the airport, even though there were lights everywhere. As we drove along, someone would single out to me a famous building, an important street, a park, a bridge that when built was thought to be a spectacle. In a daydream I used to have, all these places were points of happiness to me; all these places were lifeboats to my small drowning soul, for I would imagine myself entering and leaving them, and just that—entering and leaving over and over again—would see me through a bad feeling I did not have a name for. I only knew it felt a little like sadness but heavier than that. Now that I saw these places, they looked ordinary, dirty, worn down by so many people entering and leaving them in real life, and it occurred to me that I could not be the only person in the world for whom they were a fixture of fantasy. It was not my first bout with the disappointment of reality and it would not be my last. The undergarments that I wore were all new, bought for my journey, and as I sat in the car, twisting this way and that to get a good view of the sights before me, I was reminded of how uncomfortable the new can make you feel.

I got into an elevator, something I had never done before, and then I was in an apartment and seated at a table, eating food just taken from a refrigerator. In the place I had just come from, I always lived in a house, and my house did not have a refrigerator in it. Everything I was experiencing—the ride in the elevator, being in an apartment, eating day-old food that had been stored in a refrigerator—was such a good idea that I could imagine I would grow used to it and like it very much, but at first it was all so new that I had to smile with my mouth turned down at the corners. I slept soundly that night, but it wasn't because I was happy and comfortable—quite the opposite; it was because I didn't want to take in anything else.

That morning, the morning of my first day, the morning that followed my first night, was a sunny morning. It was not the sort of bright sun-yellow making everything curl at the edges, almost in fright, that I was used to, but a pale-yellow sun, as if the sun had grown weak from trying too hard to shine; but still it was sunny, and that was nice and made me miss my home less. And so, seeing the sun, I got up and put on a dress, a gay dress made out of madras cloth—the same sort of dress that I would wear if I were at home and setting out for a day in the country. It was all wrong. The sun was shining but the air was cold. It was the middle of January, after all. But I did not know that the sun could shine and the air remain cold; no one had ever told me. What a feeling that was! How can I explain? Something I had always known—the way I knew my skin was the color brown of a nut rubbed repeatedly with a soft cloth, or the way I knew my own name something I took completely for granted, "the sun is shining, the air is warm," was not so. I was no longer in a tropical zone, and this realization now entered my life like a flow of water dividing formerly dry and solid ground, creating two banks, one of which was my past—so familiar and predictable that, even my unhappiness then made me happy now just to think of it—the other my future, a gray blank, an overcast seascape on which rain was falling and no boats were in sight. I was no longer in a tropical zone and I felt cold inside and out, the first time such a sensation had come over me.

In books I had read—from time to time, when the plot called for it—someone would suffer from homesickness. A person would leave a not very nice situation and go somewhere else, somewhere a lot better, and then long to go back where it was not very nice. How impatient I would become with such a person, for I would feel that I was in a not very nice situation myself, and how I wanted to go somewhere else. But now I, too, felt that I wanted to be back where I came from. I understood it. I knew where I stood there. If I had had to draw a picture of my future then, it would have been a large gray patch surrounded by black, blacker, blackest.

What a surprise this was to me, that I longed to be back in the place that I came from, that I longed to sleep in a bed I had outgrown, that I longed to be with people whose smallest, most natural gesture would call up in me such a rage that I longed to see them all dead at my feet. Oh, I had imagined that with my one swift act—leaving home and coming to this new place—I could leave behind me, as if it were an old garment never to be worn again, my sad thoughts, my sad feelings, and my discontent with life in general as it presented itself to me. In the past, the thought of being in my present situation had been a comfort, but now I did not even have this to look forward to, and so I lay down on my bed and dreamt I was eating a bowl of pink mullet and green figs cooked in coconut milk, and it had been cooked by my grandmother, which was why the taste of it pleased me so, for she was the person I liked best in all the world and those were the things I liked best to eat also.

The room in which I lay was a small room just off the kitchen—the maid's room. I was used to a small room, but this was a different sort of small room. The ceiling was very high and the walls went all the way up to the ceiling, enclosing the room like a box—a box in which cargo traveling a long way should be shipped. But I was not cargo. I was only an unhappy young woman living in a maid's room, and I was not even the maid. I was the young girl who watches over the children and goes to school at night. How nice everyone was to me, though, saying that I should regard them as my family and make myself at home. I believed them to be sincere, for I knew that such a thing would not be said to a member of their real family. After all, aren't family the people who become the millstone around your life's neck? On the last day I spent at home, my cousin—a girl I had known all my life, an unpleasant person even before her parents forced her to become a Seventh Day Adventist—made a farewell present to me of her own Bible, and with it she made a little speech about God and goodness and blessings. Now it sat before me on a dresser, and I remembered how when we were children we would sit under my house and terrify and torment each other by reading out loud passages from the Book of Revelation, and I wondered if ever in my whole life a day would go by when these people I had left behind, my own family, would not appear before me in one way or another.

There was also a small radio on this dresser, and I had turned it on. At that moment, almost as if to sum up how I was feeling, a song came on, some of the words of which were "Put yourself in my place, if only for a day; see if you can stand the awful emptiness inside." I sang these words to myself over and over, as if they were a lullaby, and I fell asleep again. I dreamt then that I was holding in my hands one of my old cotton-flannel nightgowns, and it was printed with beautiful scenes of children playing with Christmas-tree decorations. The scenes printed on my nightgown were so real that I could actually hear the children laughing. I felt compelled to know where this nightgown came from, and I started to examine it furiously, looking for the label. I found it just where a label usually is, in the back, and it read "Made in Australia." I was awakened from this dream by the actual maid, a woman who had let me know right away, on meeting me, that she did not like me, and gave as her reason the way I talked. I thought it was because of something else, but I did not know what. As I opened my eyes, the word "Australia" stood between our faces, and I remembered then that Australia was settled as a prison for bad people, people so bad that they couldn't be put in a prison in their own country.

My waking hours soon took on a routine. I walked four small girls to their school, and when they returned at midday I gave them a lunch of soup from a tin, and sandwiches. In the afternoon, I read to them and played with them. When they were away, I studied my books, and at night I went to school. I was unhappy. I looked at a map. An ocean stood between me and the place I came from, but would it have made a difference if it had been a teacup of water? I could not go back.

Outside, always it was cold, and everyone said that it was the coldest winter they had ever experienced; but the way they said it made me think they said this every time winter came around. And I couldn't blame them for not really remembering each year how unpleasant, how unfriendly winter weather could be. The trees with their bare, still limbs looked dead, and as if someone had just placed them there and planned to come back and get them later; all the windows of the houses were shut tight, the way windows are shut up when a house will be empty for a long time; when people walked on the streets they did it quickly, as if they were doing something behind someone's back, as if they didn't want to draw attention to themselves, as if being out in the cold too long would cause them to dissolve. How I longed to see someone lingering on a corner, trying to draw my attention to him, trying to engage me in conversation, someone complaining to himself in a voice I could overhear about a God whose love and mercy fell on the just and the unjust.

I wrote home to say how lovely everything was, and I used flourishing words and phrases, as if I were living life in a greeting card—the kind that has a satin ribbon on it, and quilted hearts and roses, and is expected to be so precious to the person receiving it that the manufacturer has placed a leaf of plastic on the front to protect it. Everyone I wrote to said how nice it was to hear from me, how nice it was to know that I was doing well, that I was very much missed, and that they couldn't wait until the day came when I returned.

One day the maid who said she did not like me because of the way I talked told me that she was sure I could not dance. She said that I spoke like a nun, I walked like one also, and that everything about me was so pious it made her feel at once sick to her stomach and sick with pity just to look at me. And so, perhaps giving way to the latter feeling, she said that we should dance, even though she was quite sure I didn't know how. There was a little portable record-player in my room, the kind that when closed up looked like a ladies' vanity case, and she put on a record she had bought earlier that day. It was a song that was very popular at the time—three girls, not older than I was, singing in harmony and in a very insincere and artificial way about love and so on. It was very beautiful all the same, and it was beautiful because it was so insincere and artificial. She enjoyed this song, singing at the top of her voice, and she was a wonderful dancer—it amazed me to see the way in which she moved. I could not join her and I told her why: the melodies of her song were so shallow, and the words, to me, were meaningless. From her face, I could see she had only one feeling about me: how sick to her stomach I made her. And so I said that I knew songs, too, and I burst into a calypso about a girl who ran away to Port-of-Spain, Trinidad, and had a good time, with no regrets.

The household in which I lived was made up of a husband, a wife, and the four girl children. The husband and wife looked alike and their four children looked just like them. In photographs of themselves, which they placed all over the house, their six yellow-haired heads of various sizes were bunched as if they were a bouquet of flowers tied together by an unseen string. In the pictures, they smiled out at the world, giving the impression that they found everything in it unbearably wonderful. And it was not a farce, their smiles. From wherever they had gone, and they seemed to have been all over the world, they brought back some tiny memento, and they could each recite its history from its very beginnings. Even when a little rain fell, they would admire the way it streaked through the blank air.

At dinner, when we sat down at the table and did not have to say grace (such a relief; as if they believed in a God that did not have to be thanked every time you turned around)—they said such nice things to each other, and the children were so happy. They would spill their food, or not eat any of it at all, or make up rhymes about it that would end with the words "smelt bad." How they made me laugh, and I wondered what sort of parents I must have had, for even to think of such words in their presence I would have been scolded severely, and I vowed that if I ever had children I would make sure that the first words out of their mouths were bad ones.

It was at dinner one night not long after I began to live with them that they began to call me the Visitor. They said I seemed not to be a part of things, as if I didn't live in their house with them, as if they weren't like a family to me, as if I were just passing through, just saying one long Hallo!, and soon would be saying a quick Goodbye! So long! It was very nice! For look at the way I stared at them as they ate, Lewis said. Had I never seen anyone put a forkful of French-cut green beans in his mouth before? This made Mariah laugh, but almost everything Lewis said made Mariah happy and so she would laugh. I didn't laugh, though, and Lewis looked at me, concern on his face. He said, "Poor Visitor, poor Visitor," over and over, a sympathetic tone to his voice, and then he told me a story about an uncle he had who had gone to Canada and raised monkeys, and of how after a while the uncle loved monkeys so much and was so used to being around them that he found actual human beings hard to take. He had told me this story about his uncle before, and while he was telling it to me this time I was remembering a dream I had had about them: Lewis was chasing me around the house. I wasn't wearing any clothes. The ground on which I was running was yellow, as if it had been paved with cornmeal. Lewis was chasing me around and around the house, and though he came close he could never catch up with me. Mariah stood at the open windows saying, Catch her, Lewis, catch her. Eventually I fell down a hole, at the bottom of which were some silver and blue snakes.

When Lewis finished telling his story, I told them my dream. When I finished, they both fell silent. Then they looked at me and Mariah cleared her throat, but it was obvious from the way she did it that her throat did not need clearing at all. Their two yellow heads swam toward each other and, in unison, bobbed up and down. Lewis made a clucking noise, then said, Poor, poor Visitor. And Mariah said, Dr. Freud for Visitor, and I wondered why she said that, for I did not know who Dr. Freud was. Then they laughed in a soft, kind way. I had meant by telling them my dream that I had taken them in, because only people who were very important to me had ever shown up in my dreams. I did not know if they understood that.

Gary Pak

Hae Soon's Song

"What you have to do," Suzy said matter-of-factly in Korean, "is let them feel your breasts." She sipped her soft drink through a thin plastic straw, then gazed across the empty dance floor, humming a few bars of Bruce Springsteen's "Dancing in the Dark." "But what they really like is when you fondle them."

Hae Soon, sitting across the table from Suzy, bowed her head in embarrassment.

"Let them touch you a little, just enough," Suzy continued, like a well-meaning older sister. "Otherwise, they'll order one drink and leave for another place. Or worst yet, they'll give their business to one of the *other* girls." She glared at the bar where the other hostesses were gathered.

With a tilt of her head, Suzy tossed ringlets of her lightened hair from one side of her face to the other. "And why don't you go to a hairdresser and have something done to your hair? You look like a little school girl." She waited for an answer. There was none. She shook her head. "I don't get it. I don't know why you want to work here. You've worked here for a week and all you're doing is wasting your time, your money. You haven't made enough even to tip the bar and housemother or to pay the taxi fare home. This really puzzles me."

"I'm managing," Hae Soon answered quickly, also in Korean. "And I don't have to—"

"And who are you calling cheap? Not me, I hope."

"I didn't say that."

"But that's what you were going to say. Just remember that I'm showing you all this because our families come from the same province. I don't have to do this, you know."

Hae Soon lowered her eyes. "No, I didn't mean it that way," she said.

Hanging from the ceiling, a rotating disco ball was showering the dance floor with spots of bright light.

Hae Soon turned towards the bar and regarded Jimmy Choi, the tired-eyed bartender, who was leaning against the cash register and watching the television set mounted from the ceiling. His baggy eyes, his sagging cheeks—*he looks like one of those fat-faced house dogs—what did they call them?—beagles?—the kind of dog that the American colonel's wife always brought into father's shop?* She read the time on the clock, then returned to Suzy, but only for a moment, afraid that Suzy might unleash her terrible temper again. Yes, she should be fortunate that Suzy had gotten her the job. Jobs were hard to find in Hawai'i, especially if one is an immigrant with very limited English.

But she never imagined that she would be a bargirl.

They were outcasts, treated like dirt, those women in the doorways.

On the way home from school to her father's modest tailor shop that was tucked in a narrow alley, downtown Seoul, she would pass the clubs with brassy music pouring out of the doorways. Those doorways that smelled of rice wine and perfume. On slow days, the girls would gather out front, their glossy tight skirts with slits on the sides showing their sleek white thighs, their cheeks powdered and lips painted red. And when they saw Hae Soon or any of her school girlfriends, they'd call out,

"Pretty little girl! Ah! Pretty little girl!" Then, one day, one of the bargirls befriended Hae Soon—her name was Min Ja—and Min Ja gave Hae Soon a piece of wheat candy. The next day Min Ja called Hae Soon to an empty stool next to the doorway. Hae Soon sat, and they talked about Hae Soon's school, about Min Ja's home in Kwangju—they talked about Min Ja's picking of ripened persimmons and her grandmother making honeyed rice cakes—and they talked until the long shadows of passersby suggested the coming of darkness. And when Hae Soon arrived at her father's shop, she received a terrible scolding. But Hae Soon returned to that doorway and Min Ja who always had a stool and a candied treat for her. And then one time Min Ja quietly began braiding Hae Soon's hair, and after a while Hae Soon glanced back and saw that tears were in Min Ja's eyes, her eyes were blackening, dark streams of tears were dripping down her cheeks. *Why are Min Ja's tears black?*

They're bad women, her mother told her, *don't even think of looking in there. And never walk past there again. Do you know what people will say if they see you there? Do you? Do you?! If you go past there again, I will tell your father.*

So she stopped walking that route from school, for a long while. But one day she passed that doorway again. Every day she had thought about her friend Min Ja, and she missed her friend: the way Min Ja combed and braided her hair, her stories of her childhood, her soft pleasant voice. Hae Soon heard American rock 'n roll music blaring out of the dark doorway. She slowed her walk to a stop and stared into the establishment, which she had never entered, squinting her eyes at the loud and abusive music that made her ears ring. Before she could call for Min Ja, one of the other girls came out and greeted Hae Soon. *Are you looking for Min Ja? Lucky girl! She's gone off and gotten married to a rich man.*

Hae Soon ran from there, as fast as the flight of a newspaper down a gusty downtown street, *as fast as the frolicking run of a mountain stream, running over slippery rocks,* past crocks and carts of food, past the vendors' tables of bright goods, *past the darting fish,* past the scattering cats of smelly trash heaps. She didn't know why she was running. Was it because she was afraid to be caught dead in front of that house of the dark doorway? Was it because Min Ja had left without telling her? And when she was a good distance away, a block from her father's shop, she ran into a dirty, urine-smelling alley, leaned her head against the brick wall and cried.

"Look at her! Look at her, Hae Soon! Hae Soon? Hae Soon?! Look at her . . . there, at the bar. Last month she wasn't that big. Oh, my! No wonder I haven't seen her all this time. Where did she get the money to get those breasts? Her boyfriend, probably. She did it for him. Yes. He's an attorney. Hmph! So who cares?!"

Hae Soon surveyed the girl in the low-cut red evening dress. She sipped her Coke and brought her hands together on her lap, forming a folded fan.

"You know," Suzy said, narrowing her eyes, "I introduced her to him. And she took him away from me. He was *my* boyfriend."

He was a poet. His name was Yong Gil. She met him at the university where he was student of literature and modern poetics. He was young and brilliant, handsome and brave. He wrote poetry that was powerful and beautiful, each word full with lifemeaning. One day, a month after they had been going together, he presented her with a book of poems, each poem a love ode to her. He explained to her that the book was two years in the making, the time he had endured a distant, feverish love for her.

And he of course wrote other poems, mainly poems of his great love for legendary Kumgansan—the Diamond Mountains—though he had never seen them since the mountains were part of the prohibited North. *The mountains are brave mountains,* Yong Gil told her. *Kumgansan are like the Korean people, standing strong and battling invaders and destroyers of everything Korean.*

It was romantic, being with Yong Gil. Romantic.

Her father did not like him. Yong Gil was too outspoken: he openly criticized the Chun Do Hwan government as being a fascist dictatorship and a puppet of American imperialism. He was a known subversive. He had been arrested once, maybe two or three times. But Hae Soon could not listen to her father: she was in love with Yong Gil and his vision of Kumgansan. At those secret student meetings, she watched Yong Gil speak, her eyes fixed on him, her face like a flower opening to a morning sun. And in the bitter, long winter nights, their bodies as one melted the ice of the air.

"Let's go dancing tonight," Suzy said, her voice flat. She began humming the popular Korean song that was now playing on the jukebox, the song about the Man with the Yellow Shirt:

I don't know why, but I like him,
That Man with the Yellow Shirt.
I don't know why, but I like him,
That Man with the Yellow Shirt.

Hae Soon stared at Suzy, her thoughts of Yong Gil vanishing softly into the dark, empty atmosphere. "Yes? What is it?"

"There you go again," Suzy grumbled. "Always in your dream cloud. That's why the other girls out hustle you all the time. That, plus you don't put out. Do you really want to work here?"

Hae Soon straightened up. "Have some customers come in?"

"No—no—silly! How are we going to have customers on a dead night like tonight?" She looked away, shaking her head. "Look. Let's go dancing tonight. We could go down to Seoul Palace. I know the bartender there. He and I used to work at the Bluebird Lounge on Ke'eaumoku. He's really nice. And he has a cute brother working with him. Maybe I could introduce you . . ."

Hae Soon shook her head.

"Oh! You're no fun!" Suzy folded her arms over her chest and sank as low as she could in her seat. "I don't know why you work here. All you do is sit around and sip your Coke. And dream. How do you expect to make a living in Hawai'i? And you with a child to support. You have to hustle. Work hard. Oh . . . I don't know why I talk to you."

Hae Soon's eyes moistened. Gently she dabbed her eyes with a paper napkin so as not to smear the mascara.

"Oh, I'm sorry," Suzy offered. "You know me. When it gets slow like tonight, I get this way. You're my friend. Our families come from the same province. It's like we know each other for a long time. Right?" She paused to check on an entering customer. Without looking around, the older local Asian man sat at the bar. "Look. I'm sorry I told you these things. All right? You forgive me?"

Hae Soon forced a smile and nodded her head. "It's all right. I know . . . I've . . . I've been stubborn."

"We're all like that. And we're all in this same disgusting boat. *Aiigoo!*"

"Maybe we can go dancing tonight?"

Suzy's eyes lit up. "All right . . . if you want to. And I'll introduce you to Tong Sul's cute brother."

Hae Soon waved off the match-making suggestion, shaking her head. "No—no arrangement. All right? Please?"

"You're still in love with him, aren't you?"

Hae Soon nodded, a shy smile rising to her face.

"Oh . . . come on," Suzy said, taking Hae Soon's hand. "You can be honest with me. I can understand. I was in love once, too." Suzy's eyes became distant. She let Hae Soon's hand go. "Sometimes . . . I wonder what is it like to be in love again. It's been such a long time." Suzy's eyes reached across the dance floor for the country love song playing on the jukebox. "What is his name again?"

"Yong Gil."

It was spring, and they had eloped. It was a beautiful time of the year. The air was warm and the earth fecund, and the blossoms on the apple and persimmon trees threw their ripe redolence into the air. And those wonderfully romantic and hectic days of love and lust and demonstrations against the ruling order lasted for all that spring and into an eruptive summer.

They had fallen asleep after a night of lovemaking when the police broke down their door. They beat a bewildered, naked and struggling Yong Gil, then handcuffed him. They grabbed her womanparts and came near raping her with their batons in front of Yong Gil with his mouth of broken teeth when their professor-friend, from whom they rented the small cottage, came storming out of the main house and demanded that the police leave immediately. They threw Hae Soon down on the floor, even with her showing five-months, and started on the professor, slashing a baton across his face, then smashing his face into a whimpering mess. But they left without further touching her: maybe they were overdue at the station, perhaps they had to hustle up more radicals for their nightly quota. *Those dogs! They dragged Yong Gil clutching only a blanket for cover.*

"Yong Gil," Suzy mused. "That's a nice name. Of course, he must be very handsome. You say he is very smart, too?"

> Yong Gil. I will love no one else but you. Forever.
> Willow weeps like a thousand cranes
> With heads bowed
> *And legs crossed:*
> A hunger for fish they feel.
> We hide under its branches,
> Hear its weeping

And feel our hunger
Cursed from birth.

But far away loom majestic mountains
Of diamond spires and sides of jade
And topped with emeralds.
We may be careless,
Wounded birds of love,
Pushed to and fro by cold harsh winds,
But when we reach the jeweled mountains,
The ugly scars from hate
Will disappear.
We'll love again:
Love seeds new love.

"What did you say?" Suzy asked, her eyes wide with curiosity.

"Huh? Oh . . . Yong Gil. His name is Yong Gil."

"Yes, you told me that. But what was it you were saying after that?"

"Oh, I don't know." Hae Soon shook her head with embarrassment. "I don't remember."

Suzy frowned. "All right, you don't have to tell me. But tell me this. Why did you come to Hawai'i where there are no good jobs? The only thing a woman can do here is to work in a bar."

"I told you before."

"But I want to hear it again. Besides, what else is there to talk about? Is there any excitement in our lives?" Suzy spun a hard look over the crowdless room.

"I had to leave," Hae Soon said, biting her words.

"But you said you were a high school teacher. You had a good job in Seoul. You leave a good job to come here to make money hustling in a bar? You had a future in Korea. And anyway, what good is a teacher in America who can't speak English?"

"Let's go dancing tonight!"

Suzy threw her hands in the air. "All right. If you don't want to talk about it. You just get me all upset. You don't even confide in me. After all, I'm your only friend in Hawai'i."

Yes, a good friend in Hawai'i. But you wouldn't understand. You can't understand.

A customer staggered into the lounge, an old gray man, local Oriental. Immediately Suzy jumped up to greet him before the other girls could slide off their stools. Holding the old man's hand, she led him to a dim corner of the lounge and sat him down. Shortly after, she ordered at the bar, plunked a few quarters into the jukebox and made her selection of popular Japanese songs. Then she glided over to Hae Soon.

"The old man says that his friends are going to join him in a little while. When they come, join us. I've been with them before. They like to touch a lot, but they're big spenders."

Hae Soon watched Suzy's lean swaying hips as she sashayed to the bar to pick up the order.

Maybe I should walk like her. No. What am I saying?

She regarded the large digital clock behind the bar. Time was hardly passing tonight. And how long ago was it when she left Korea and Yong Gil? Seven months ago? A year? Ten years?

Why did she leave?

That ancient bronze bell used to resound over the university campus, signaling the end of the class period. She would wait for him down by the ancient royal fishponds, and there they'd walk hand-in-hand, something they couldn't do in public. And the nights they'd spend locked up in one of the stuffy study rooms in the library: alone, trusting, warm skin on warm skin.

Oh, Yong Gil! Why did they take you away? Do you think about our son? How we live our lives so—

"Hae Soon! Hae Soon!" Suzy shook Hae Soon on the shoulder. "What's the matter with you?"

Hae Soon straightened up and blinked, startled by Suzy's round, piercing eyes.

"Come on, Hae Soon. His friends are here. Quickly—before the others beat you to them!"

Hae Soon fumbled for her handbag—*oh, it's behind the bar, I forgot*—then sidled out of the booth. Straightening her dress borrowed from Suzy's copious and silky wardrobe, she followed her friend obediently, past empty booths to the carousing men. Suzy glanced over her shoulders, gave Hae Soon a look of warning, then wiggled and smiled and laughed as she joined the men, settling herself between two of them.

Hae Soon found herself smiling. And, mildly surprised that the effort was easier than she thought, she was copying Suzy's waltzing steps. The noticing men rejoiced with her arrival. One of them flashed his gold teeth, which shone dull and warm in the semi-darkness. Hae Soon sat down in the booth across from Suzy. The table was covered with bottles of beer and platters of food. She poured beer into the glass of the strongly cologne-scented man sitting next to her.

"What's your name?" the man asked.

"My nam-ah? Oh—Hae Soon."

"No!" interrupted Suzy, emphatically shaking her head, then smiling. "Her name ez—her name ez—eh—Eva."

"How are you, Eva?" the man said with a smile. "How come you dunno yo' name?" The men laughed. "Eva, how 'bout you bring me and my friends one 'nother round?"

"Go to Jimmy and order three Budweisers," Suzy interpreted in Korean.

Hae Soon nodded her head and went to the bar. She gave the order to Jimmy Choi, then turned to the other hostesses and smiled. They were whispering among themselves, avoiding eye contact with her. Hae Soon paid Jimmy, then returned to the table with the order.

Suzy was in the arms of the grayish man, playfully diverting his hands from entering the openings of her dress.

Hae Soon looked away and served the beer. The strongly scented man patted the empty seat next to him. Reluctantly, she sat down, folding her arms across her chest.

"You pretty," the man said. "How long you stay here in Hawai'i?"

She shrugged her shoulders. Suzy tapped Hae Soon in the shin with the toe of her shoe, then translated into Korean the question for her.

"Oh—I t'ink so—fo' month-soo—already."

"You speak good English. My friends and me, all the time we come dis bar, but first time we see you. How long you been working here?"

She nodded, though not understanding what he had said.

He put his arm around her shoulders. Hae Soon shivered. "You have beautiful skin." He ran his hand up and down her arm.

Hae Soon looked at Suzy for help, but the grayish man's hand was all over Suzy's chest now, and Suzy's hand was lowered somewhere in his groin, out of Hae Soon's view. She closed her eyes, wishing she was imagining what she was seeing. Then the man next to her slipped his hand under her arms. She resisted, shaking off the advance. He grinned, snickered, and pursued more, his other hand gripping her outside shoulder, bringing her tighter into his snare. The man persisted, and she refused him, but finally, finally, she let him in, loosening the lock of her arms though not dropping them. The man found a breast and squeezed it. It hurt her. He kissed her on the cheek, his alcoholic breath burning her skin, that thick cologne smell rubbing off on her face. She trembled. She fought back a cry.

"You're very pretty."

"I—come back—hokay?"

"No," the man said, holding her down. "I like you here. You stay here and take care of me, and I take care of you." He pointed with his eyes to a small pile of money at the edge of the table.

Suzy was laughing. "Isn't this fun?" she said in Korean. "This old man is so small, but he's so funny."

The men finished their beers and asked for another round. Hae Soon leaped out of the booth, straightening her bra, and went to the bar before Suzy could unstrap the gray man's arms. She put in the order. The girls on the stools were giggling at her. Embarrassed, Hae Soon looked the other way, towards the open front door. It was raining outside. She thought of walking out.

They were walking in the rain the day she told him that she was pregnant. He was silent for a long while, his face furrowed with anxiety. Then, suddenly, he leaped ahead of her, jumping up and down while clapping his hands and shouting to the world, "I'm going to be a father! I'm going to be a father!" He dropped to his knees and begged her to marry him.

She could not answer. She was crying. She had never seen before Yong Gil so deliriously happy. It shook her. But she took his head and pressed it against her womb.

Can you feel our baby breathe, my love?
Can you feel our baby move?
Can you hear the beating heart
Like wings fluttering,
A thousand doves
Descending from the Heavens?

Hae Soon glanced back at the booth. Suzy was laughing with the men. Hae Soon didn't want to return. But the money. The money.

His face was battered, though his eyes were alert and filled with anger.
"Yong Gil!!"

"Shut up, whore! Hurry up! Get him out of here."

"And the other?" Pointing to the professor unconscious on the ground.

"Leave him. Hurry up! Let's go!"

His mouth opened, but his words were broken, unspeakable. He spat out a bloody tooth, then another. Coughed. In desperation he made weak gestures—his hands, arms, head—trying to convey the message to her: *Stomach?—Baby?—Are you all right?*

They handcuffed him and dragged him out the door on his bare ass.

Yong Gil, please understand. It's all for little Yong Gil, little one. So he can grow up big and strong, return home to find his father. And he'll get back at them, those bastards, sons of bastard pigs, for humiliating his father—

"Hae Soon?! What are you doing?" Suzy. "They're waiting and waiting for their drinks. Are you dreaming again?"

"I—I'm coming."

"And call yourself *Eva*. Don't you like that name?"

Jimmy Choi stared at her, then grinned at the other girls: What's wrong with this bitch?

"Oh—yes—"

"Come on. They're waiting." Suzy scurried back to the table.

Hae Soon paid the bartender, then hurried back to the booth.

"How come took you so long?" the cologne man asked.

Hae Soon forced a smile.

The man said something to his friend. They looked at her and grinned.

"Charlie says he like to date you," the man said. "But I tol' him fo' get lost. You mine tonight, eh, sweetheart?"

The man smiled broadly, showing his gold teeth. He corralled her with a large arm and kissed her on the cheek. He tried to touch her breast again, but Hae Soon pushed his thick calloused hands away. He forced his hand up her dress and grabbed her crotch. She shrieked, squirmed out of his grasp and jumped out of the booth. She grabbed an empty bottle from the table and broke it on his face.

"Hae Soon!!"

She grabbed the money and threw it at the men.

Suzy leaped out of her seat and tangled her arms with Hae Soon's. "Stop it!! Hae Soon!!"

The bottle had cut the man's cheek. Blood was streaming out of the wound. With anger and disbelief, the man stared at the blood dripping on his hand, then cautiously touched his face. He lunged out of the booth.

"You cunt!"

He grabbed Suzy, who was in the way, by the hair and tossed her to the side where she fell like a crumpled puppet.

"You cunt!"

A blow sent Hae Soon flying into another table. The man lifted her and beat her with an open hand until Jimmy Choi and the man's drinking partners could restrain him.

"You cunt!"

From the floor, numbed of pain, she watched the struggle, the commotion, the madness, as if she was an outsider looking in. Two girls from the bar began mothering her, trying to help her up. She pushed them away, then shakily pulled herself up. She grabbed her handbag from the back of the bar and started towards the door. But she stopped halfway across the dance floor. With the swirling spots of light covering her, she glared at the dogs, spat at them, then marched out of the lounge.

The rain had stopped. The air was cool. The boulevard was empty of cars. She gazed at the dark sky and took a deep breath before taking off her shoes and nylons. A block from the lounge a taxi slowed down beside her. She waved it away. She had no money for a cab, nothing for food and rent that was due in another week. How could she and little

Yong Gil survive? On Yong Gil's thin volume of poetry? On sympathy from the dogs?

I don't know why, but I like him,
That Man with the Yellow Shirt.
I don't know why, but I like him,
That Man with the Yellow Shirt.

Judith Ortiz Cofer

Exile

I left my home behind me
but my past clings to my fingers
so that every word I write bears
the mark like a cancelled postage stamp
of my birthplace.
There was no angel to warn me
of the dangers of looking back.
Like Lot's wife, I would trade
my living blood for one last look
at the house where each window held
a face framed as in a family album.
And the plaza lined with palms
where my friends and I strolled in our pink
and yellow and white Sunday dresses, dreaming
of husbands, houses, and orchards where
our children would play in the leisurely summer
of our future. Gladly would I spill

my remaining years like salt upon the ground,
to gaze again on the fishermen of the bay
dragging their catch in nets glittering
like pirate gold, to the shore.
Nothing remains of that world, I hear,
but the skeletons of houses, all colors
bled from the fabric of those
who stayed behind
inhabiting the dead cities
like the shadows of Hiroshima.

Chang-rae Lee

from *Native Speaker*

I steadily entrenched myself in the routines of Kwang's office. When I wasn't out working with Janice, I was the willing guy Friday. I let the staffers know through painstaking displays of competence and efficiency that I was serious about the work however menial and clerical, and that I was ready to do what anyone of authority required. I was just the person they were looking for. I answered phones and made plasticene overheads and picked up dry cleaning and kids from day care. I had to show the staff that I possessed native intelligence but not so great a one or of a certain kind that it impeded my sense of duty.

This is never easy; you must be at once convincing and unremarkable. It takes long training and practice, an understanding of one's self-control and self-proportion: you must know your effective size in a given situation, the tenor at which you might best speak. Hoagland would talk for hours on the subject. He bemoaned the fact that Americans generally made the worst spies. Mostly he meant whites. Even with methodical training they were inclined to run off at the mouth, make unnecessary displays of themselves, unconsciously slip in the tiniest flourish that could scare off a nervous contact. An off-color anecdote, a laugh in the wrong place. They felt this subcutaneous aching to let everyone know they were a spook, they couldn't help it, it was like some charge or vanity of the culture, a la James Bond and Maxwell Smart.

"If I were running a big house like the CIA," Hoagland said to me once, "I'd breed agents by raising white kids in your standard Asian household. Discipline farms."

His Boys from Bushido.

I told him go ahead. Incubate. See what he got. He'd have platoons of guys like Pete Ichibata deployed about the globe, each too brilliant for his own good, whose primary modes were sorrow and parody. Then, too, regret. Pete makes a good spook but a good spook has no brothers, no sisters, no father or mother. He's intentionally lost that huge baggage, those encumbering remnants of blood and flesh, and because of this he carries no memory of a house, no memory of a land, he seems to have emerged from nowhere. He's brought himself forth, self-cesarean. If I see him at all. It is the picture of him silently whittling down fruitwood dowels into the most refined sets of chopsticks, the used-up squares of finishing sandpaper petaling about his desk amid the other detritus of peanut shells and wood shavings and peels of tangerine, the skins of everything he touches compulsively mined, strip-searched.

His friendly advice on how to handle Luzan was that I actively seek out his weaknesses, expose and use them to take him apart, limb from limb, cell by cell. Pete was a kind of anti-therapist, a professional who steadily ruined you session by session. He was a one-man crisis of faith. He was skilled enough in our work that he didn't simply listen, watch, wait; he poked and denuded and uncovered secrets while still remaining unextraordinary to the subject, making the subjects dismantle themselves through his care and guidance without their ever realizing it.

As part of my initial training I watched him work a Chinese graduate student at Columbia. The student was starting a doctorate in electrical engineering. He also organized rallies against the hard-liners in Beijing in the flag plaza of the UN.

Pete and I were supposedly working with a Japanese daily, the something something *Shimbun,* Pete the reporter and me in tow taking pictures. Wen Zhou, our subject, his face fleshy like a boy's, sat quietly for us in his tiny, orderly studio apartment in Morningside Heights. As my rented Nikkormat clicked and whirred, Pete plied him with the expected questions but then in a filial tone smattered with perfect Mandarin asked after his family and his studies and the long way he must feel from home. Pete then smoked a cigarette with him. I kept working the shutter, getting angles we didn't need, even though I'd long run out of film. The two of them joked about American girls. Pete tried to get me involved but I just grunted when he asked what I thought. Wen shyly said he didn't know any well but wouldn't mind meeting one. A date would be fun. He confessed to a fancy for those with reddish hair. Pete laughed and told him he knew a few and they ought to go drinking together and have a fun time, and then he asked Wen if he wasn't concerned for the safety of his loved ones back in China, with his face and name in the news. Wen said no one immediate, they were all living in Kowloon now, or some other place, but that yes there was one person, a young woman he'd befriended at the national university, a bright and ambitious girl from the southern provinces. He said he had stopped writing to her, so she wouldn't have any trouble.

Pete kept on him, talking so gently and sweetly that he seemed all the more furious in his discipline, and I thought he had to be murdering himself inside to hold the line like that. We had been there nearly an hour. In the second hour Wen broke. He opened like the great gates of the Forbidden City. Pete led us inside the walls. We got whole scrolls of names, people both here and in China, and even names of contributors (all of them minor, not even the stuff of trivia) who helped the students by paying for flyers and banners and the renting of meeting halls.

I was enjoying myself. I was thrilled with what we were doing, as with a discovery, like finding a new place you like, or a good book. I felt explicitly that secret living I'd known throughout my life, but now for the first time it took the form of a bizarre sanction being with Pete and even Wen. We laughed heartily together. We three thieves American. Wen was soon talking without prompts from Pete about his giant China, about the provinces, and poverty, the backwardness of people and leaders. It was both stony and nostalgic, the whole messy text of his homesickness. He liked New York City. The only other place he had been was West Lafayette, Indiana, doing a term of research at Purdue. "I guess I am a Boilermaker."

He spoke the sweetest, halting English. Caesurae abounding. He kept saying, "America and Japan strong, but China is the future place." He retrieved an album from below his sofa bed and showed us pictures of a collective farm where his father grew up, a full page of his grandmother, a shrunken woman with three teeth and skin the color of chestnuts, his mother and father and sister in the middle of Hong Kong harbor on a tour junk, overdressed, looking seagreen. And I thought I heard Pete say to him, "And you'll be back someday."

But then Wen said the name of the girl he loved. I knew immediately that she was doomed. I don't remember her name, maybe I forgot it instantly when he volunteered the thing. Rather what I recall exactly was Pete's face, which I caught reconfiguring, lamping up with the day's first piece of truly useful information. There was a joy there, if oblique, left-handed, and Wen probably thought here was a man with whom he could share a longing. I noticed earlier that Pete hadn't asked after her when Wen first brought her up. Of course he wasn't missing anything. Not a step. It's the simplest finesse, Dennis Hoagland lesson number one, and only effective with virginals like Wen, who would never imagine anything beyond a simple polarity to the world. Positive and negative. You couldn't fault him, for why would an immense China ever need a third party to reach a person like him, the tiniest of the tiny, so easily forgotten, whom no one ever listened to anyway?

The Kwang job was different. Nobody in the office was a cherry. This was street-level urban politics, conducted house by house, block by block, the work sweaty and inglorious. You could get mugged or beaten up if you strayed down an alley, or knocked on the wrong door. Bravery didn't matter. Nor raw smarts. You had to be tactical. Suspicious. Ready to admit your losses. Careful with the tongue.

And as Hoagland always said, "Brave like the gazelle."

In truth the setup was perfect for me. I had to agree with Dennis on that one. I didn't have to manufacture the circumstances in which I could ask questions that would get worthwhile answers. I didn't have to push too hard. Each day brought scores of regular people and visitors through the offices, and with all the lesser meetings and speeches Kwang attended to weekly, the countless minor moments, I witnessed what ertswhile observers—anthropologists and pundits alike—might have called his natural state.

His human clues. I'd sit in one corner of his office during the three hours on Wednesdays that he opened his door to speak with "walk-ins," the sundry visitors and neighborhood groups. By noon they'd be lined up in skeins outside the building, all kinds of people, people holding bags and children, people in suits, in smocks.

I sat in on the meetings with him and took notes. He wanted a record of each person and his or her concerns, and afterward I had to quickly interview them myself for their personal and biographical information. The office kept an electronic database of every voter and potential voter we encountered, and then those that it reached through regular mailers. With this body of files we could sift and sort through the population of the district by gender, race, ethnicity, party affiliation, occupation. We had names and birth dates of their children and relatives. Data on weekly income, what they paid in rent, in utilities, if they were on public assistance, how long. If they had been victims of crime. Their houses of worship. The languages they spoke, in rank of proficiency. The list always growing, profligate. Almost biblical.

On Fridays, John Kwang took home a stack of double-wide green-and-white printouts to commit to memory. It was something you eventually learned when you worked here: John Kwang was a devotee of memory. I thought it strange, first on the obvious level of why a busy and ambitious politician would devote any amount of time to memorizing lists of people he'd never need to know. Then I wondered if he wasn't simply odd, nervous. An uptight Korean man. What I eventually saw was that he never intended to know each live body in the district, his purpose wasn't statistical mastery, although that certainly happened. The memorizing was more a discipline for him, like a serious craft or martial art, a chosen kind of suffering involving hours of practice and concentration by which you gradually came to know yourself.

Late in the afternoon one Friday I was printing out the newest records in the war room. Kwang must have heard the whine of the machine and looked in. He caught me scanning the sheets. I was always good at memory games, and as a boy I annoyed my father by beating him if he slipped just once. But now, serene with Hoagland's method, my memory is fantastic, near diabolic. It arrests whatever appears before my eyes. I don't memorize anymore. I simply see.

When the printing was done I folded the sheaf in half so it would fit inside his briefcase. He took it graciously. He said nothing as I helped him with his light overcoat. I was ready for him to ask me what my interest in the printout was but instead he said if I wasn't busy he would like me to come have drink and good food with him. That was how he said it, drink and good food. Certain things he still expressed with a foreigner's simplicity. May and the boys were upstate for the week at their house on Cayuga Lake, and he said he wasn't in the mood to eat by himself. It was a strange thing to hear from a Korean man, and I wondered what circumstance would have had to arise for my father to profess openly a feeling like that.

"Learning the business, I see," John finally said, affably. We were walking outside. "In past times, a person's education was a matter of what he could remember. It still is in Korea and Japan. I must assume in China as well. Americans like to believe this is the great failing of Asia. Why the Japanese are good at copying and not inventing, which is no longer really true, if it ever was. I had a teacher who made us memorize scores of classical Chinese and Korean poems. We had to recite any one of them on command. He was hoping to give us knowledge, but what he actually impressed upon us was a legacy. He would smack the top of your head if you hadn't perfectly prepared the assignment, but then later in the class he could be overcome after reading a poem aloud."

He stopped to unlock the door for me. He drove a new Lincoln Continental. I noticed that he drove several different cars as well, and then only American models; a politician, especially an Asian-American one, doesn't have a choice in the matter. He had interests in car dealerships and a local chain of electronics stores, in addition to his core business of selling high-end dry-cleaning equipment.

"Young Master Lim," he said. "He was becoming a respected writer when the war broke out. We later heard that he was killed in the fighting. Sometime before the school was closed he said it was our solemn duty to act as vessels for our country and civilization, that we must give ourselves over to what had come before us, as much to literature as we did to our parents and ancestors. You look like him, I think. Around the eyes. Thick lidded."

"My mother's," I said.

"Ah. You know, Henry, why they're so? They're thick to keep the spirit warm and contented."

"I don't know if my mother would have said they worked," I told him.

"How about for you?" he asked.

I laughed a little bit and said, "They work perfectly."

We joked a little more, I thought like regular American men, faking, dipping, juking. I found myself listening to us. For despite how well he spoke, how perfectly he moved through the sounds of his words, I kept listening for the errant tone, the flag, the minor mistake that would tell of his original race. Although I had seen hours of him on videotape, there was something that I still couldn't abide in his speech. I couldn't help but think there was a mysterious dubbing going on, the very idea I wouldn't give quarter to when I would speak to strangers, the checkout girl, the mechanic, the professor, their faces dully awaiting my real speech, my truer talk and voice. When I was young I'd look in the mirror and address it, as if daring the boy there; I would say something dead and normal, like, "Pleased to make your acquaintance," and I could barely convince myself that it was I who was talking.

We hit the Friday night street traffic on 39th Avenue going west toward Corona. The restaurant was a dozen or so blocks farther than that, near Elmhurst, a new Korean barbecue house. He talked steadily through the stop and go, freely using his hands to punctuate his speech, the movements subtle but stylized, what I recognized as Anglo. The boycotts of Korean grocers were spreading from Brooklyn to other parts of the city, to black neighborhoods in the Bronx and even in his home borough, in the Williamsburg section, and then also in upper Manhattan. Though he wasn't having trouble in his own neighborhoods, he was being hounded by the media for statements and opinions on the mayor's handling of them, particularly the first riot in Brownsville, where a mostly black crowd, watched over by a handful of police, looted and arsoned a Korean-owned grocery.

"De Roos has positioned himself in the situation very skillfully," he said. "He denounces the violence but has Chillingsworth nearby to take the heat for letting things get out of hand. He has his lieutenants leak his concern about Chillingsworth's decision-making but then in public says he stands behind 'the commissioner's expertise and judgment.' "

Roy Chillingsworth was the police commissioner. He'd worked in New Orleans and Dade County, Florida, before being hired by De Roos early in the present term. He was a prosecuting attorney by training. He had a reputation for being tough on drug dealers and gangs and illegal immigrants. And he was black.

"No one ultimately faults the commissioner," Kwang said. "There weren't any deaths or injuries. Given that, it's almost acceptable that he didn't order in more police to arrest his own people. The mayor himself didn't lose any black confidence or votes. Perhaps he even gained some. All along, he offered himself as a model of liberal reaction, which is initially fascination and disdain, but then relief. It's a race war everyone can live with. Blacks and Koreans somehow seem meant for trouble in America. It was long coming. In some ways we never had a chance. But then, Henry, I imagine that you know these difficulties firsthand."

He knew my father had run vegetable stores in the city. I knew that Kwang might hear of this when I told Eduardo, given how close they seemed to be. I wasn't overly concerned in the beginning—nor were Dennis and Jack, for that matter—that I was employing my own life as material for my alter identity. Though to a much lesser extent, a certain borrowing is always required in our work. But this assignment made it, in fact, quite necessary to allow for more than the usual trade. When the line between identities is fine (and the situation is not dangerous), it's preferable not to build up a whole other, nearly parallel legend.

This, Jack had once told me, was the source of my troubles with Emile Luzan. Inconsistencies began to arise in crucial details, all of which I inexplicably confused and alternated. From the soft stuffed chair of his office I told the kind brown-faced doctor that my son had suffocated while playing alone with a plastic garbage bag, or that my American girlfriend was conducting extended research in Europe, or that my father had recently taken a second wife; and then in another session, in another week, I might tell him another set of near-truths, forget my conflations and hidings and offer him whatever lay immediately within my grasp.

Luzan himself was afraid I was unraveling. He held my hand to comfort me. He eventually recommended a course of medication. But for me it was simply loose, terrible business. The kind of display my father would not have tolerated in any member of his family. It would have sickened him.

Nobody give two damn about your problem or pain, he might say. *You just take care yourself. Keep it quiet.*

I didn't have to tell John Kwang the first thing about my father and our life, at least in relation to what he was talking about. I told him what my *ah-boh-jee* had done for work. Simply, it felt good not having to explain any further. To others you need to explain so much to get across anything worthwhile. It's not like a flavor that you can offer and have someone simply taste. The problem, you realize, is that while you have been raised to speak quietly and little, the notions of where you come from and who you are need a maximal approach. I used to wish that I were more like my Jewish and Italian friends, or even the black kids who hung out in front of my father's stores; I was envious of how they'd speak so confidently, so jubilantly celebrate the fact with their hands and hips and tongues, letting it all hang out (though of course in different ways) for anybody who'd look and listen.

As we passed the rows of Korean stores on the boulevard, John could tell me the names of the owners and previous owners. Mr. Kim, before him Park, Hong, then Cho, Im, Noh, Mrs. Yi. He himself once ran a wholesale shop on this very row, long before all of it became Korean in the 1980s. He sold and leased dry cleaning machines and commercial washers and dryers, only high-end equipment. He expanded quickly from the little neighborhood business, the street-front store, for he had mastered enough language to deal with non-Korean suppliers and distributors in other cities and Europe. Other Koreans depended on him to find good deals and transact them. Suddenly, he existed outside the intimate community of his family and church and the street where he conducted his commerce. He wasn't bound to 600 square feet of ghetto retail space like my father, who more or less duplicated the same basic store in various parts of the city. Those five stores defined the outer limit of his ambition, the necessary end of what he could conceive for himself. I am not saying that my father was not a remarkable and clever man, though I know of others like him who have reached farther into the land and grabbed hold of every last advantage and opportunity. My father simply did his job. Better than most, perhaps.

Kwang, though, kept pushing, adding to his wholesale stores by eventually leasing plants in North Carolina to assemble in part the machines he sold for the Italian and German manufacturers. He bought into car and electronics dealerships, too, though it was known that some of the businesses had been troubled in recent years, going without his full attention. The rumor was that he'd lost a few million at least. But he seemed to have plenty left. At the age of forty-one he started attending Fordham full-time for his law and business degrees. I have seen pictures of the graduation day hung about his house, Kwang and his wife, May, smiling in the bright afternoon light, bear-hugging each other. He passed the bar immediately, though I know he never intended to practice the law or big corporate business. He wanted the credentials. But that sounds too cynical of him, which would be all wrong. He wasn't vulnerable to that kind of pettiness. He was old-fashioned enough that he believed he needed proper intellectual training and expertise before he could serve the public.

"Henry," he said, "over there, on the far corner." There were two men talking and pointing at each other in the open street display of a wristwatch and handbag store. The lighted sign read H&J ENTER-PRISES, with smaller Korean characters on the ends. He pulled us over and I followed him out.

The owner recognized Kwang immediately, and stopped arguing with the other man and quickly bowed. The man was shaking a gold-toned watch: it had stopped working and he wanted his money back. The Korean explained to us that he only gave exchanges, no refunds, he seemed to say again for all, pointing continually at the sign that said so by the door. Besides, he told Kwang in Korean, this man bought the watch many months ago, during the winter, and he was being generous enough in offering him another one. He added, *You know how these blacks are, always expecting special treatment.*

Kwang let the statement pass. He introduced himself to the man, telling him he was a councilman. He asked the man if he had bought other things at the store.

"I stop here every couple weeks," the man answered. "Maybe pick out something for my wife."

"One time a *muhnt!*" the Korean insisted.

The man shook his head and mouthed, "Bullshit." He explained he'd originally come to get an exchange, but the owner was so rude and hard to understand (intentionally, he thought) that he decided to demand a full refund instead. He wasn't going to leave until he got one. He showed us the receipt. Kwang nodded and then gestured for the storekeeper to speak with him inside the store. I waited outside with the customer. I remember him particularly well because his name, Henry, was embossed on a tag clipped to his shirt pocket. When I told him my name he smiled weakly and looked in the store for Kwang. I didn't say anything else and he coughed and adjusted his glasses and said he was tired and frustrated and just wanted his money or an exchange so he could get on home. He was a salesman at the big discount office furniture store off 108th Street.

"I don't know why I keep shopping here," he said to me, searching the wares in the bins. "It's mostly junk anyway. My wife kind of enjoys the jewelry, though, and it's pretty inexpensive, I suppose. Buying a watch here was my mistake. I should know better. Thirteen ninety-nine. And I know I wasn't born yesterday."

We laughed a little. Henry explained that it was easy to stop here on

Fridays to buy something for his wife, a pair of earrings or a bracelet. "She works real hard all week and I like to give her a little present, to let her know I know what's going on." She was a registered nurse. He showed me a five-dollar set of silver earrings. "I was gonna buy these, but I don't know, you don't expect anybody to be *nice* anymore, but that man in there, he can be cold."

I didn't try to explain the store owner to Henry, or otherwise defend him. I don't know what stopped me. Maybe there was too much to say. Where to begin?

Certainly my father ran his stores with an iron attitude. It was amazing how successful he still was. He generally saw his customers as adversaries. He disliked the petty complaints about the prices, especially from the customers in Manhattan. "Those millionaires is biggest trouble," he often said when he got home. "They don't like anybody else making good money." He hated explaining to them why his prices were higher than at other stores, even the other Korean ones, though he always did. He would say without flinching that his produce was simply the best. The freshest. They should shop at other stores and see for themselves. He tried to put on a good face, but it irked him all the same.

With blacks he just turned to stone. He never bothered to explain prices to them. He didn't follow them around the aisles like some store-keepers do, but he always let them know there wasn't going to be any funny business here. When a young black man or woman came in—old people or those with children in tow didn't seem to alarm him—he took his broom and started sweeping at the store entrance very slowly, deliberately, not looking at the floor. He wouldn't make any attempt to hide what he was doing. At certain stores there were at least two or three incidents a day. Shoplifting, accusations of shoplifting, complaints and arguments. Always arguments.

To hear those cries now: the scene a stand of oranges, a wall of canned ham. I see my father in his white apron, sleeves rolled up. A woman in a dirty coat. They lean in and let each other have it, though the giving is almost in turns. It's like the most awful and sad opera, the strong music of his English, then her black English; her colorful, almost elevated, mocking of him, and his grim explosions. They fight like lovers, scarred, knowing. Their song circular and vicious. For she always comes back the next day, and so does he. It's like they are here to torture each other. He can't afford a store anywhere else but where she lives, and she has no other place to buy a good apple or a fresh loaf of bread.

In the end, after all those years, he felt nothing for them. Not even pity. To him a black face meant inconvenience, or trouble, or the threat of death. He never met any blacks who measured up to his idea of decency; of course he'd never give a man like Henry half a chance. It was too risky. He personally knew several merchants who had been killed in their stores, all by blacks, and he knew of others who had shot or killed someone trying to rob them. He had that one close call himself, of which he never spoke.

For a time, he tried not to hate them. I will say this. In one of his first stores, a half-wide fruit and vegetable shop on 173rd Street off Jerome in the Bronx, he hired a few black men to haul and clean the produce. I remember my mother looking worried when he told her. But none of them worked out. He said they either came to work late or never and when they did often passed off fruit and candy and six-packs of beer to their friends. Of course, he never let them work the register.

Eventually, he replaced them with Puerto Ricans and Peruvians. The "Spanish" ones were harder working, he said, because they didn't speak English too well, just like us. This became a kind of rule of thumb for him, to hire somebody if they couldn't speak English, even blacks from Haiti or Ethiopia, because he figured they were new to the land and understood that no one would help them for nothing. The most important thing was that they hadn't been in America too long.

I asked Henry instead if he had known of Kwang before. He didn't, not caring much for politics or politicians. "But you know," he said, "he's not like all the other Koreans around here, all tense and everything."

When they returned, the shop owner approached Henry and nodded very slightly, in the barest bow, and offered him another watch, this one boxed in clear plastic. "I give you betteh one!" he said, indicating the higher price on the sticker. "Puh-rease accept earring too. Pfor your wifuh. No chargeh!"

Henry looked confused and was about to decline when John Kwang reached over and vigorously shook his hand, pinning the jewelry there. "This is a gift," he said firmly. "Mr. Baeh would like you to accept it."

Henry shook our hands and left for home. As we waited for the traffic to pass so we could pull away from the curb, I saw Baeh inside his tiny store shaking his head as he quickly hung handbags. Every third or fourth one he banged hard against the plastic display grid. He wouldn't look back out at us. Kwang saw him, too. We drove a few blocks before he said anything.

"He knows what's good for us is good for him," Kwang said grimly. "He doesn't have to like it. Right now, he doesn't have any choice."

At the time I didn't know what Kwang meant by that last notion, what kind of dominion or direct influence he had over people like Baeh. I only considered the fact of his position and stature in the community as what had persuaded the storekeeper to deal fairly with Henry. I assumed Baeh was honoring the traditional Confucian structure of community, where in each village a prominent elder man heard the townspeople's grievances and arbitrated and ruled. Though in that world Baeh would have shown displeasure only in private. He would have acted as the dutiful younger until the wise man was far down the road.

But respect is often altered or lost in translation. Here on 39th Avenue of old Queens, in the mixed lot of peoples, respect (and honor and kindness) is a matter of margins, what you can clear on a $13.99 quartz watch, or how much selling it takes to recover when you give one away.

I knew that Mr. Baeh would stay open late tonight, maybe for no more of a chance than to catch the dance club overflow a full five hours later, drunk and high kids who might blow a few bucks on one of his gunmetal rings or satin scarves or T-shirts. The other merchants on the block would do the same. The Vietnamese deli, the West Indian takeout. Stay open. Keep the eyes open. You are your cheapest labor. Here is the great secret, the great mystery to an immigrant's success, the dwindle of irredeemable hours beneath the cheap tube lights. Pass them like a machine. Believe only in chronology. This will be your coin-small salvation.

Helena María Viramontes

The
Cariboo Cafe

I

They arrived in the secrecy of night, as displaced people often do, stopping over for a week, a month, eventually staying a lifetime. The plan was simple. Mother would work, too, until they saved enough to move into a finer future where the toilet was one's own and the children needn't be frightened. In the meantime, they played in the back alleys, among the broken glass, wise to the ways of the streets. Rule one: never talk to strangers, not even the neighbor who paced up and down the hallways talking to himself. Rule two: the police, or "polie" as Sonya's popi pronounced the word, was La Migra in disguise and thus should always be avoided. Rule three: keep your key with you at all times—the four walls of the apartment were the only protection against the streets until Popi returned home.

Sonya considered her key a guardian saint and she wore it around her neck as such until this afternoon. Gone was the string with the big knot. Gone was the key. She hadn't noticed its disappearance until she picked up Macky from Mrs. Avila's house and walked home. She remembered playing with it as Ama walked her to school. But lunch break came, and Lalo wrestled her down so that he could see her underwear, and it probably fell somewhere between the iron rings and sandbox. Sitting on the front steps of the apartment building, she considered how to explain the missing key without having to reveal what Lalo had seen, for she wasn't quite sure which offense carried the worse penalty.

She watched people piling in and spilling out of the buses, watched an old man asleep on the bus bench across the street. He resembled a crumbled ball of paper, huddled up in the security of a tattered coat. She became aware of their mutual loneliness and she rested her head against her knees, blackened by the soot of the playground asphalt.

The old man eventually awoke, yawned like a lion's roar, unfolded his limbs and staggered to the alley where he urinated between two trash bins. (She wanted to peek, but it was Macky who turned to look.) He zipped up, drank from a paper bag, and she watched him until he disappeared around the corner. As time passed, buses came less frequently, and every other person seemed to resemble Popi. Macky became bored. He picked through the trash barrel; later, and to Sonya's fright, he ran into the street after a pigeon. She understood his restlessness, for waiting was as relentless as long lines to the bathroom. When a small boy walked by, licking away at a scoop of vanilla ice cream, Macky ran after him. In his haste to outrun Sonya's grasp, he fell and tore the knee of his denim jeans. He began to cry, wiping snot against his sweater sleeve.

"See?" she asked, dragging him back to the porch steps by his wrist. "See? God punished you!" It was a thing she always said because it seemed to work. Terrified by the scrawny tortured man on the cross, Macky wanted to avoid His wrath as much as possible. She sat him on the steps in one gruff jerk. Seeing his torn jeans and her own scraped knees, she wanted to join in his sorrow and cry. Instead, she snuggled so close to him she could hear his stomach growling.

"Coke," he said. Mrs. Avila gave him an afternoon snack which usually held him over until dinner. But sometimes Macky got lost in the midst of her own six children and . . .

Mrs. Avila! It took Sonya a few moments to realize the depth of her idea. They could wait there, at Mrs. Avila's. And she'd probably have a stack of flour tortillas, fresh off the *comal,* ready to eat with butter and salt. She grabbed his hand. "Mrs. Avila has Coke."

"Coke!" He jumped up to follow his sister. "Coke," he cooed.

At the major intersection, Sonya quietly calculated their next move while the scores of adults hurried to their own destinations. She scratched one knee as she tried retracing her journey home in the labyrinth of her memory. Things never looked the same when backwards and she searched for familiar scenes. She looked for the newspaperman who sat in a little house with a little T.V. on and sold magazines with naked girls holding beach balls. But he was gone. What remained was a little closet-like shed with chains and locks, and she wondered what happened to him, for she thought he lived there with the naked ladies.

They finally crossed the street at a cautious pace, the colors of the streetlights brighter as darkness descended, a stereo store blaring music from two huge, blasting speakers. She thought it was the disco store she passed, but she didn't remember if the sign was green or red. And she didn't remember it flashing like it was now. Studying the neon light, she bumped into a tall, lanky dark man. Maybe it was Raoul's popi. Raoul was a dark boy in her class that she felt sorry for because everyone called him spongehead. Maybe she could ask Raoul's popi where Mrs. Avila lived, but before she could think it all out, red sirens flashed in their faces and she shielded her eyes to see the polie.

The polie are men in black who get kids and send them to Tijuana, says Popi. Whenever you see them, run, because they hate you, says Popi. She grabs Macky by his sleeve and they crawl under a table of bargain cassettes. Macky's nose is running, and when he sniffles, she puts her finger to her lips. She peeks from behind the poster of Vincente Fernandez to see Raoul's father putting keys and stuff from his pockets onto the hood of the polie car. And it's true, they're putting him in the car and taking him to Tijuana. Popi, she murmured to herself. Mama.

"Coke." Macky whispered, as if she had failed to remember.

"Ssssh. Mi'jo, when I say run, you run, okay?" She waited for the tires to turn out, and as the black and white drove off, she whispered "Now," and they scurried out from under the table and ran across the street, oblivious to the horns.

They entered a maze of alleys and dead ends, the long, abandoned warehouses shadowing any light. Macky stumbled and she continued to drag him until his crying, his untied sneakers, and his raspy breathing finally forced her to stop. She scanned the boarded-up boxcars, the rows of rusted rails to make sure the polie wasn't following them. Tired, her heart bursting, she leaned him against a tall chain-link fence. Except for the rambling of some railcars, silence prevailed, and she could hear Macky sniffling in the darkness. Her mouth was parched and she swallowed to rid herself of the metallic taste of fear. The shadows stalked them, hovering like nightmares. Across the tracks, in the distance, was a room with a yellow glow, like a beacon light at the end of a dark sea. She pinched Macky's nose with the corner of her dress, took hold of his sleeve. At least the shadows will be gone, she concluded, at the zero-zero place.

II

Don't look at me. I didn't give it the name. It was passed on. Didn't even know what it meant until I looked it up in some library dictionary. But I kinda liked the name. It's, well, romantic, almost like the name of a song, you know, so I kept it. That was before JoJo turned fourteen even. But now if you take a look at the sign, the paint's peeled off 'cept for the two O's. The double zero cafe. Story of my life. But who cares, right? As long as everyone 'round the factories knows I run an honest business.

The place is clean. That's more than I can say for some people who walk through that door. And I offer the best prices on double-burger deluxes this side of Main Street. Okay, so it's not pure beef. Big deal, most meat markets do the same. But I make no bones 'bout it. I tell them up front, "yeah, it ain't dogmeat, but it ain't sirloin either." Cause that's the sort of guy I am. Honest.

That's the trouble. It never pays to be honest. I tried scrubbing the stains off the floor, so that my customers won't be reminded of what happened. But they keep walking as if my cafe ain't fit for lepers. And that's the thanks I get for being a fair guy.

Not once did I hang up all those stupid signs. You know, like "We reserve the right to refuse service to anyone," or "No shirt, no shoes, no service." To tell you the truth—which is what I always do though it don't pay—I wouldn't have nobody walking through that door. The streets are full of scum, but scum gotta eat too is the way I see it. Now, listen. I ain't talkin 'bout out-of-luckers, weirdos, whores, you know. I'm talking 'bout five-to-lifers out of some tech. I'm talking Paulie.

I swear Paulie is thirty-five, or six. JoJo's age if he were still alive, but he don't look a day over ninety. Maybe why I let him hang out is 'cause he's JoJo's age. Shit, he's okay as long as he don't bring his wigged-out friends whose voices sound like a record at low speed. Paulie's got too many stories and they all get jammed up in his mouth so I can't make out what he's saying. He scares the other customers, too, acting like he is shadow boxing, or like a monkey hopping on a frying pan. You know, nervous, jumpy, his jaw all falling and his eyes bulgy and dirt-yellow. I give him the last booth, coffee, and yesterday's donut holes to keep him quiet. After a few minutes, out he goes, before lunch. I'm too old, you know, too busy making ends meet to be nursing the kid. And so is Delia.

That Delia's got these unique titties. One is bigger than the other. Like an orange and grapefruit. I kid you not. They're like that on account of when she was real young she had some babies, and they all sucked only one favorite tittie. So one is bigger than the other, and when she used to walk in with Paulie, huggy-huggy and wearing those tight leotard blouses that show the nipple dots, you could see the difference. You could tell right off that Paulie was proud of them, the way he'd hang his arm over her shoulder and squeeze the grapefruit. They kill me, her knockers. She'd come in real queenlike, smacking gum and chewing the fat with the illegals who work in that garment warehouse. They come in real queenlike, too, sitting in the best booth near the window, and order Cokes. That's all. Cokes. Hey, but I'm a nice guy. So what if they mess up my table, bring their own lunches and only order small Cokes, leaving a dime as tip? So sometimes the place ain't crawling with people, you comprende, buddy? A dime's a dime as long as its in my pocket.

Like I gotta pay my bills, too, I gotta eat. So like I serve anybody whose got the greens, including that crazy lady and the two kids that started all the trouble. If only I had closed early. But I had to wash the dinner dishes on account of I can't afford a dishwasher. I was scraping off some birdshit glue stuck to this plate, see, when I hear the bells jingle against the door. I hate those fucking bells. That was Nell's idea. Nell's my wife; my ex-wife. So people won't sneak up on you, says my ex. Anyway, I'm standing behind the counter staring at this short woman. Already I know that she's bad news because she looks street to me. Round face, burnt-toast color, black hair that hangs like straight ropes. Weirdo, I've had enough to last me a lifetime. She's wearing a shawl and a dirty slip is hanging out. Shit if I have to dish out a free meal. Funny thing, but I didn't see the two kids 'til I got to the booth. All of a sudden I see these big eyes looking over the table's edge at me. It shook me up, the way they kinda appeared. Aw, maybe they were there all the time.

The boy's a sweetheart. Short Order don't look nothing like his mom. He's got dried snot all over his dirty cheeks and his hair ain't seen a comb for years. She can't take care of herself, much less him or the doggie of a sister. But he's a tough one, and I pinch his nose 'cause he's a real sweetheart like JoJo. You know, my boy.

It's his sister I don't like. She's got these poking eyes that follow you 'round 'cause she don't trust no one. Like when I reach for Short Order, she flinches like I'm 'bout to tear his nose off, gives me a nasty, squinty look. She's maybe five, maybe six, I don't know, and she acts like she owns him. Even when I bring the burgers, she doesn't let go of his hand. Finally, the fellow bites it and I wink at him. A real sweetheart.

In the next booth, I'm twisting the black crud off the top of the ketchup bottle when I hear the lady saying something in Spanish. Right off I know she's illegal, which explains why she looks like a weirdo. Anyway, she says something nice to them 'cause it's in the same tone that Nell used when I'd rest my head on her lap. I'm surprised the illegal's got a fiver to pay, but she and her tail leave no tip. I see Short Order's small bites on the bun.

You know, a cafe's the kinda business that moves. You get some regulars, but most of them are on the move, so I don't pay much attention to them. But this lady's face sticks like egg yolk on a plate. It ain't 'til I open a beer and sit in front of the B & W to check out the wrestling matches that I see this news bulletin 'bout two missing kids. I recognize the mugs right away. Short Order and his doggie sister. And all of a sudden her face is out of my mind. Aw, fuck, I say, and put my beer down so hard that the foam spills onto last month's Hustler. Aw, fuck.

See, if Nell was here, she'd know what to do: call the cops. But I don't know. Cops ain't exactly my friends, and all I need is for bacon to be crawling all over my place. And seeing how her face is vague now, I decide to wait 'til the late news. Short Order don't look right neither. I'll have another beer and wait for the late news.

The alarm rings at four and I have this headache, see, from the six-pack, and I gotta get up. I was supposed to do something, but I got all suck-faced and forgot. Turn off the TV, take a shower, but that don't help my memory any.

Hear sirens near the railroad tracks. Cops. I'm supposed to call the cops. I'll do it after I make the coffee, put away the eggs, get the donuts out. But Paulie strolls in looking partied out. We actually talk 'bout last night's wrestling match between BoBo Brazil and the Crusher. I slept through it, you see. Paulie orders an OJ on account of he's catching a cold. I open up my big mouth and ask about De. Drinks the rest of his OJ, says real calmlike, that he caught her eaglespread with the vegetable fatso down the block. Then, very polite like, Paulie excuses himself. That's one thing I gotta say about Paulie. He may be one big Fuck-Up, but he's got manners. Juice gave him shit cramps, he says.

Well, leave it to Paulie. Good ole Mr. Fuck-Up himself to help me with the cops. The prick OD's in my crapper; vomits and shits are all over—I mean all over the fuckin' walls. That's the thanks I get for being Mr. Nice Guy. I had the cops looking up my ass for the stash. Says one, the one wearing a mortician's suit, *We'll be back, we'll be back when you ain't looking.* If I was pushing, would I be burning my goddamn balls off with spitting grease? So fuck 'em, I think. I ain't gonna tell you nothing 'bout the lady. Fuck you, I say to them as they drive away. Fuck your mother.

That's why Nell was good to have 'round. She could be a pain in the ass, you know, like making me hang those stupid bells, but mostly she knew what to do. See, I go bananas. Like my mind fries with the potatoes and by the end of the day, I'm deader than dogshit. Let me tell you what I mean. A few hours later, after I swore I wouldn't give the fuckin' pigs the time of day, the green vans roll up across the street. While I'm stirring the chili con carne, I see all these illegals running out of the factory to hide, like roaches when the lightswitch goes on. I taste the chili, but I really can't taste nothing on account of I've lost my appetite after cleaning out the crapper, when three of them run into the Cariboo. They look at me as if I'm gonna stop them, but when I go on stirring the chili, they run to the bathroom. Now look, I'm a nice guy, but I don't like to be used, you know? Just 'cause they're regulars don't mean jackshit. I run an honest business. And that's what I told them agents. See, by that time, my stomach being all dizzy, and the cops all over the place, and the three illegals running in here, I was all confused, you know. That's how it was, and well, I haven't seen Nell for years, and I guess that's why I pointed to the bathroom.

I don't know. I didn't expect handcuffs and them agents putting their hands up and down their thighs. When they walked passed me, they didn't look at me. That is, the two young ones. The older one, the one that looked silly in the handcuffs on account of she's old enough to be my grandma's grandma, looks straight at my face with the same eyes Short Order's sister gave me yesterday. What a day. Then, to top off the potatoes with the gravy, the bells jingle against the door and in enters the lady again with the two kids.

III

He's got lice. Probably from living in the detainers. Those are the rooms where they round up the children and make them work for their food. I saw them from the window. Their eyes are cut glass, and no one looks for sympathy. They take turns, sorting out the arms from the legs, heads from the torsos. Is that one your mother? one guard asks, holding a mummified head with eyes shut tighter than coffins. But the children no longer cry. They just continue sorting as if they were salvaging cans from a heap of trash. They do this until time is up and they drift into a tunnel, back to the womb of sleep, while a new group comes in. It is all very organized. I bite my fist to keep from retching. Please, God, please don't let Geraldo be there.

For you see, they took Geraldo. By mistake, of course. It was my fault. I shouldn't have sent him out to fetch me a mango. But it was just to the corner. I didn't even bother to put his sweater on. I hear his sandals flapping against the gravel. I follow him with my eyes, see him scratching his buttocks when the wind picks up swiftly, as it often does at such unstable times, and I have to close the door.

The darkness becomes a serpent's tongue, swallowing us whole. It is the night of La Llorona. The women come up from the depths of sorrow to search for their children. I join them, frantic, desperate, and our eyes become scrutinizers, our bodies opiated with the scent of their smiles. Descending from door to door, the wind whips our faces. I hear the wailing of the women and know it to be my own. Geraldo is nowhere to be found.

Dawn is not welcomed. It is a drunkard wavering between consciousness and sleep. My life is fleeing, moving south towards the sea. My tears are now hushed and faint.

The boy, barely a few years older than Geraldo, lights a cigarette, rests it on the edge of his desk, next to all the other cigarette burns. The blinds are down to keep the room cool. Above him hangs a single bulb that shades and shadows his face in such a way as to mask his expressions. He is not to be trusted. He fills in the information, for I cannot write. Statements delivered, we discuss motives.

"Spies," says he, flicking a long burning ash from the cigarette onto the floor, then wolfing the smoke in as if his lungs had an unquenchable thirst for nicotine. "We arrest spies. Criminals." He says this with cigarette smoke spurting out from his nostrils like a nosebleed.

"Spies? Criminal?" My shawl falls to the ground. "He is only five and a half years old." I plead for logic with my hands. "What kind of crimes could a five year old commit?"

"Anyone who so willfully supports the Contras in any form must be arrested and punished without delay." He knows the line by heart.

I think about moths and their stupidity. Always attracted by light, they fly into fires, or singe their wings with the heat of the single bulb and fall on his desk, writhing in pain. I don't understand why nature has been so cruel as to prevent them from feeling warmth. He dismisses them with a sweep of a hand. "This," he continues, "is what we plan to do with the Contras and those who aid them." He inhales again.

"But, Señor, he's just a baby."

"Contras are tricksters. They exploit the ignorance of people like you.

Perhaps they convinced your son to circulate pamphlets. You should be talking to them, not us." The cigarette is down to his yellow finger tips, to where he can no longer continue to hold it without burning himself. He throws the stub on the floor, crushes it under his boot. "This," he says, screwing his boot into the ground, "is what the Contras do to people like you."

"Señor. I am a washerwoman. You yourself see I cannot read or write. There is my X. Do you think my son can read?" How can I explain to this man that we are poor, that we live as best we can? "If such a thing has happened, perhaps he wanted to make a few centavos for his mama. He's just a baby."

"So you are admitting his guilt?"

"So you are admitting he is here?" I promise, once I see him, hold him in my arms again, I will never, never scold him for wanting more than I can give. "You see, he needs his sweater..." The sweater lies limp on my lap.

"Your assumption is incorrect."

"May I check the detainers for myself?"

"In time."

"And what about my Geraldo?"

"In time." He dismisses me, placing the forms in a big envelope crinkled by the day's humidity.

"When?" I am wringing the sweater with my hands.

"Don't be foolish, woman. Now off with your nonsense. We will try to locate your Pedro."

"Geraldo."

Maria came by today with a bowl of hot soup. She reports, in her usual excited way, that the soldiers are now eating the brains of their victims. It is unlike her to be so scandalous. So insane. Geraldo must be cold without his sweater.

"Why?" I ask as the soup gets cold. I will write Tavo tonight.

At the plaza, a group of people are whispering. They are quiet when I pass, turn to one another and put their finger to their lips to cage their voices. They continue as I reach the church steps. To be associated with me is condemnation.

Today I felt like killing myself, Lord. But I am too much of a coward. I am a washerwoman, Lord. My mother was one, and hers, too. We have lived as best we can, washing other people's laundry, rinsing off other people's dirt until our hands crust and chap. When my son wanted to hold my hand, I held soap instead. When he wanted to play, my feet were in pools of water. It takes such little courage, being a washerwoman. Give me strength, Lord.

What have I done to deserve this, Lord? Raising a child is like building a kite. You must bend the twigs enough, but not too much, for you might break them. You must find paper that is delicate and light enough to wave on the breath of the wind, yet must withstand the ravages of a storm. You must tie the strings gently but firmly so that it may not fall apart. You must let the string go, eventually, so that the kite will stretch its ambition. It is such delicate work, Lord, being a mother. This I understand, Lord, because I am. But you have snapped the cord, Lord. It was only a matter of minutes and my life is lost somewhere in the clouds. I don't know, I don't know what games you play, Lord.

These four walls are no longer my house; the earth beneath it, no longer my home. Weeds have replaced all good crops. The irrigation ditches are clodded with bodies. No matter where we turn, there are rumors facing us, and we try to live as best we can under the rule of men who rape women then rip their fetuses from their bellies. Is this our home? Is this our country? I ask Maria. Don't these men have mothers, lovers, babies, sisters? Don't they see what they are doing? Later, Maria says, these men are babes farted out from the Devil's ass. We check to make sure no one has heard her say this.

Without Geraldo, this is not my home; the earth beneath it, not my country. This is why I have to leave. Maria begins to cry. Not because I am going, but because she is staying.

Tavo. Sweet Tavo. He has sold his car to send me the money. He has just married and he sold his car for me. Thank you, Tavo. Not just for the money. But also for making me believe in the goodness of people again. . . . The money is enough to buy off the border soldiers. The rest will come from the can. I have saved for Geraldo's schooling and it is enough for a bus ticket to Juárez. I am to wait for Tavo there.

I spit. I do not turn back.

Perhaps I am wrong in coming. I worry that Geraldo will not have a home to return to, no mother to cradle his nightmares away, soothe the scars, stop the hemorrhaging of his heart. Tavo is happy I am here, but it is crowded with the three of us, and I hear them arguing behind their closed door. There is only so much a nephew can provide. I must find work. I have two hands willing to work. But the heart. The heart wills only to watch the children playing in the street.

The machines, their speed and dust, make me ill. But I can clean. I clean toilets, dump trash cans, sweep. Disinfect the sinks. I will gladly do whatever is necessary to repay Tavo. The baby is due any time and money is tight. I volunteer for odd hours, weekends, since I really have very little to do. When the baby comes, I know Tavo's wife will not let me hold it, for she thinks I am a bad omen. I know it.

Why would God play such a cruel joke, if he isn't my son? I jumped the curb, dashed out into the street, but the street is becoming wider and wider. I've lost him once and can't lose him again and to hell with the screeching tires and the horns and the headlights barely touching my hips. I can't take my eyes off him because, you see, they are swift and cunning and can take your life with a snap of a finger. But God is a just man and His mistakes can be undone.

My heart pounds in my head like a sledgehammer against the asphalt. What if it isn't Geraldo? What if he is still in the detainer waiting for me? A million questions, one answer: Yes. Geraldo, yes. I want to touch his hand first, have it disappear in my own because it is so small. His eyes look at me in total bewilderment. I grab him because the earth is crumbling beneath us and I must save him. We both fall to the ground.

A hot meal is in store. A festival. The cook, a man with shrunken cheeks and the hands of a car mechanic, takes a liking to Geraldo. It's like birthing you again, mi'jo. My baby.

I bathe him. He flutters in excitement, the water gray around him. I scrub his head with lye to kill off the lice, comb his hair out with a fine-tooth comb. I wash his rubbery penis, wrap him in a towel, and he stands in front of the window, shriveling and sucking milk from a carton, his hair shiny from the dampness.

He finally sleeps. So easily, she thinks. On her bed next to the open window he coos in the night. Below, the sounds of the city become as monotonous as the ocean waves. She rubs his back with warm oil, each stroke making up for the days of his absence. She hums to him softly so that her breath brushes against his face, tunes that are rusted and crack in her throat. The hotel neon shines on his back and she covers him.

All the while the young girl watches her brother sleeping. She removes her sneakers, climbs into the bed, snuggles up to her brother, and soon her breathing is raspy, her arms under her stomach.

The couch is her bed tonight. Before switching the light off, she checks once more to make sure this is not a joke. Tomorrow she will make arrangements to go home. Maria will be the same, the mango stand on the corner next to the church plaza will be the same. It will all be the way it was before. But enough excitement. For the first time in years, her mind is quiet of all noise and she has the desire to sleep.

The bells jingle when the screen door slaps shut behind them. The cook wrings his hands in his apron, looking at them. Geraldo is in the middle, and they sit in the booth farthest away from the window, near the hall where the toilets are, and right away the small boy, his hair now neatly combed and split to the side like an adult, wrinkles his nose at the peculiar smell. The cook wipes perspiration off his forehead with the corner of his apron, finally comes over to the table.

She looks so different, so young. Her hair is combed slick back into one thick braid and her earrings hang like baskets of golden pears on her finely sculptured ears. He can't believe how different she looks. Almost beautiful. She points to what she wants on the menu with a white, clean fingernail. Although confused, the cook is sure of one thing—it's Short Order all right, pointing to him with a commanding finger, saying his only English word: Coke.

His hands tremble as he slaps the meat on the grill; the patties hiss instantly. He feels like vomiting. The chili overboils and singes the fires, deep red trail of chili crawling to the floor and puddling there. He grabs the handles, burns himself, drops the pot on the wooden racks of the floor. He sucks his fingers, the patties blackening and sputtering grease. He flips them, and the burgers hiss anew. In some strange way he hopes they have disappeared, and he takes a quick look only to see Short Order's sister, still in the same dress, still holding her brother's hand. She is craning her neck to peek at what is going on in the kitchen.

Aw, fuck, he says, in a fog of smoke, his eyes burning tears. He can't believe it, but he's crying. For the first time since JoJo's death, he's crying. He becomes angry at the lady for returning. At JoJo. At Nell for leaving him. He wishes Nell here, but doesn't know where she's at or what part of Vietnam JoJo is all crumbled up in. Children gotta be with their parents, family gotta be together, he thinks. It's only right. The emergency line is ringing.

Two black and whites roll up and skid the front tires against the curb. The flashing lights carousel inside the cafe. She sees them opening the screen door, their guns taut and cold like steel erections. Something is wrong, and she looks to the cowering cook. She has been betrayed, and her heart is pounding like footsteps running, faster, louder, faster, and she can't hear what they are saying to her. She jumps up from the table, grabs Geraldo by the wrist, his sister dragged along because, like her, she refuses to release his hand. Their lips are mouthing words she can't hear, can't comprehend. Run, Run is all she can think of to do, Run through the hallway, out to the alley, Run because they will never take him away again.

But her legs are heavy and she crushes Geraldo against her, so tight, as if she wants to conceal him in her body again, return him to her belly so that they will not castrate him and hang his small blue penis on her door, not crush his face so that he is unrecognizable, not bury him among the heaps of bones, and ears, and teeth, and jaws, because no one but she cared to know that he cried. For years he cried and she could hear him day and night. Screaming, howling, sobbing, shriveling and crying because he is only five years old, and all he wanted was a mango.

But the crying begins all over again. In the distance, she hears crying.

She refuses to let go. For they will have to cut her arms off to take him, rip her mouth off to keep her from screaming for help. Without thinking, she reaches over to where two pots of coffee are brewing and throws the steaming coffee into their faces. Outside, people begin to gather, pressing their faces against the window glass to get a good view. The cook huddles behind the counter, frightened, trembling. Their faces become distorted and she doesn't see the huge hand that takes hold of Geraldo and she begins screaming all over again, screaming so that the walls shake, screaming enough for all the women of murdered children, screaming, pleading for help from the people outside, and she pushes an open hand against an officer's nose, because no one will stop them and he pushes the gun barrel to her face.

And I laugh at his ignorance. How stupid of him to think that I will let them take my Geraldo away just because he waves that gun like a flag. Well, to hell with you, you pieces of shit, do you hear me? Stupid, cruel pigs. To hell with you all, because you can no longer frighten me. I will fight you for my son until I have no hands left to hold a knife. I will fight you all because you're all farted out of the Devil's ass, and you'll not take us with you. I am laughing, howling at their stupidity because they should know by now that I will never let my son go. And then I hear something crunching like broken glass against my forehead and I am blinded by the liquid darkness. But I hold onto his hand. That I can feel, you see, I'll never let go. Because we are going home. My son and I.

Nola Kambanda

My
New World
Journey

The anticipation of coming to this great country and all of its physical, social, and economic capacity was overwhelming. It made me feel like a toddler in a toy store, unable to decide which adventure to tackle first. Coming to California from Burundi—a place that I had come to call home, a place that was so very different in every aspect from the United States—I was in complete awe. The first thing that hit me was the speed with which everything was going. It seemed too fast paced. The movement of the people was rushed, and no one was looking anywhere else except where they were going; the cars moved too fast; there were too many lights, too many buttons to press, too many escalators. I was suddenly asking myself if these people ever stopped talking to one another. The longing to be back home suddenly came upon me. The need for some kind of familiarity was so strong and yet I had just stepped off the plane.

In many ways, I have lived my life as an immigrant of one sort or another. I was born in Burundi to Rwandese parents who had each left the country in the early '60s as a political refugee to escape the ethnic cleansing which was going on. Despite the fact that they met, married, created a home, and had all seven of their children in Burundi, my parents never considered themselves anything other than Rwandese. There was no such thing as assimilation, as becoming a citizen of Burundi. As such, they raised their children to identify themselves as Rwandese. So I grew up with the understanding that where you were born has little, if any, bearing on who you are, let alone what you will become. You will always be followed by the shadow of your heritage and of ancestry.

All refugees grow up with this understanding. You grow up knowing that you do not automatically belong, that you always have to prove yourself, earn your place in the society which has so graciously allowed you the freedom of life. In my household, it was just assumed that we would do well in school. There was no room for failure, for being anything other than the best. I, like all my siblings, excelled in my academics. I left Bujumbura, the capital city, to complete my secondary education at an all-girls boarding school in Kiganda, a small countryside town.

I had always wanted to be in a boarding school. My friends and the various acquaintances I met who had attended and/or graduated from boarding school told me about the lifelong bonds that were developed by the girls, about how it was an experience that had forever changed their sense of who they were as women. Though relatively unexciting, my first year at school in Kiganda was pleasant enough. My second year, however, was another story. A story that my parents, having left the violence of their homeland behind, had hoped I would never be able to tell.

Not so unlike the rival gang warfare I have grown accustomed to hearing about in Los Angeles, the territory of Central Africa where I am from is marred by tribal warfare. The two main tribes in both Burundi and Rwanda are the Hutus and the Tutsis. The hatred and rivalry between the tribes has existed from the beginning of this century's colonial occupation of these two countries. Even though most of the world has recently appealed to both the Tutsi and the Hutu tribes to put an end to the genocide, it will most likely continue into the next millenium. It is hard to change when you know no other way of life.

I suppose that this was the case with the young Hutu student at the boarding school who was plotting to have me, a Tutsi, killed. Actually, she and a small group of her Hutu friends were planning to extinguish all the Tutsi students. I just happened to be at the top of the list—literally. Mine was the first name on a list of over thirty names that the administration discovered. After the girls were found out and threatened with expulsion, they quickly abandoned their murderous plans. But for me, it was a serious reminder that I was a refugee and that meant I was never safe, always susceptible. I was never truly home. When I told my parents what had happened, their reaction only cemented this. "This is what you have to live with, Nola," they said. "This is who you are."

So there I was, at the Los Angeles International Airport, just one short taxi ride away from meeting the family with whom I'd be living. My aunt and cousin from Swaziland, where I had been living for most of the previous year, accompanied me on this, my first trip to America. More specifically, to what would be my new home—at least while I was attending school. While I was standing there outside the airport watching cars and buses of all shapes and sizes drive by, I thought about how I had reached this point in my life. I realized the sacrifice that not only my parents but also my siblings were making to send me out here. I was the first one of all seven of my parents' children to move so far away from Burundi. I should have felt privileged. I should have been excited and on top of the world about coming to America—the country I had been made to believe was the richest and most technologically advanced of them all.

But a sense of guilt was washing over me, one which became more pronounced as I kept thinking of the economic burden it would place on my father. An economic burden which I felt was too large for him to bear in order to accommodate just one child. The guilt and the realization that stemmed from it brought on a tremendous sense of responsibility for me. Even more so than in Burundi, failure was unacceptable. I could not fail here in America. I was going to have to be the best. I was going to have to do extremely well in school so that I could go on to get a decent job so that I would be able to contribute financially to my family's well-being.

The family that I was going to be living with in Los Angeles were strangers. They were well acquainted with my uncle and aunt who had come to vacation in the States each year. But I had never met them before. I wondered how awkward it would be to live with people I had never met before. When I walked into their house they greeted me very warmly. The sound of their voices calling me by name was not strange but, rather, familiar. It eased the pain of separation that I had been feeling from the moment our plane landed at the airport. I felt at home in their home.

Even still, I found myself growing ever-conscious of the way I spoke. This was the beginning of what would be my lengthy battle to translate myself in a language not my own, to communicate in English—not just any English, but *American* English. It seemed like I would never be able to speak as fast and as well as these people. I would never be able to say and remember their names, names I was not used to, as easily as they seemed to be able to say and remember mine. I wondered if they were, in meeting me, as aware of our differences as I was in meeting them. How did I seem to them? Did I seem too soft? Too slow? Too self-conscious? I must not have, because my new family—a Jewish-American social activist, a Jamaican-American actress-cum-writer and their prepubescent daughter—were very caring and hospitable. They never made me feel like I didn't fit in just right. I felt, in their eyes and in their home, like myself, like an individual, not a representative of Burundi, Rwanda, or Africa at large.

This was not the case with other people I met. I couldn't believe the questions that were posed to me. Questions about my country and about Africa—although in many cases there was no real distinction because so many people think that Africa is just one big country, not a continent with many, many countries in it. People would ask me if I spoke "African," if I could speak a little "African" for them to hear. One day while I was visiting the elementary school that the family's daughter was attending, one student asked me—with genuine sincerity—if we rode on elephants in Africa as a means of transportation. That blew me away.

When I went to apply for my Social Security card, the clerk looked at my passport, pointed to the printed name of my country, and asked, "Where is that?" Upon being told by me that I had recently arrived from Burundi, by way of Swaziland, a young man asked, "How did you get here from there?" The thought that I could have flown in a commercial airplane from there to here did not seem to ever cross his curious mind. At times, I received these questions with humor. At times, I received them with confusion and took great offense. Why didn't these people know anything about Africa and its people, its geography? Why was there such a deep pit of ignorance? Where was the knowledge and wisdom and greatness I imagined everyone in America would have?

Surprisingly, most Americans I met in Los Angeles had no concept of African modernity. They still thought of Africans as people who lived in a jungle, people who had no access to airplanes, cars, televisions, telephones, CD players, or any of the other household appliances and urban facilities that I grew up enjoying in Burundi. The fact that these Americans were not aware of African modernity was not as surprising as my discovery of the fact that they also knew very little about American history. In Burundi, geography, history, and anthropology were a critical part of our educational curriculum. And not just our geography, our history, and the study of our culture. We learned about the entire world. By the time I finished secondary school, I knew all the significant details of all the countries in all the continents. I knew the capitals of all the states in America, I knew who the presidents of the country were. Living in the glamour of Los Angeles and not knowing what a Tutsi or a Hutu is, not knowing where Burundi or Rwanda is can somehow be rationalized. Not knowing who Andrew Jackson was or where the capital of California is, cannot. This is how my romanticized idea of America died and the recognition of my journey into *a* new world—not *the* New World—began to take form.

The world I eventually came to embrace in America, in Los Angeles, and in the home where I was living was both comfortable and complicated. Even though my new family made it as painless as possible for me to emerge into their way of life, there were many things I had to learn. The differences in our cultures and lifestyles continued to display themselves as the days went by. Everything was rushed, was too this or too that, was always being pushed to the extreme. There just seemed to be a ton of information to recall. Where had all the simple things gone?

I had used a telephone plenty of times before and I had always thought of it as a pretty basic unit. You pick up the phone, you dial who you're calling, they answer it and you talk. No interruptions, no complexities. Until I learned that there was such thing as call waiting. And then three-way calling. And call forwarding. And single telephone units with multiple lines. What was all this? Was it all really necessary?

I wondered about the level of sophistication toward which everything seemed to be aspiring. It was a sophistication intended to facilitate, to make life simpler. But how is it possible to be simple and sophisticated at the same time? Take, for instance, the washing machine. I had neither seen nor used one before. You put your dirty clothes and some soap into a machine, close the lid, press a button and within minutes your clothes were done—clean and ready to be placed in yet another machine to be dried!?! Back at home, in Burundi, we would put our dirty clothes in a basin, soak them a bit, hand wash them with soap, and then hang them up to line dry. I will admit that the American way is definitely more convenient. But it lacks a certain ritual of intimacy. There is a care that I like to put into the cleaning of my clothes, those things that cover and protect my body, so I still invariably find myself hand washing.

Only recently did I realize that the majority of these cultural contrasts stemmed from the same root, the concept of time. Americans have a way of wanting to accomplish as much as possible in as little time as possible. Even something as sacred as eating. Fast food. It was amazing how many fast-food restaurants there were in Los Angeles, even in just our small neighborhood. Everyone ate at fast-food restaurants. I noticed how many ate while driving or being driven. I had not seen anything like this in my country. We ate three meals a day—breakfast, lunch, and dinner; and this was rarely done outside of either your own home or someone else's home. Eating out was a very formal affair. People didn't go out to eat by themselves. It was what you did in large numbers, something the whole family did together. Regardless of whether it was done in the home or out, dining required time. Food was never fast.

*   *   *

It didn't take long for me to catch on, for me to grab a hold of America. Especially after I had started doing what I came here to do—go to school. Once I started going to school and working a part-time job, I knew the meaning of busy. I knew why people ate and talked on the phone while driving from one place to another. Before long I started doing it myself. I'd never gone to school and worked at the same time. I don't think I'd ever known anyone in my life, certainly not in Burundi, who was working and going to school at the same time. School was your job. You were obligated to study and do well until you were finished because only then would you be qualified for employment. That was our incentive. Nobody wanted to hold a job for which you didn't need qualifications. Those petty positions were for the uneducated, for those who couldn't finish secondary school or university. Education was something that was taken seriously in Burundi. If you failed a class, you were not only castigated and harshly punished for it, you would also have to repeat the entire year of school before being allowed to move on the next grade level. Out of fear for authority and all elders in society, we gave our professors the ultimate respect.

When I began attending Los Angeles City College, I was completely thrown off by the casual relationships between professors and students. The students appeared confident of their circumstances, unafraid of any consequences. The school was overflowing with options and choices. You could decide what classes you wanted to take, how many, and when you wanted to take them. You could miss a class and still make up for it. You could miss a class and never make up for it and still graduate.

Working and going to school was grueling, but I managed to do it because that was why I had come to America to begin with. I had to prove myself. There would be no reason to return to Burundi without a degree. Any of the students back home would have killed to be in my shoes. So why not use them to carry me someplace, somewhere of significance? After I completed my studies at the community college, I transferred to California State University—Los Angeles. I declared electrical engineering as my major. It did not go by unnoticed—by me or anyone else—that I happened to be the only black person, not to mention black woman, sitting in most of my classes. My strong accent made every verbal answer I gave a staring session for the rest of my classmates as they tried to figure out my words. The same is true of my present coworkers.

After receiving my degree, I was immediately offered the opportunity to begin my career. I took a position at Boeing Reusable Space Systems, where I am, again, one of a small few. It seems that I have always stood out. In Burundi. In America. My parents were right when they urged me to become used to the fact that I would always be the "other." Everywhere I go I come back to their words. "This is what you have to live with, Nola. This is who you are."

No doubt I am not American. I am a Rwandese Tutsi refugee who is becoming more and more understanding and appreciative of America each day I am here. The appreciativeness and understanding creates an awareness that makes me unique in every circle I could possibly travel in. It keeps me on my toes. If I was still in Burundi, I would also be busy, but not in the same way I am in America. I would probably be married with a couple of children. I would be busy with the kids, busy tending to the housework, busy taking care of my extended family and local community, busy helping my husband with his career and his dreams. I would be busy being a typical Rwandese housewife.

Sometimes I do think about going home. I think about the rewards of having an extended family and a local community that depends and insists upon my involvement. I think about finding a mate, that person I have not yet been able to find in the United States, the one who will be able to accept and relate to all aspects of my background and my culture. I think about the food, about the *cassava* leaves and the fried green bananas. I miss what I used to have, and what I used to want, who I thought I would become. Then again, I don't.

Sometimes I am not sure whether home is behind me or in front of me. I am not so sure this longing is really recognizable. I might just be attaching it to those things that are familiar to me. Home might very well be a place that I have not yet discovered, that I have not yet created. Or it might not be a place at all. After all, Rwanda, that place that I have called home all my life, is a place I have visited for only one month. I don't know its rivers, its mountains, intimately. All I know of Rwanda is its people, my family. So home might be family, and nothing more. It might be the people who make me feel. The people who define and occupy and receive my emotions, the people who reciprocate, who give me the most sought after, most valuable and intangible gifts—acceptance, trust, laughter, comfort, love. In that case, Burundi is home. And so is Swaziland. And so is America.

Agha Shahid Ali

Snow on the Desert

"Each ray of sunshine is seven minutes old,"
Serge told me in New York one December night.

"So when I look at the sky, I see the past?"
"Yes, Yes," he said, "especially on a clear day."

On January 19, 1987,
as I very early in the morning
drove my sister to Tucson International,

suddenly on Alvernon and 22nd Street
the sliding doors of the fog were opened,

and the snow, which had fallen all night, now
sun-dazzled, blinded us, the earth whitened

out, as if by cocaine, the desert's plants,
its mineral-hard colors extinguished,
wine frozen in the veins of the cactus.

        *   *   *

The Desert Smells Like Rain: in it I read:
The syrup from which sacred wine is made

is extracted from the saguaros each
summer. The Papagos place it in jars,

where the last of it softens, then darkens
into a color of blood though it tastes

strangely sweet, almost whiter, like a dry wine.
As I tell Sameetah this, we are still

seven miles away. "And you know the flowers
of the saguaros bloom only at night?"

We are driving slowly, the road is glass.
"Imagine where we are was a sea once.

Just imagine!" The sky is relentlessly
sapphire, and the past is happening quickly:

the saguaros have opened themselves, stretched
out their arms to rays millions of years old,

in each ray a secret of the planet's
origin, the rays hurting each cactus

into memory, a human memory—
for they are humans, the Papagos say:

not only because they have arms and veins
and secrets. But because they too are a tribe

vulnerable to massacre. "It is like
the end, perhaps the beginning of the world,"

Sameetah says, staring at their snow-sleeved
arms. And we are driving by the ocean

that evaporated here, by its shores,
the past now happening so quickly that each

stoplight hurts us into memory, the sky
taking rapid notes on us as we turn

at Tucson Boulevard and drive into
the airport, and I realize that the early

is thawing from longing into longing and
that we are being forgotten by those arms.

*   *   *

At the airport I stared after her plane
till the window was

        again a mirror,
As I drove back into the foothills, the fog

shut its doors behind me on Alvernon,
and I breathed the seas

the earth had lost,
their forsaken shores. And I remembered

another moment that refers only
to itself:

in New Delhi one night
as Begum Akhtar sang, the lights went out.

It was perhaps during the Bangladesh War,
perhaps there were sirens,

air-raid warnings.
But the audience, hushed, did not stir.

The microphone was dead, but she went
singing, and her voice

was coming from far
away, as if she had already died.

And just before the lights did flood here
again, melting the frost

of her diamond
into rays, it was, like this turning dark

of fog, a moment when only a lost sea
can be heard, a time

to recollect
every shadow, everything the earth was losing,

a time to think of everything the earth
and I had lost, of all

that I would lose,
of all that I was losing.

Achy Obejas

from *We Came All the Way from Cuba So You Could Dress Like This?*

I'm wearing a green sweater. It's made of some synthetic material, and it's mine. I've been wearing it for two days straight and have no plans to take it off right now.

I'm ten years old. I just got off the boat—or rather, the ship. The actual boat didn't make it: We got picked up halfway from Havana to Miami by a gigantic oil freighter to which they then tied our boat. That's how our boat got smashed to smithereens, its wooden planks breaking off like toothpicks against the ship's big metal hull. Everybody talks about American ingenuity, so I'm not sure why somebody didn't anticipate that would happen. But they didn't. So the boat that brought me and my parents most of the way from Cuba is now just part of the debris that'll wash up on tourist beaches all over the Caribbean.

As I speak, my parents are being interrogated by an official from the office of Immigration and Naturalization Services. It's all a formality because this is 1963, and no Cuban claiming political asylum actually gets turned away. We're evidence that the revolution has failed the middle class and that communism is bad. My parents—my father's an accountant and my mother's a social worker—are living, breathing examples of the suffering Cubans have endured under the tyranny of Fidel Castro.

The immigration officer, a fat Hungarian lady with sparkly hazel eyes and a perpetual smile, asks my parents why they came over, and my father, whose face is bright red from spending two days floating in a little boat on the Atlantic Ocean while secretly terrified, points to me— I'm sitting on a couch across the room, more bored than exhausted— and says, We came for her, so she could have a future.

The immigration officer speaks a halting Spanish, and with it she tells my parents about fleeing the Communists in Hungary. She says they took everything from her family, including a large country estate, with forty-four acres and two lakes, that's now being used as a vocational training center. Can you imagine that, she says. There's an official presidential portrait of John F. Kennedy behind her, which will need to be replaced in a week or so.

I fold my arms in front of my chest and across the green sweater. Tonight the U.S. government will put us up in a noisy transient hotel. We'll be allowed to stay there at taxpayer expense for a couple of days until my godfather—who lives with his mistress somewhere in Miami comes to get us.

*   *   *

Leaning against the wall at the processing center, I notice a volunteer for Catholic Charities who approaches me with gifts: oatmeal cookies, a plastic doll with blond hair and a blue dress, and a rosary made of white plastic beads. She smiles and talks to me in incomprehensible English, speaking unnaturally loud.

My mother, who's watching while sitting nervously next to my father as we're being processed, will later tell me she remembers this moment as something poignant and good.

All I hold onto is the feel of the doll—cool and hard—and the fact that the Catholic volunteer is trying to get me to exchange my green sweater for a little gray flannel gym jacket with a hood and an American flag logo. I wrap myself up tighter in the sweater, which at this point still smells of salt and Cuban dirt and my grandmother's house, and the Catholic volunteer just squeezes my shoulder and leaves, thinking, I'm sure, that I've been traumatized by the trip across the choppy waters. My mother smiles weakly at me from across the room.

I'm still clutching the doll, a thing I'll never play with but which I'll carry with me all my life, from apartment to apartment, one move after the other. Eventually, her little blond nylon hairs will fall off and, thirty years later, after I'm diagnosed with cancer, she'll sit atop my dresser, scarred and bald like a chemo patient.

*   *   *

Is life destiny or determination?

For all the blond boyfriends I will have, there will be only two yellow-haired lovers. One doesn't really count—a boy in a military academy who subscribes to Republican politics like my parents, and who will try, relatively unsuccessfully, to penetrate me on a south Florida beach. I will squirm away from underneath him, not because his penis hurts me but because the stubble on his face burns my cheek.

The other will be Martha, perceived by the whole lesbian community as a gold digger, but who will love me in spite of my poverty. She'll come to my one-room studio on Saturday mornings when her rich lover is still asleep and rip tee-shirts off my shoulders, brutally and honestly.

One Saturday we'll forget to set the alarm to get her back home in time, and Martha will have to dress in a hurry, the smoky smell of my sex all over her face and her own underwear tangled up in her pants leg. When she gets home, her rich lover will notice the weird bulge at her calf and throw her out, forcing Martha to acknowledge that without a primary relationship for contrast, we can't go on.

It's too dangerous, she'll say, tossing her blond hair away from her face.

Years later, I'll visit Martha, now living seaside in Provincetown with her new lover, a Kennedy cousin still in the closet who has a love of dogs, and freckles sprinkled all over her cheeks.

*   *   *

At the processing center, the Catholic volunteer has found a young Colombian woman to talk to me. I don't know her name, but she's pretty and brown, and she speaks Spanish. She tells me she's not Catholic but that she'd like to offer me Christian comfort anyway. She smells of violet water.

She pulls a Bible from her big purse and asks me, Do you know this, and I say, I'm Catholic, and she says that, well, she was once Catholic, too, but then she was saved and became something else. She says everything will change for me in the United States, as it did for her.

Then she tells me about coming here with her father and how he got sick and died, and she was forced to do all sorts of work, including what she calls sinful work, and how the sinful work taught her so much about life, and then how she got saved. She says there's still a problem, an impulse, which she has to suppress by reading the Bible. She looks at me as if I know what she's talking about.

Across the room, my parents are still talking to the fat Hungarian lady, my father's head bent over the table as he fills out form after form.

Then the Catholic volunteer comes back and asks the Colombian girl something in English, and the girl reaches across me, pats my lap, and starts reading from her Spanish language Bible: Your breasts are like two fawns, twins of a gazelle that feed upon the lilies. Until the day breathes and the shadows flee, I will tie me to the mountain of myrrh and the hill of frankincense. You are all fair, my love; there is no flaw in you.

*   *   *

Here's what my father dreams I will be in the United States of America: A lawyer, then a judge, in a system of law that is both serious and just.

Not that he actually believes in democracy—in fact, he's openly suspicious of the popular will—but he longs for the power and prestige such a career would bring, and which he can't achieve on his own now that we're here, so he projects it all on me. He sees me in courtrooms and lecture halls, at libraries and in elegant restaurants, the object of envy and awe.

My father does not envision me in domestic scenes. He does not imagine me as a wife or mother because to do so would be to imagine someone else closer to me than he is, and he cannot endure that. He will never regret not being a grandfather; it was never part of his plan.

Here's what my mother dreams I will be in the United States of America: The owner of many appliances and a rolling green lawn; mother of two mischievous children; the wife of a boyishly handsome North American man who drinks Pepsi for breakfast; a career woman with a well-paying position in local broadcasting.

My mother pictures me reading the news on TV at four and home at the dinner table by six. She does not propose that I will actually do the cooking, but rather that I'll oversee the undocumented Haitian woman my husband and I have hired for that purpose. She sees me as fulfilled, as she imagines she is.

All I ever think about are kisses, not the deep throaty kind but quick pecks all along my belly just before my lover and I dissolve into warm blankets and tangled sheets in a bed under an open window. I have no view of this scene from a distance, so I don't know if the window frames tall pine trees or tropical bushes permeated with skittering gray lizards.

*   *   *

It's hot and stuffy in the processing center, where I'm sitting under a light that buzzes and clicks. Everything smells of nicotine. I wipe the shine off my face with the sleeve of my sweater. Eventually, I take off the sweater and fold it over my arm.

My father, smoking cigarette after cigarette, mutters about communism and how the Dominican Republic is next and then, possibly, someplace in Central America.

My mother has disappeared to another floor in the building, where the Catholic volunteer insists that she look through boxes filled with clothes donated by generous North Americans. Later, my mother will tell us how the Catholic volunteer pointed to the little gray flannel gym jacket with the hood and the American flag logo, how she plucked a bow tie from a box, then a black synthetic teddy from another and laughed, embarrassed.

My mother will admit she was uncomfortable with the idea of sifting through the boxes, sinking arm-deep into other people's sweat and excretions, but not that she was afraid of offending the Catholic volunteer and that she held her breath, smiled, and fished out a shirt for my father and a light blue cotton dress for me, which we'll never wear.

*   *   *

My parents escaped from Cuba because they did not want me to grow up in a communist state. They are anti-Communists, especially my father.

It's because of this that when Martin Luther King, Jr., dies in 1968 and North American cities go up in flames, my father will gloat. King was a Communist, he will say; he studied in Moscow, everybody knows that.

I'll roll my eyes and say nothing. My mother will ask him to please finish his *café con leche* and wipe the milk moustache from the top of his lip.

Later, the morning after Bobby Kennedy's brains are shot all over a California hotel kitchen, my father will greet the news of his death by walking into our kitchen wearing a "Nixon's the One" button.

There's no stopping him now, my father will say; I know, because I was involved with the counterrevolution, and I know he's the one who's going to save us, he's the one who came up with the Bay of Pigs which would have worked, all the experts agree, if he'd been elected instead of Kennedy, that coward.

My mother will vote for Richard Nixon in 1968, but in spite of his loud support my father will sit out the election, convinced there's no need to become a citizen of the United States (the usual prerequisite for voting) because Nixon will get us back to Cuba in no time, where my father's dormant citizenship will spring to life.

Later that summer, my father, who has resisted getting a television set (too cumbersome to be moved when we go back to Cuba, he will tell us), suddenly buys a huge Zenith color model to watch the Olympics broadcast from Mexico City.

I will sit on the floor, close enough to distinguish the different colored dots, while my father sits a few feet away in a LA-Z-BOY chair and roots for the Cuban boxers, especially Teofilo Stevenson. Every time Stevenson wins one—whether against North Americans or East Germans or whomever my father will jump up and shout.

Later, when the Cuban flag waves at us during the medal ceremony, and the Cuban national anthem comes through the TV's tinny speakers, my father will stand up in Miami and cover his heart with his palm just like Fidel, watching on his own TV in Havana.

When I get older, I'll tell my father a rumor I heard that Stevenson, for all his heroics, practiced his best boxing moves on his wife, and my father will look at me like I'm crazy and say, Yeah, well, he's a Communist, what did you expect, huh?

*   *   *

In the processing center, my father is visited by a Cuban man with a large camera bag and a steno notebook into which he's constantly scribbling. The man has green Coke-bottle glasses and chews on a pungent Cuban cigar as he nods at everything my father says.

My mother, holding a brown paper bag filled with our new (used) clothes, sits next to me on the couch under the buzzing and clicking lights. She asks me about the Colombian girl, and I tell her she read me parts of the Bible, which makes my mother shudder.

The man with the Coke-bottle glasses and cigar tells my father he's from Santiago de Cuba in Oriente province, near Fidel's hometown, where he claims nobody ever supported the revolution because they knew the real Fidel. Then he tells my father he knew his father, which makes my father very nervous.

The whole northern coast of Havana Harbor is mined, my father says to the Cuban man as if to distract him. There are *milicianos* all over the beaches, he goes on; it was a miracle we got out, but we had to do it for her, and he points my way again.

Then the man with the Coke-bottle glasses and cigar jumps up and pulls a giant camera out of his bag, covering my mother and me with a sudden explosion of light.

*   *   *

In 1971, I'll come home for Thanksgiving from Indiana University where I have a scholarship to study optometry. It'll be the first time in months I'll be without an antiwar demonstration to go to, a consciousness-raising group to attend, or a Gay Liberation meeting to lead.

Alaba'o, I almost didn't recognize you, my mother will say, pulling on the fringes of my suede jacket, promising to mend the holes in my floor sweeping bell-bottom jeans. My green sweater will be somewhere in the closet of my bedroom in their house.

We left Cuba so you could dress like this? my father will ask over my mother's shoulder.

And for the first and only time in my life, I'll say, Look, you didn't come for me, you came for you; you came because all your rich clients were leaving, and you were going to wind up a cashier in your father's hardware store if you didn't leave, okay?

My father, who works in a bank now, will gasp—*¿Qué qué?*—and step back a bit. And my mother will say, Please, don't talk to your father like that.

And I'll say, It's a free country, I can do anything I want, remember? Christ, he only left because Fidel beat him in that stupid swimming race when they were little.

And then my father will reach over my mother's thin shoulders, grab me by the red bandanna around my neck, and throw me to the floor, where he'll kick me over and over until all I remember is my mother's voice pleading, Please stop, please, please, please stop.

*   *   *

We leave the processing center with the fat Hungarian lady, who drives a large Ford station wagon. My father sits in the front with her, and my mother and I sit in the back, although there is plenty of room for both of us in the front as well. The fat Hungarian lady is taking us to our hotel, where our room will have a kitchenette and a view of an alley from which a tall black transvestite plies her night trade.

Eventually, I'm drawn by the lights of the city, not just the neon streaming by the car windows but also the white globes on the street lamps, and I scamper to the back where I can watch the lights by myself. I close my eyes tight, then open them, loving the tracers and star bursts on my private screen.

Up in front, the fat Hungarian lady and my father are discussing the United States' many betrayals, first of Eastern Europe after World War II, then of Cuba after the Bay of Pigs invasion.

My mother, whom I believe is as beautiful as any of the palm trees fluttering on the median strip as we drive by, leans her head against the car window, tired and bereft. She comes to when the fat Hungarian lady, in a fit of giggles, breaks from the road and into the parking lot of a supermarket so shrouded in light that I'm sure it's a flying saucer docked here in Miami.

We did this when we first came to America, the fat Hungarian lady says, leading us up to the supermarket. And it's something only people like us can appreciate.

My father bobs his head up and down and my mother follows, her feet scraping the ground as she drags me by the hand.

We walk through the front door and then a turnstile, and suddenly we are in the land of plenty—row upon row of cereal boxes, TV dinners, massive displays of fresh pineapple, crate after crate of oranges, shelves of insect repellent, and every kind of broom. The dairy section is jammed with cheese and chocolate milk.

There's a butcher shop in the back, and my father says, Oh my God, look, and points to a slab of bloody red ribs thick with meat. My God my God my God, he says, as if he's never seen such a thing, or as if we're on the verge of starvation.

Calm down, please, my mother says, but he's not listening, choking back tears and hanging off the fat Hungarian lady who's now walking him past the sausages and hot dogs, packaged bologna and chipped beef.

All around us people stare, but then my father says, We just arrived from Cuba, and there's so much here!

The fat Hungarian lady pats his shoulder and says to the gathering crowd, Yes, he came on a little boat with his whole family; look at his beautiful daughter who will now grow up well-fed and free.

I push up against my mother, who feels as smooth and thin as a palm leaf on Good Friday. My father beams at me tears in his eyes. All the while, complete strangers congratulate him on his wisdom and courage, give him hugs and money, and welcome him to the United States.

*　　*　　*

There are things that can't be told.

Things like when we couldn't find an apartment, everyone's saying it was because landlords in Miami didn't rent to families with kids, but knowing, always, that it was more than that.

Things like my doing very poorly on an IQ test because I didn't speak

English, and getting tossed into a special education track, where it took until high school before somebody realized I didn't belong there.

Things like a North American hairdresser telling my mother she didn't do her kind of hair.

Like my father, finally realizing he wasn't going to go back to Cuba anytime soon, trying to hang himself with the light cord in the bathroom while my mother cleaned rooms at a nearby luxury hotel, but falling instead and breaking his arm.

Like accepting welfare checks, because there really was no other way.

Like knowing that giving money to exile groups often meant helping somebody buy a private yacht for Caribbean vacations, not for invading Cuba, but also knowing that refusing to donate only invited questions about our own patriotism.

And knowing that Nixon really wasn't the one, and wasn't doing anything, and wouldn't have done anything, even if he'd finished his second term, no matter what a good job the Cuban burglars might have done at the Watergate Hotel.

*   *   *

What if we'd stayed? What if we'd never left Cuba? What if we were there when the last of the counterrevolution was beaten, or when Mariel Harbor leaked thousands of Cubans out of the island, or when the Pan-American Games came? What if we'd never left?

All my life, my father will say I would have been a young Communist, falling prey to the revolution's propaganda. According to him, I would have believed ice-cream treats came from Fidel, that those hairless Russians were our friends, and that my duty as a revolutionary was to turn him in for his counterrevolutionary activities—which he will swear he'd never have given up if we'd stayed in Cuba.

My mother will shake her head but won't contradict him. She'll say the revolution uses people, and that I, too, would probably have been used, then betrayed, and that we'll never know, but maybe I would have wound up in jail whether I ever believed in the revolution or not, because I would have talked back to the wrong person, me and my big mouth.

I wonder, if we'd stayed then who, if anyone—if not Martha and the boy from the military academy—would have been my blond lovers, or any kind of lovers at all.

*   *   *

And what if we'd stayed, and there had been no revolution?

My parents will never say, as if somehow they know that their lives were meant to exist only in opposition.

I try to imagine who I would have been if Fidel had never come into Havana sitting triumphantly on top of that tank, but I can't. I can only think of variations of who I am, not who I might have been.

In college one day, I'll tell my mother on the phone that I want to go back to Cuba to see, to consider all these questions, and she'll pause, then say, What for? There's nothing there for you, we'll tell you whatever you need to know, don't you trust us?

Over my dead body, my father will say, listening in on the other line.

Years later, when I fly to Washington, D.C., and take a cab straight to the Cuban Interests Section to apply for a visa, a golden-skinned man with the dulled eyes of a bureaucrat will tell me that because I came to the U.S. too young to make the decision to leave for myself—that it was in fact my parents who made it for me—the Cuban government does not recognize my U.S. citizenship.

You need to renew your Cuban passport, he will say. Perhaps your parents have it, or a copy of your birth certificate, or maybe you have a relative or friend who could go through the records in Cuba for you.

I'll remember the passport among my mother's priceless papers, handwritten in blue ink, even the official parts. But when I ask my parents for it, my mother will say nothing, and my father will say, It's not here anymore, but in a bank box, where you'll never see it. Do you think I would let you betray us like that?

*   *   *

The boy from the military academy will say oh baby baby as he grinds his hips into me. And Martha and all the girls before and after her here in the United States will say ooohhh ooooohhhhh oooooooohhhhhhhh as my fingers explore inside them.

But the first time I make love with a Cuban, a politically controversial exile writer of some repute, she will say, *Aaaaaqyyyyyyaaaaaqyyyyaaaaay* and lift me by my hair from between her legs, strings of saliva like sea foam between my mouth and her shiny curls. Then she'll drop me onto her mouth where our tongues will poke each other like wily porpoises.

In one swift movement, she'll flip me on my back, pillows falling every which way from the bed, and kiss every part of me, between my breasts and under my arms, and she'll suck my fingertips, and the inside of my elbows. And when she rests her head on my belly, her ear listening not to my heartbeat but to the fluttering of palm trees, she'll sit up, place one hand on my throat, the other on my sex, and kiss me there, under my rib cage, around my navel, where I am softest and palest.

The next morning, listening to her breathing in my arms, I will wonder how this could have happened, and if it would have happened at all if we'd stayed in Cuba. And if so, if it would have been furtive or free, with or without the revolution. And how—knowing now how cataclysmic life really is, I might hold on to her for a little while longer.

*   *   *

When my father dies of a heart attack in 1990 (it will happen while he's driving, yelling at somebody, and the car will just sail over to the sidewalk and stop dead at the curb where he'll fall to the seat and his arms will somehow fold over his chest, his hands set in prayer), I will come home to Florida from Chicago, where I'll be working as a photographer for the *Tribune*. I won't be taking pictures of murder scenes or politicians then but rather rock stars and local performance artists.

I'll be living in Uptown, in a huge house with a dry darkroom in one of the bedrooms, now converted and sealed black, where I cut up negatives and create photomontages that are exhibited at the Whitney Biennial and hailed by the critics as filled with yearning and hope.

When my father dies, I will feel sadness and a wish that certain things had been said, but I will not want more time with him. I will worry about my mother, just like all the relatives who predict she will die of heartbreak within months (she has diabetes and her vision is failing). But she will instead outlive both him and me.

I'll get to Miami Beach, where they've lived in a little coach house off Collins Avenue since their retirement, and find cousins and aunts helping my mother go through insurance papers and bank records, my father's will, his photographs and mementos: his university degree, a faded list of things to take back to Cuba (including Christmas lights), a jaundiced clipping from *Diario de las Americas* about our arrival which quotes my father as saying that Havana Harbor is mined, and a photo of my mother and me, wide-eyed and thin, sitting on the couch in the processing center.

My father's funeral will be simple but well attended, closed casket at my request, but with a moment reserved for those who want a last look. My mother will stay in the room while the box is pried open (I'll be in the lobby smoking a cigarette, a habit I despised in my father but which I'll pick up at his funeral) and tell me later she stared at the cross above the casket, never registering my father's talcumed and perfumed body beneath it.

I couldn't leave, it wouldn't have looked right, she'll say. But thank God I'm going blind.

Then a minister who we do not know will come and read from the Bible and my mother will reach around my waist and hold onto me as we listen to him say, When all these things come upon you, the blessing and the curse . . . and you call them to mind among all the nations where the Lord your God has driven you, and return to the Lord your God, you and your children, and obey his voice . . . with all your heart and with all your soul; then the Lord your God will return your fortunes, and have compassion upon you, and he will gather you again from all the peoples where the Lord your God has scattered you.

*   *   *

There will be a storm during my father's burial, which means it will end quickly. My mother and several relatives will go back to her house, where a TV will blare from the bedroom filled with bored teenage cousins, the women will talk about how to make picadillo with low-fat ground turkey instead of the traditional beef and ham, and the men will sit outside in the yard, drinking beer or small cups of Cuban coffee, and talk about my father's love of Cuba, and how unfortunate it is that he died just as Eastern Europe is breaking free, and Fidel is surely about to fall.

Three days later, after taking my mother to the movies and the mall, church and the local Social Security office, I'll be standing at the front gate with my bags, yelling at the cab driver that I'm coming, when my mother will ask me to wait a minute and run back into the house, emerging minutes later with a box for me that won't fit in any of my bags.

A few things, she'll say, a few things that belong to you that I've been meaning to give you for years and now, well, they're yours.

I'll shake the box, which will emit only a muffled sound, and thank her for whatever it is, hug her and kiss her and tell her I'll call her as soon as I get home. She'll put her chicken bone arms around my neck, kiss the skin there all the way to my shoulders, and get choked up, which will break my heart.

Sleepy and tired in the cab to the airport, I'll lean my head against the window and stare out at the lanky palm trees, their brown and green leaves waving good-bye to me through the still coming drizzle. Everything will be damp, and I'll be hot and stuffy, listening to car horns detonating on every side of me. I'll close my eyes, stare at the blackness, and try to imagine something of yearning and hope, but I'll fall asleep instead, waking only when the driver tells me we've arrived, and that he'll get my bags from the trunk, his hand outstretched for the tip as if it were a condition for the return of my things.

When I get home to Uptown I'll forget all about my mother's box until one day many months later when my memory's fuzzy enough to let me be curious. I'll break it open to find grade-school report cards, family pictures of the three of us in Cuba, a love letter to her from my father (in which he talks about wanting to kiss the tender mole by her mouth), Xeroxes of my birth certificate, copies of our requests for political asylum, and my faded blue-ink Cuban passport (expiration date: June 1965), all wrapped up in my old green sweater.

When I call my mother—embarrassed about taking so long to unpack her box, overwhelmed by the treasures within it—her answering machine will pick up and, in a bilingual message, give out her beeper number in case of emergency.

A week after my father's death, my mother will buy a computer with a Braille keyboard and a speaker, start learning how to use it at the community center down the block, and be busy investing in mutual funds at a profit within six months.

*   *   *

But this is all a long way off, of course. Right now, we're in a small hotel room with a kitchenette that U.S. taxpayers have provided for us.

My mother, whose eyes are dark and sunken, sits at a little table eating one of the Royal Castle hamburgers the fat Hungarian lady bought for us. My father munches on another, napkins spread under his hands. Their heads are tilted toward the window which faces an alley. To the far south edge, it offers a view of Biscayne Boulevard and a magically colored thread of night traffic. The air is salty and familiar, the moon brilliant hanging in the sky.

I'm in bed, under sheets that feel heavy with humidity and the smell of cleaning agents. The plastic doll the Catholic volunteer gave me sits on my pillow.

Then my father reaches across the table to my mother and says, We made it, we really made it.

And my mother runs her fingers through his hair and nods, and they both start crying, quietly but heartily, holding and stroking each other as if they are all they have.

And then there's a noise—a screech out in the alley followed by what sounds like a hyena's laughter—and my father leaps up and looks out the window, then starts laughing, too.

Oh my God, come here, look at this, he beckons to my mother, who jumps up and goes to him, positioning herself right under the crook of his arm. Can you believe that, he says.

Only in America, echoes my mother.

And as I lie here wondering about the spectacle outside the window and the new world that awaits us on this and every night of the rest of our lives, even I know we've already come a long way. What none of us can measure yet is how much of the voyage is already behind us.

Tato Laviera

AmeRícan

we gave birth to a new generation,
AmeRícan, broader than lost gold
never touched, hidden inside the
puerto rican mountains.

we gave birth to a new generation,
AmeRícan, it includes everything
imaginable you-name-it-we-got-it
society.

we gave birth to a new generation,
AmeRícan salutes all folklores,
european, indian, black, spanish,
and anything else compatible:

AmeRícan, singing to composer pedro flores' palm
     trees high up in the universal sky!

AmeRícan, sweet soft spanish danzas gypsies
        moving lyrics la espanola cascabelling
        presence always singing at our side!

AmeRícan, beating jibaro modern troubadours
        crying guitars romantic continental
        bolero love songs!

AmeRícan, across forth and across back
        back across and forth back
        forth across and back and forth
        our trips are walking bridges!

        it all dissolved into itself, the attempt
        was truly made, the attempt was truly
        absorbed, digested, we spit out
        the poison, we spit out the malice,
        we stand, affirmative in action,
        to reproduce a broader answer to the
        marginality that gobbled us up abruptly!

AmeRícan, walking plena-rhythms in new york,
        strutting beautifully alert, alive,
        many turning eyes wondering,
        admiring!

AmeRícan, defining myself my own way any way many
ways Am e Rican, with the big R and the
accent on the i!

AmeRícan, like the soul gliding talk of gospel
        boogie music!

AmeRícan, speaking new words in spanglish tenements
      fast tongue moving street corner "que
      corta" talk being invented at the insistence
      of a smile!

AmeRícan, abounding inside so many ethnic english
      people, and out of humanity, we blend
      and mix all that is good!

AmeRícan, integrating in new york and defining our
      own destino, our own way of life,

AmeRícan, defining the new america, humane america,
      admired america, loved america, harmonious
      america, the world in peace, our energies
      collectively invested to find other civili-
      zations, to touch God, further and further,
      to dwell in the spirit of divinity!

AmeRícan, yes, for now, for i love this, my second
      land, and i dream to take the accent from
      the altercation, and be proud to call
      myself AmeRícan, in the U.S. sense of the
      word, AmeRícan, America!

Vijay Seshadri

Made in the Tropics

Bobby Culture ("Full of Roots and Culture")
and Ranking Joe ("Man Make You Widdle
Pon Your Toe") shift down
in the gloaming, snap off
their helmets, kill their engines, park
one thousand cubic centimeters
of steeled precision Japanese art.
Their bands drive up
in fur-trimmed vans, unload and unwrap
the hundred watt speakers, thousand-watt amps,
mikes and mike stands,
guitars, cymbals, steel cans,
at the Blue Room Lawn on Gun Hill Road
by the Bronx botanical gardens.
The sun over Jersey
kicks and drops
into the next of its ready-made slots,
and, like a dark lotion
from a pitcher poured, night fills

the concrete hollows, and the grass
cools in the projects,
the glowing lakes contract
around their artificial islands,
the gardens breathe
easier in the dwindling fever
of today's unbearable summer.
They say the tropics
are moving north,
the skullcap of ice melting
from both the pole now pointed
toward the sun
and the one pointing away.
But what they say is hardly heard here,
where the cooling brick-work
engine red Edwardian
railroad flats empty
their tenants, who gather
in twos and threes, float down
from the stations,
and congregate at the Blue Room Lawn
to celebrate Independence
Day in Jamaica.
The bass line fires up.
From Savanna-La-Mar to Gun Hill Road
the backwash of reggae spirals
to its perch, ripples
and flares its solar wings
along the upended moving limbs,
as if a chain were passed through every wrist,
as if a chain were tied from hip to hip.
The sun does what it does because the earth tilts.

Maxine Hong Kingston

Absorption
of Rock

We bought from Laotian refugees a cloth
that in war a woman sewed, appliquéd
700 triangles—mountain ranges
changing colors with H'Mong suns and seasons,
white and yellow teeth, black arrows,
or sails. They point in at an embroidery,
whose mystery seems the same as that posed
by face cards. Up close, the curls and x's do
not turn plainer; a green strand runs through
the yellow chains, and black between the white.
Sometimes caught from across the room, twilighted,
the lace in the center smokes, and shadows move
over the red background, which should shine.
One refugee said, "This old woman's design."

We rented a room to a Vietnam vet,
who one Saturday night ran back to it—

thrashed through bamboo along the neighborhood
stream, then out on to sidewalk, lost the police,
though he imprinted the cement with blood
from his cut foot. He came out of the bathroom
an unidentifiable man. His strange
jagged wound yet unstaunched, he had shaved.
Yellow beard was mixed with blood and what
looked like bits of skin in the tub and toilet.
On the way to the hospital, he said, "Today
the M.C. raised his finger part way.
They're just about ready to gong my act."

We search out facts to defend a Vietnamese,
who has allegedly shot to death a Lao
in Stockton, outside a bar. It was in fear,
we hear him say, of a cantaloupe or rock
that the Lao man had caused to appear
inside him. One anthropologist testifies
that Vietnamese driving in the highlands
rolled up the windows against the H'mong air.
The H'mong in Fairfield were not indicted for
their try at family suicide, there was a question
of a Lao curse or want of a telephone.
Three translators have run away—this fourth
does not say enough words.

Li-Young Lee

The
Cleaving

He gossips like my grandmother, this man
with my face, and I could stand
amused all afternoon
in the hon kee grocery,
amid hanging meats he
chops: roast pork cut
from a hog hung
by nose and shoulders,
her entire skin burnt
crisp, flesh I know
to be sweet,
her shining
face grinning
up at ducks
dangling single file,
each pierced by black
hooks through breast, bill,

and steaming from a hole
stitched shut at the ass.
I step to the counter, recite,
and he, without even slightly
varying the rhythm of his current confession or harangue,
scribbles my order on a greasy receipt,
and chops it quick.

Such a sorrowful Chinese face,
nomad, Gobi, Northern
in its boniness
clear from the high
warlike forehead
To the sheer edge of the jaw.
He could be my brother, but finer,
and, except for his left forearm, which is engorged,
sinewy from his daily grip and
wield of a two-pound tool,
he's delicate, narrow-
waisted, his frame
so slight a lover, some
rough other
might break it down
its smooth, oily length.
In his light-handed calligraphy
on receipts and in his
moodiness, he is
a Southerner from a river-province;
suited for scholarship, his face poised
above an open book, he'd mumble
his favorite passages.
He could be my grandfather;

come to America to get a Western education
in 1917, but too homesick to study,
he sits in the park all day reading poems
and writing letters to his mother.

He lops the head off, chops
the neck of the duck
into six, slits
the body
open, groin
to breast, and drains
the scalding juices,
then quarters the carcass
with two fast hacks of the cleaver,
old blade that has worn
into the surface of the round
foot-thick chop-block
a scoop that cradles precisely the curved steel.

The head, flung from the body, opens
down the middle where the butcher
cleanly halved it between
the eyes, and I
see, foetal-crouched
inside the skull, the homunculus,
gray brain grainy
to eat.
Did this animal, after all, at the moment
its neck broke,
image the executioner
shrinks from his own death?
Is this how

I, too, recoil from my day?
See how this shape
hordes itself, see how
little it is.
See its grease on the blade.
is this how I'll be found
when judgement is passed, when names
are called, when crimes are tallied?
This is also how I looked before I tore my mother open.
Is this how I presided over my century, is this how
I regarded the murderers?
This is also how I prayed.
Was it me in the Other
I prayed to when I prayed?
This too was how I slept, clutching my wife.
Was it me in the other I loved
when I love another?
The butcher sees me eye this delicacy.
With a finger, he picks it
out of the skull-cradle
and offers it to me.
I take it gingerly between my fingers
and suck it down.
I eat my man.

The noise the body makes
when the body meets
the soul over the soul's ocean and penumbra
is the sound of up-and-down, in-and-out,
a lump of muscle chug-chugging blood
into the ear; a lover's
heart-shaped tongue;

flesh rocking flesh until flesh comes;
the butcher working
at his block and blade to marry their shapes
by violence and time;
an engine crossing,
recrossing salt water, hauling
immigrants and the junk
of the poor. These
are the faces I love, the bodies
and scents of bodies
for which I long
in various ways, at various times,
thirteen gathered around the redwood,
happy, talkative, voracious
at day's end,
eager to eat
four kinds of meat
prepared four different ways,
numerous plates and bowls of rice and vegetables,
each made by distinct affections
and brought to table by many hands.
Brothers and sisters by blood and design,
who sit in separate bodies of varied shapes,
we constitute a many-membered
body of love.
in a world of shapes
of my desires, each one here
is a shape of one of my desires, and each
is known to me and dear by virtue
of each one's unique corruption
of those texts, the face, the body:
that jut jaw

to gnash tendon;
that wide nose to meet the blows
a face like that invites;
those long eyes closing on the seen;
those thick lips
to suck the meat of animals
or recite 300 poems of the T'ang;
these teeth to bite my monosyllables;
these cheekbones to make
those syllables sing the soul.
Puffed or sunken
according to the life,
dark or light, according
to the birth, straight
or humped, whole, manqué, quasi, each pleases, verging
on utter grotesquery.
All are beautiful by variety.
The soul too
is a debasement
of a text, but, thus, it
acquires salience, although a
human salience, but
inimitable, and hence, memorable.
God is the text.
The soul is a corruption
and a mnemonic.

A bright moment,
I hold up an old head
from the sea and admire the haughty
down-curved mouth
that seems to disdain

all the eyes are blind to,
including me, the eater.
Whole unto itself, complete
without me, yet its
shape complements the shape of my mind.
I take it as text and evidence
of the world's love for me,
and I feel urged to utterance,
urged to read the body of the world, urged
to say it
in human terms,
my reading a kind of eating, my eating
a kind of reading,
my saying a diminishment, my noise
a love-in-answer.
What is it in me would
devour the world to utter it?
What is it in me will not let
the world be, would eat
not just this fish,
but the one who killed it,
the butcher who cleaned it.
I would eat the way he
squats, the way he
reaches into the plastic tubs
and pulls out a fish, clubs it, takes it
to the sink, guts it, drops it on the weighing pan.

I would eat that thrash
and plunge of the watery body
in the water, that liquid violence
between the man's hands,

I would eat
the gutless twitching on the scales,
three pounds of dumb
nerve and pulse, I would eat it all
to utter it.
The deaths at the sinks, those bodies prepared
for eating, I would eat,
and the standing deaths
at the counters in the aisles,
the walking deaths in the streets,
the death-far-from-home, the death-
in-a-strange-land, these Chinatown
deaths, these American deaths.
I would devour this race to sing it,
this race that according to Emerson
managed to preserve to a hair
for three or four thousand years
the ugliest features in the world.
I would eat these features, eat
the last three or four thousand years, every hair.
And I would eat Emerson, his transparent soul, his
soporific transcendence.
I would eat his head,
glazed in pepper-speckled sauce,
the cooked eyes opaque in their sockets.
I would bring it to my mouth and—
that way I was taught, the way I've watched
others before me do—
with a stiff tongue lick out
the cheek meat and the meat
over the armored jaw, my eating
its sensual, salient nowness,

punctuating the void
from which such hunger springs and to which it proceeds.

And what
is this
I excavate
with my mouth?
What is the
plated, ribbed, hinged
architecture, *this carp head,*
but one more
articulation of a single nothing
severally manifested?
What is my eating,
rapt as it is,
but another
shape of going,
my immaculate expiration?

O, nothing is so
steadfast it won't go
the way the body goes.
The body goes.
The body's grave,
so serious
in its dying,
arduous as martyrs
in that task and as
glorious. It goes
empty always
and announces its going
be spasms and groans, farts and sweats.

Crossing into America

What I thought were the arms
aching *cleave,* were the knees trembling *leave.*
What I thought were the muscles
insisting *resist, persist, exist,*
were the pores
hissing *mist* and *waste.*
What I thought was the body humming *reside, reside,*
was the body sighing *revise, revise.*
O, the murderous deletions, the keening
down to nothing, the cleaving.
All of the body's revisions end
in death.
All of the body's revisions end.

Bodies eating bodies, heads eating heads,
we are nothing eating nothing,
and though we feast,
are filled, overfilled,
we go famished.
We gang the doors of death.
That I, our deaths are fed
that we may continue our daily dying,
our bodies going
down, while the plates-soon-empty
are passed around, that true
direction of our true prayers,
while the butcher spells
his message, manifold,
in the mortal air.
He coaxes, cleaves, brings change
before our very eyes, and at every
moment of our being.

As we eat we're eaten.
Else what is this
violence, this salt, this
passion, this heaven?

I thought the soul an airy thing.
I did not know the soul
is cleaved, so that the soul might be restored.
Live wood hewn,
its sap springs from a sticky wound.
No seed, no egg has he
whose business calls for an axe.
In the trade of my soul's shaping,
he traffics in hews and hacks.

No easy thing, violence.
One of its names? Change. Change
resides in the embrace
of the effaced and the effacer,
in the covenant of the opened and the opener;
the axe accomplishes it on the soul's axis.
What then may I do
but cleave to what cleaves me.
I kiss the blade and eat my meat.
I think the wielder and receive,
while terror spirits
my change, sorrow also.
The terror the butcher
scripts in the unhealed
air, the sorrow of his Shang
dynasty face,
African face with slit eyes, he is

ter, this
utiful Bedouin, this Shulamite,
keeper of sabbaths, diviner
of holy texts, this dark
dancer, this Jew, this Asian, this one
with the Cambodian face, Vietnamese face, this Chinese
I daily face,
this immigrant,
this man with my own face.

Richard Rodriguez

Mexico's
Children

When I was a boy it was still possible for Mexican farmworkers in California to commute between the past and the future.

The past returned every October. The white sky clarified to blue and fog opened white fissures in the landscape.

After the tomatoes and the melons and the grapes had been picked, it was time for Mexicans to load up their cars and head back into Mexico for the winter.

The schoolteacher said aloud to my mother what a shame it was the Mexicans did that—took their children out of school.

Like wandering Jews, Mexicans had no true home but the tabernacle of memory.

The schoolteacher was scandalized by what she took as the Mexicans' disregard of their children's future. The children failed their tests. They made no friends. What did it matter? Come November, they would be gone to some bright world that smelled like the cafeteria on Thursdays— Bean Days. Next spring they would be enrolled in some other school, in some other Valley town.

choolroom myth of America described an ocean—immigrants
g behind several time zones and all the names for things.

Mexican-American memory described proximity. There are large
Mexican-American populations in Seattle and Chicago and Kansas City,
but the majority of Mexican Americans live, where most have always
lived, in the Southwestern United States, one or two hours from Mexico,
which is within the possibility of recourse to Mexico or within the sound
of her voice.

My father knew men in Sacramento who had walked up from Mexico.

There is confluence of earth. The cut of the land or its fold, the
bleaching sky, the swath of the wind, the length of shadows—all these
suggested Mexico. Mitigated was the sense of dislocation otherwise familiar to immigrant experience.

By November the fog would thicken, the roads would be dangerous.
Better to be off by late October. Families in old trucks and cars headed
south down two-lane highways, past browning fields. Rolls of toilet paper
streaming from rolled-down windows. After submitting themselves to
the vegetable cycle of California for a season, these Mexicans were free.
They were Mexicans! And what better thing to be?

HAIIII-EEE. HAI. HAI. HAI.

There is confluence of history.

Cities, rivers, mountains retain Spanish names. California was once
Mexico.

The fog closes in, condenses, and drips day and night from the bare
limbs of trees. And my mother looks out the kitchen window and cannot
see the neighbor's house.

Amnesia fixes the American regard of the past. I remember a graduate
student at Columbia University during the Vietnam years; she might have
been an ingenue out of Henry James. "After Vietnam, I'll never again
believe that America is the good and pure country I once thought it to
be," the young woman said.

Whereas Mexican Americans have paid a price for the clarity of their past.

Consider my father: when he decided to apply for American citizenship, my father told no one, none of his friends, those men with whom he had come to this country looking for work. American citizenship would have seemed a betrayal of Mexico, a sin against memory. One afternoon, like a man with something to hide, my father slipped away. He went downtown to the Federal Building in Sacramento and disappeared into America.

Now memory takes her revenge on the son.

*   *   *

VETE PERO NO ME OLVIDES.

Go, but do not forget me, someone has written on the side of a building near the border in Tijuana.

Mexicans may know their souls are imperiled in America but they do not recognize the risk by its proper name.

Two Mexican teenagers say they are going to *los Estados Unidos* for a job. Nothing more.

For three or four generations now, Mexican villages have lived under the rumor of America, a rumor vaguer than paradise. America exists in thousands of maternal prayers and in thousands of pubescent dreams. Everyone knows someone who has been. Everyone knows someone who never came back.

What do you expect to find?

The answer is always an explanation for the journey: "I want money enough to be able to return to live with my family in Mexico."

Proofs of America's existence abound in Mexican villages—stereo equipment, for example, or broken-down cars—but these are things Americans picked up or put down, not America.

Mexicans know very little of the United States, though they have seen

America, the TV show, and America, the movie. Mexico's preeminent poet, Octavio Paz, writes of the United States as an idea of no characteristic mansion or spice. Paz has traveled and taught in America, but his writings relegate America to ineluctability—a jut of optimism, an aerodynamic law.

To enter America, which is invisible, Mexicans must become invisible. Tonight, a summer night, five hundred Mexicans will become invisible at 8:34 P.M. While they wait, they do not discuss Tom Paine or Thomas Jefferson or the Bill of Rights. Someone has an uncle in Los Angeles who knows a peach farmer near Tracy who always hires this time of year.

Compared with pulpy Mexico, grave Mexico, sandstone Mexico, which takes the impression of time, the United States and its promise of the future must seem always hypothetical—occasion more than place.

I once had occasion to ask a middle-class Mexican what he admires about the United States (a provocative question because, according to Mexican history and proverb, there is nothing about the United States to admire). He found only one disembodied word: "organization." When I pressed the man to anthropomorphize further he said, "Deliveries get made, phones are answered, brakes are repaired" (indirect constructions all, as if by the consent of unseen hands).

Coming from Mexico, a country that is so thoroughly *there,* where things are not necessarily different from when your father was your age, Mexicans are unable to puncture the abstraction. For Mexicans, even death is less abstract than America.

Mexican teenagers waiting along the levee in Tijuana are bound to be fooled by the United States because they do not yet realize the future will be as binding as the past. The American job will introduce the Mexican to an industry, an optimism, a solitude nowhere described in Mexico's theology.

How can two Mexican teenagers know this, clutching the paper bags their mamas packed for them this morning? The past is already the future, for the bags contain only a change of underwear. These two may have seen *Dallas* on TV and they may think they are privy to the logic and locution of America. But that is not the same thing as having twenty American dollars in their own pockets.

*   *   *

Mexico, mad mother. She still does not know what to make of our leaving. For most of this century Mexico has seen her children flee the house of memory. During the Revolution 10 percent of the population picked up and moved to the United States; in the decades following the Revolution, Mexico has watched many more of her children cast their lots with the future; head north for work, for wages; north for life. Bad enough that so many left, worse that so many left her for the gringo.

America wanted cheap labor. American contractors reached down into Mexico for men to build America. Sons followed fathers north. It became a rite of passage for the poor Mexican male.

I will send for you or I will come home rich.

I would see them downtown on Sundays—men my age drunk in Plaza Park. I was still a boy at sixteen, but I was an American. At sixteen, I wrote a gossip column, "The Watchful Eye," for my school paper.

Or they would come into town on Monday nights for the wrestling matches or on Tuesday nights for boxing. They worked on ranches over in Yolo County. They were men with time on their hands. They were men without women. They were Mexicans without Mexico.

On Saturdays, Mexican men flooded the Western Union office, where they sent money—money turned into humming wire and then turned back into money—all the way down into Mexico. America was a monastery. America was a vow of poverty. They kept themselves poor for Mexico.

Fidel, the janitor at church, lived over the garage at the rectory. Fidel spoke Spanish and was Mexican. He had a wife down there, people said; some said he had grown children. But too many years had passed and he didn't go back. Fidel had to do for himself. Fidel had a clean piece of linoleum on the floor; he had an iron bed; he had a table and a chair; he had a frying pan and a knife and a fork and a spoon. Everything else Fidel sent back to Mexico. Sometimes, on summer nights, I would see his head through the bars of the little window over the garage of the rectory.

My parents left Mexico in the twenties: she as a girl with her family; he as a young man, alone. To tell different stories. Two Mexicos. At some celebration—we went to so many when I was a boy—a man in the crowd filled his lungs with American air to crow over all, ¡VIVA MEXICO! Everyone cheered. My parents cheered. The band played louder. Why VIVA MEXICO? The country that had betrayed them? The country that had forced them to live elsewhere?

I remember standing in the doorway of my parents' empty bedroom.

Mexico was memory—not mine. Mexico was mysteriously both he and she, like this, like my parents' bed. And over my parents' bed floated the Virgin of Guadalupe in a dimestore frame. In its most potent guise, Mexico was a mother like this queen. Her lips curved like a little boat. *Tú. Tú.* The suspirate vowel. *Tú.* The ruby pendant. The lemon tree. The song of the dove. Breathed through the nose, perched on the lips. Two voices, two pronouns were given me as a child, like good and bad angels, like sweet and sour milks, like rank and clement weathers; one yielding, one austere.

In the sixteenth century, Spain bequeathed to Mexico two forms of address, two versions of "you": In Mexico there is *tú* and there is *usted.*

In Sacramento, California, everything outside our house was English, was "you"—hey you. My dog was you. My parents were you. The nuns were you. My best friend, my worst enemy was you. God was You.

Whereas the architecture of Mexico is the hardened shell of a Spanish distinction.

Treeless, open plazas abate at walls; walls yield to refreshment, to interior courtyards, to shuttered afternoons.

At the heart there is *tú*—the intimate voice—the familiar room in a world full of rooms. *Tú* is the condition, not so much of knowing, as of being known; of being recognized. *Tú* belongs within the family. *Tú* is spoken to children and dogs, to priests; among lovers and drunken friends; to servants; to statues; to the high court of heaven; to God Himself.

The shaded arcade yields once more to the plaza, to traffic and the light of day. *Usted,* the formal, the bloodless, the ornamental you, is spoken to the eyes of strangers. By servants to masters. *Usted* shows deference to propriety, to authority, to history. *Usted* is open to interpretation; therefore it is subject to corruption, a province of politicians. *Usted* is the language outside Eden.

*   *   *

In Mexico, one is most oneself in private. The very existence of *tú* must undermine the realm of *usted.* In America, one is most oneself in public.

In order to show you America I would have to take you out. I would take you to the restaurant—OPEN 24 HOURS—alongside a freeway, any freeway in the U.S.A. The waitress is a blond or a redhead—not the same color as at her last job. She is divorced. Her eyebrows are jet-black migraines painted on, or relaxed, clownish domes of cinnamon brown. Morning and the bloom of youth are painted on her cheeks. She is at once antimaternal—the kind of woman you're not supposed to know— and supramaternal, the nurturer of lost boys.

She is the priestess of the short order, curator of the apple pie. She administers all the consolation of America. She has no illusions. She knows the score; she hands you the Bill of Rights printed on plastic, decorated with an heraldic tumble of French fries and drumsticks and steam.

Your table may yet be littered with bitten toast and spilled coffee and a dollar tip. Now you will see the greatness of America. As one complete gesture, the waitress pockets the tip, stacks dishes along one strong forearm, produces a damp rag soaked in lethe water, which she then passes over the Formica.

There! With that one swipe of the rag, the past has been obliterated. The Formica gleams like new. You can order anything you want.

If I were to show you Mexico, I would take you home; with the greatest reluctance I would take you home, where family snapshots crowd upon the mantel. For the Mexican, the past is firmly held from within. While outside, a few miles away in the American city, there is only loosening, unraveling; generations living apart. Old ladies living out their lives in fiercely flowered housedresses. Their sons are divorced; wear shorts, ride bikes; are not men, really; not really. Their granddaughters are not fresh, are not lovely or keen, are not even nice.

Seek the Mexican in the embrace of the family, where there is much noise. The family stands as a consolation, because in the certainty of generation there is protection against an uncertain future. At the center of this gravity the child is enshrined. He is not rock-a-bye baby at the very top of the family tree, as it is with American families. The child does not represent distance from the past, but reflux. She is not expected to fly away, to find herself. He is not expected to live his own life.

I will send for you or I will come home rich.

The culture of *tú* is guarded by the son, desired by the son, enforced by the son. Femininity is defined by the son as motherhood. Only a culture so cruel to the wife could sustain such a sentimental regard for *mamacita*. By contrast, much license is appropriated by the Mexican male. If the brother is taught to hover—he is guarding his sister's virginity— the adolescent male is otherwise, elsewhere, schooled in seduction. For the male as for the female, sexuality is expressed as parenthood. The male, by definition, is father. The husband is always a son.

It is not coincidental that American feminists have borrowed the Spanish word *macho* to name their American antithesis. But in English, the macho is publicly playful, boorish, counterdomestic. American macho is drag—the false type for the male—as Mae West is the false type for the female.

Machismo in Mexican Spanish is more akin to the Latin *gravitas*. The male is serious. The male provides. The Mexican male never abandons those who depend upon him. The male remembers.

Mexican *machismo,* like Mexican politics, needs its mise-en-scène. In fair Verona, in doublet and hose, it might yet play. The male code derives less from efficacy than from valor. *Machismo* is less an assertion of power or potency than it is a rite of chivalry.

The *macho* is not urbane Gilbert Roland or the good guy Lee Trevino; he is more like Bobby Chacon, the slight, leathery middle-aged boxer, going twelve rounds the night after his wife commits suicide. The macho holds his own ground. There is sobriety in the male, and silence, too—a severe limit on emotional range. The male isn't weak. The male wins a Purple Heart or he turns wife beater. The male doesn't cry.

Men sing in Mexico. In song, the male can admit longing, pain, desire, weakness.

HAIII-EEEE.

A cry like a comet rises over the song. A cry like mock-weeping tickles the refrain of Mexican love songs. The cry is meant to encourage the balladeer—it is the raw edge of his sentiment. HAI-II-EEE. It is the man's sound. A ticklish arching of semen, a node wrung up a guitar string, until it bursts in a descending cascade of mockery. HAI. HAI. HAI. The cry of the jackal under the moon, the whistle of the phallus, the maniacal song of the skull.

So it may well be Mama who first realizes the liberation of the American "you," the American pan-*usted,* the excalibur "I" which will deliver her from the Islamic cloister of Mexico. (*Tú.*)

*   *   *

A true mother, Mexico would not distinguish among her children. Her protective arm extended not only to the Mexican nationals working in the United States, but to the larger number of Mexican Americans as well. Mexico was not interested in passports; Mexico was interested in blood. No matter how far away you moved, you were still related to her.

In 1943, American sailors in Los Angeles ventured into an evil vein of boredom. They crashed the east side of town, where they beat up barrio teenagers dressed in the punk costume of their day. "The Zoot Suit Riots" lasted several nights. City officials went to bed early, and the Los Angeles press encouraged what it termed high-spirited sailors. It required the diplomatic protest of the Mexican ambassador and the consequent intervention of the U.S. secretary of state to end the disturbances.

Mexico sent cables of protest to Washington whenever she heard of the mistreatment of Mexican nationals. In a city as small as Sacramento in the 1950s, there was a Mexican consulate—a small white building downtown, in all ways like an insurance office, except for the seal of Mexico over the door. For decades, at offices like this one, Mexicans would find a place of defense in the U.S.A.

In 1959, Octavio Paz, Mexico's sultan son, her clever one philosopher, poet, statesman—published *The Labyrinth of Solitude,* his reflections on Mexico. Within his labyrinth, Paz places as well the Mexican American. He writes of the *pachuco,* the teenage gang member, and, by implication, of the Mexican American: "The *pachuco* does not want to become a Mexican again; at the same time he does not want to blend into the life of North America. His whole being is sheer negative impulse, a tangle of contradictions, an enigma."

This was Mother Mexico talking, her good son; this was Mexico's metropolitan version of Mexican Americans. Mexico had lost language, lost gods, lost ground. Mexico recognized historical confusion in us. We were Mexico's Mexicans.

When we return to Mexico as *turistas,* with our little wads of greenbacks, our credit cards, our Japanese cameras, our Bermuda shorts, our pauses for directions and our pointing fingers, Mexico condescends to take our order (our order in halting Spanish), *claro* señor. But the table is not cleared; the table will never be cleared. Mexico prefers to reply in English, as a way of saying:

¡Pocho!

The Mexican American who forgets his true mother is a *pocho,* a person of no address, a child of no proper idiom. But blood is blood, or perhaps, in this case, language is blood. Mexico worried. Mexico had seen her children lured by the gringo's offer of work. During the Great Depression, as the gringo's eyes slowly drained of sugar, thousands of Mexicans in the United States were rounded up and deported.

In 1938, my mother's brother returned to Mexico with only a curse for the United States of America. He had worked at construction sites throughout California and he was paid less than he had contracted for. At his stupefaction—the money in his hand—the contractor laughed.

What's the matter, babe, can't you Mesicans count?

And who took him back, shrieks Mexico, thumping her breast. Who?

No wonder that Mexico would not entertain the idea of a "Mexican American" except as a fiction, a bad joke of history. And most Mexican Americans lived in barrios, apart from gringos; many retained Spanish, as if in homage to her. We were still her children.

As long as we didn't marry.

*   *   *

His coming of age.

From his bed he watches Mama moving back and forth under the light. Outside, the bells of the church fly through the dark. Mama crosses herself. He pushes back the plastic curtain until his nostril catches air. He turns toward Mama. He studies her back—it is like a loaf of bread—as she bends over the things she is wrapping for him to take.

Today he becomes a man. His father has sent for him. His father has sent an address in the American city. That's what it means. His father is in the city with his uncle. He remembers his uncle remembering snow with his beer.

The boy dresses in the shadows. Then he moves toward the table, the circle of light. He sits down. He forces himself to eat. Mama stands over him to make the sign of the cross with her thumb on his forehead. He smiles for her. She puts a bag of food in his hands. She says she has told La Virgen to watch over him.

Yes, and he leaves quickly. Outside it is gray. He hears a little breeze. Or is it the rustle of old black Dueña, the dog—yes, it is she—taking her shortcuts through the weeds, crazy Dueña, her pads through the dust, following him. He passes the houses of the village; each window has a proper name. He passes Muñoz, the store. Old Rosa, the bar. The lighted window of the clinic where the pale medical student from Monterrey lives alone and reads his book full of sores late into the night.

The boy has just passed beyond the cemetery. His guardian breeze has died. The sky has begun to lighten. He turns and throws a rock back at La Dueña—it might be his heart that he throws. But no need. She will not go past the cemetery, not even for him. She will turn in circles like a loca and bite herself, Old Dueña, saying her rosary.

The dust takes on gravel, the path becomes a rutted road which leads to the highway. He walks north. The sky has turned white. Insects click in the fields. In time, there will be a bus.

*   *   *

The endurance of Mexico may be attributed to the realm of *tú* wherein the family, the village, is held in immutable suspension; whereby the city—the government—is held in contempt.

Mexicans will remember this century as the century of loss. The land of Mexico will not sustain Mexicans. For generations, from Mexico City, came promises of land reform. *The land will be yours.*

What more seductive promise could there be to a nation haunted by the memory of dispossession?

The city broke most of its promises.

The city represents posture and hypocrisy to the average Mexican. The average Mexican imagination will weigh the city against the village and come up short. But the city represents the only possibility for survival. In the last half of this century, Mexicans have abandoned the village. And there is no turning back. After generations of ancestors asleep beneath the earth and awake above the sky, after roosters and priests and sleeping dogs, there is only the city.

The Goddess of Liberty—that stony schoolmarm—may well ask Mexicans why they are so resistant to change, to the interesting freedoms she offers. Mexicans are notorious in the United States for their skepticism regarding public life. Mexicans don't vote. Mexicans drop out of school.

Mexicans live in superstitious fear of the American diaspora. Mexican Americans are in awe of education, of getting too much schooling, of changing too much, of moving too far from home.

Well, now. Never to be outdone, Mother Mexico has got herself up in goddess cloth. She carries a torch, too, and it is the torch of memory. She is searching for her children.

A false mother, Mexico cares less for her children than for her pride. The exodus of so many Mexicans for the U.S. is not evidence of Mexico's failure; it is evidence, rather, of the emigrant's failure. After all, those who left were of the peasant, the lower classes—those who could not make it, in Mexico.

The government of hurt pride is not above political drag. The government of Mexico impersonates the intimate genius of matriarchy in order to justify a political stranglehold.

In its male, in its public, in its city aspect, Mexico is an arch-transvestite, a tragic buffoon. Dogs bark and babies cry when Mother Mexico walks abroad in the light of day. The policeman, the Marxist mayor—Mother Mexico doesn't even bother to shave her mustachios. Swords and rifles and spurs and bags of money chink and clatter beneath her skirts. A chain of martyred priests dangles from her waist, for she is an austere, pious lady. Ay, how much—clutching her jangling bosoms; spilling cigars—how much she has suffered!

REMEMBER. THE STRENGTH OF MEXICO IS THE FAMILY.
(A government billboard.)

*   *   *

In his glass apartment overlooking the Polanco district of Mexico City, the journalist says he does not mind in the least that I call myself an American. "But when I hear Mexicans in the United States talk about George Washington as the father of their country," he exhales a florid ellipsis of cigarette smoke.

*   *   *

America does not lend itself to sexual metaphor as easily as Mexico does. George Washington is the father of the country, we say. We speak of Founding Fathers. The legend ascribed to the Statue of Liberty is childlessness.

America is an immigrant country. Motherhood—parenthood—is less our point than adoption. If I had to assign gender to America, I would notice the consensus of the rest of the world. When America is burned in effigy, a male is burned. Americans themselves speak of Uncle Sam. Uncle Sam is the personification of conscription.

During World War II, hundreds of thousands of Mexican Americans were drafted to fight in Europe and in Asia. And they went, submitting themselves to a commonweal. Not a very Mexican thing to do, for Mexico had taught us always that we lived apart from history in the realm of *tú*.

It was Uncle Sam who shaved the sideburns from that generation of Mexican Americans. Like the Goddess of Liberty, Uncle Sam has no children of his own. In a way, Sam represents necessary evil to the American imagination. He steals children to make men of them, mocks all reticence, all modesty, all memory. Uncle Sam is a hectoring Yankee, a skinflint uncle, gaunt, uncouth, unloved. He is the American Savonarola—hater of moonshine, destroyer of stills, burner of cocaine. Free enterprise is curiously an evasion of Uncle Sam, as is sentimentality. Sam has no patience with mamas' boys. That includes Mama Mexico, ma'am.

You betray Uncle Sam by favoring private over public life, by seeking to exempt yourself. By cheating on your income taxes, by avoiding jury duty, by trying to keep your boy on the farm. These are legal offenses.

Betrayal of Mother Mexico, on the other hand, is a sin against the natural law, a failure of memory.

When the war was over, Mexican Americans returned home to a GI Bill and with the expectation of an improved future. By the 1950s, Mexican Americans throughout the Southwest were busy becoming middle-class. I would see them around Sacramento: a Mexican American dentist; a shoe salesman at Weinstock's; the couple that ran the tiny Mexican food store that became, before I graduated from high school, a block-long electrified MEXICATESSEN. These were not "role models," exactly; they were people like my parents, making their way in America.

*   *   *

When I was in grammar school, they used to hit us for speaking Spanish.
THEY.

Mexican Americans forfeit the public experience of America because we fear it. And for decades in the American Southwest, public life was withheld from us. America lay north of *usted,* beyond even formal direct address. America was the realm of *los norteamericanos*—They. We didn't have an adequate name for you. In private, you were the gringo. The ethnic albino. The goyim. The ghost. You were not us. In public we also said "Anglo"—an arcane usage of the nineteenth century—you-who-speak-English. If we withdrew from directly addressing you, you became *ellos*—They—as in: They kept us on the other side of town. They owned the land. They owned the banks. They ran the towns they and their wives in their summer-print dresses. They kept wages low. They made us sit upstairs in the movie houses. Or downstairs.

Thus spoken memory becomes a kind of shorthand for some older, other outrage, the nineteenth-century affront. The land stolen. The Mexican scorned on land he had named. Spic. Greaser. Spanish, the great metropolitan language, reduced to a foreign tongue, a language of the outskirts, the language of the gibbering poor, thus gibberish; English, the triumphal, crushing metaphor.

I know Mexican Americans who have lived in this country for forty or fifty years and have never applied for citizenship or gathered more than a Montgomery Ward sense of English. Their refusal, lodged between *How much* and *Okay,* is not a linguistic dilemma primarily.

On the other hand, when we call ourselves Mexican Americans, Mexico is on the phone, long-distance: *So typical of the gringo's arrogance to appropriate the name of a hemisphere to himself—yes? But why should you repeat the folly?*

Mexico always can find a myth to account for us: Mexicans who go north are like the Chichimeca—a barbarous tribe antithetical to Mexico. But in the United States, Mexican Americans did not exist in the national imagination until the 1960s—years when the black civil rights movement prompted Americans to acknowledge "invisible minorities" in their midst. Then it was determined statistically that Mexican Americans constituted a disadvantaged society, living in worse conditions than most other Americans, having less education, facing bleaker sidewalks or Safeways.

Bueno. (Again Mother Mexico is on the phone.) *What kind of word is that—"minority"? Was the Mexican American*—she fries the term on the skillet of her tongue—*was the Mexican American content to say that his association with Mexico left him culturally disadvantaged?*

The sixties were years of romance for the American middle class. Americans competed with one another to play the role of society's victim. It was an age of T-shirts.

In those years, the national habit of Americans was to seek from the comparison with blacks a kind of analogy. Mexican American political activists, especially student activists, insisted on a rough similarity between the two societies—black, Chicano—ignoring any complex factor of history or race that might disqualify the equation.

Black Americans had suffered relentless segregation and mistreatment, but blacks had been implicated in the public life of this country from the beginning. Oceans separated the black slave from any possibility of rescue or restoration. From the symbiosis of oppressor and the oppressed, blacks took a hard realism. They acquired the language of the white man, though they inflected it with refusal. And because racism fell upon all blacks, regardless of class, a bond developed between the poor and the bourgeoisie, thence the possibility of a leadership class able to speak for the entire group.

Mexican Americans of the generation of the sixties had no myth of themselves as Americans. So that when Mexican Americans won national notoriety, we could only refer the public gaze to the past. We are people of the land, we told ourselves. Middle-class college students took to wearing farmer-in-the-dell overalls and they took, as well, a rural slang to name themselves: Chicanos.

Chicanismo blended nostalgia with grievance to reinvent the mythic northern kingdom of Atzlán as corresponding to the Southwestern American desert. Just as Mexico would only celebrate her Indian half, Chicanos determined to portray themselves as Indians in America, as indigenous people, thus casting the United States in the role of Spain.

Chicanos used the language of colonial Spain to declare to America that they would never give up their culture. And they said, in Spanish, that Spaniards had been oppressors of their people.

Left to ourselves in a Protestant land, Mexican Americans shored up our grievances, making of them altars to the past. *May my tongue cleave to my palate if I should forget thee. (Tú.)*

Ah, Mother, can you not realize how Mexican we have become?

But she hates us, she hates us.

Chicanismo offended Mexico. It was one thing for Mexico to play the victim among her children, but Mexico did not like it that Chicanos were playing the same role for the gringos.

By claiming too many exemptions, Chicanos also offended Americans. Chicanos seemed to violate a civic agreement that generations of other immigrants had honored: My grandparents had to learn English. . . .

Chicanos wanted more and less than they actually said. On the one hand, Chicanos were intent upon bringing America (as a way of bringing history) to some Act of Contrition. On the other hand, Chicanos sought pride, a restoration of face in America. And America might provide the symbolic solution to a Mexican dilemma: if one could learn public English while yet retaining family Spanish, *usted* might be reunited with *tú,* the future might be reconciled with the past.

Mexicans are a people of sacraments and symbols. I think few Chicanos ever expected Spanish to become a public language coequal with English. But by demanding Spanish in the two most symbolic places of American citizenship—the classroom and the voting booth—Chicanos were consoling themselves that they need not give up the past to participate in the American city. They were not less American for speaking Spanish; they were not less Mexican for succeeding in America.

America got bored with such altars—too Catholic for the likes of America. Protestant America is a literal culture.

SAY WHAT YOU WANT.

What was granted was a bureaucratic bilingualism—classrooms and voting booths—pragmatic concessions to a spiritual grievance.

I end up arguing about bilingualism with other Mexican Americans, middle-class like myself. As I am my father's son, I am skeptical, like Mexico; I play the heavy, which is to say I play America. We argue and argue, but not about pedagogy. We argue about desire's reach; we exchange a few platitudes (being richer for having two languages; being able to go home again). In the end, the argument reduces to somebody's childhood memory.

When I was in school, they used to hit us for speaking Spanish.

My father says the trouble with the bilingual voting ballot is that one ends up voting for the translator.

*   *   *

In the late 1960s, when César Chávez made the cover of *Time* as the most famous Mexican American anyone could name, he was already irrelevant to Mexican-American lives insofar as 90 percent of us lived in cities and we were more apt to work in construction than as farmworkers. My mother, who worked downtown, and my father, who worked downtown, nevertheless sent money to César Chávez, because the hardness of his struggle on the land reminded them of the hardness of their Mexican past.

I remember the farmworkers' "Lenten Pilgrimage" through California's Central Valley in 1966. Lines of men, women, and children passed beneath low, rolling clouds, beneath the red and black union flags and the flapping silk banners of the Virgin of Guadalupe. Their destination was the state capital, Sacramento, the city, Easter. They were private people praying in public. Here were the most compelling symbols of the pastoral past: life on the land (the farmworker); the flag, the procession in song (a people united, the village); the Virgin Mary (her consolation in sorrow).

Chávez wielded a spiritual authority that, if it was political at all, was not mundane and had to be exerted in large, priestly ways or it was squandered. By the late 1970s, Chávez had spent his energies in legislative maneuvers. His union got mixed up in a power struggle with the Teamsters. Criticized in the liberal press for allowing his union to unravel, Chávez became a quixotic figure; Gandhi without an India.

César Chávez was a folk hero. But the political example for my generation was Mayor Henry Cisneros of San Antonio. As a man of the city, Cisneros reflected our real lives in the America of *usted*. Cisneros attempted a reconciliation between the private and the public, between the family and the world. On the one hand, he belonged to the city. He spoke a metropolitan English, as well as Old Boy English; Cisneros spoke an international Spanish, as well as Tex-Mex. He chose to live in his grandfather's house on Monterey Street. The fiction was that he had never left home. Well, no the fiction was that he had gone very far, but come home unchanged.

My mother saw Henry Cisneros twice on *60 Minutes*. My mother said she would vote for Cisneros for any office.

The career of Henry Cisneros magnified the dilemma of other Mexican Americans within that first generation of affirmative action. Had it not been for *CBS News,* my mother would never have heard of Henry Cisneros. Though his success was unique—though his talent is personal—my mother assumed that his career was plural, that he represented Mexican Americans because that is what he was—and that is what he was because he was the first. Groomed for leadership by an Ivy League college and by Democratic Party officials, Cisneros was then unveiled to the constituency he was supposed already to represent. He must henceforward use the plural voice on committees and boards and at conferences. We want. We need. The problem, in this case, is not with the candidate; it is with the constituency. Who are we? We who have been to Harvard? Or we who could not read English? Or we who could not read? Or we who have yet to take our last regard of the lemon tree in our mother's Mexican garden?

Politics can easily override irony. But, by the 1980s, the confusing "we" of Mexican Americanism was transposed an octave higher to the "we" of pan-American Hispanicism.

In the late 1980s, Henry Cisneros convened a conference of Hispanic leaders to formulate a national Hispanic political agenda.

Mexican Americans constituted the majority of the nation's Hispanic population. But Mexican Americans were in no position to define the latitude of the term "Hispanic"—the tumult of pigments and altars and memories there. "Hispanic" is not a racial or a cultural or a geographic or a linguistic or an economic description. "Hispanic" is a bureaucratic integer—a complete political fiction. How much does the Central American refugee have in common with the Mexican from Tijuana? What does the black Puerto Rican in New York have in common with the white Cuban in Miami? Those Mexican Americans who were in a position to speak for the group—whatever the group was—that is, those of us with access to microphones because of affirmative action, were not even able to account for our own success. Were we riding on some clement political tide? Or were we advancing on the backs of those who were drowning?

Think of earlier immigrants to this country. Think of the Jewish immigrants or the Italian. Many came, carefully observing Old World distinctions and rivalries. German Jews distinguished themselves from Russian Jews. The Venetian was adamant about not being taken for a Neapolitan. But to America, what did such claims matter? All Italians looked and sounded pretty much the same. A Jew was a Jew. And now America shrugs again. Palm trees or cactus, it's all the same. Hispanics are all the same.

I saw César Chávez again, a year ago, at a black-tie benefit in a hotel in San Jose. The organizers of the event ushered him into the crowded ballroom under a canopy of hush and tenderness and parked him at the center table, where he sat blinking. How fragile the great can seem. How much more substantial we of the ballroom seemed, the Mexican-American haute bourgeoisie, as we stood to pay our homage—orange women in fur coats, affirmative-action officers from cigarette companies, filmmakers, investment bankers, fat cats and stuffed shirts and bleeding hearts—stood applauding our little saint. César Chávez reminded us that night of who our grandparents used to be.

Then Mexican waiters served champagne.

Success is a terrible dilemma for Mexican Americans, like being denied some soul-sustaining sacrament. Without the myth of victimization—who are we? We are no longer Mexicans. We are professional Mexicans. We hire Mexicans. After so many years spent vainly thinking of ourselves as exempt from some common myth of America, we might as well be Italians.

*   *   *

I am standing in my sister's backyard.

They are away. The air is golden; the garden is rising green, but beginning to fall. There is my nephew's sandbox, deserted, spilled. And all his compliant toys fallen where he threw them off after his gigantic lovemaking. Winnie-the-Pooh. The waistcoated frog. Refugees of some long English childhood have crossed the Atlantic, attached themselves to the court of this tyrannical dauphin.

Aserrín aserrán
Something something de San Juan . . .

I can remember sitting on my mother's lap as she chanted that little faraway rhyme.

Piden pan. No les dan. . . .

The rhyme ended with a little tickle under my chin. Whereas my nephew rides a cockhorse to Banbury Cross.

My youngest nephew. He has light hair; he stares at me with dark eyes. I think it is Mexico I see in his eyes, the unfathomable regard of the past, while ahead of him stretches Sesame Street. What will he know of his past, except that he has several? What will he know of Mexico, except that his ancestors lived on land he will never inherit?

The knowledge Mexico bequeaths to him passes silently through his heart, something to take with him as he disappears, like my father, into America.

Martín Espada

Thanksgiving

This was the first Thanksgiving with my wife's family,
sitting at the stained pine table in the dining room.
The wood stove coughed during her mother's prayer:
Amen and the gravy boat bobbing over fresh linen.
Her father stared into the mashed potatoes
and saw a white battleship floating in the gravy.
Still staring at the mashed potatoes, he began a soliloquy
about the new Navy missiles fired across miles of ocean,
how they could jump into the smokestack of a battleship.
"Now in Korea," he said, "I was a gunner, and the people there
ate kimch'i, and it really stinks." Mother complained
that no one was eating the creamed onions. *"Eat, Daddy."*
The creamed onions look like eyeballs, I thought,
and then said, "I wish I had missiles like that."
Daddy laughed a 1950s' horror movie mad scientist laugh,
then told me he didn't have a missile, but he had his own cannon.

"Daddy, eat the candied yams," Mother hissed, as if
he were a liquored CIA spy telling military secrets
to some Puerto Rican janitor he met in a bar. "I'm a toolmaker.
I made the cannon myself," Daddy said, and left the table.
"Daddy's family has been here in the Connecticut Valley since
    1680,"
Mother said. "There were Indians here once, but they left."
When I started dating her daughter, Mother called me a half-black,
but now she spooned candied yams on my plate. I nibbled
at the candied yams. I remembered my own Thanksgivings
in the Bronx, turkey with arroz y habichuelas and plátanos,
and countless cousins swaying to bugalú on the record player
or roaring at my grandmother's Spanish punchlines in the kitchen,
the glowing of her cigarette like a firefly lost in the city. For years
I thought everyone ate rice and beans with turkey at Thanksgiving.
Daddy returned to the table with a cannon, steering the black
iron barrel. "Does that cannon go boom?" I asked. "I fire it
in the backyard at the tombstones," Daddy said. "That cemetery
bought all our land during the Depression. Now we only have
the house." He stared and said nothing, then glanced up suddenly,
like a ghost had tickled his ear. "Want to see me fire it?" he grinned.
"Daddy, fire the cannon after dessert," Mother said. "If I fire
the cannon, I have to take out the cannonballs first," he told me.
He tilted the cannon downward, and cannonballs dropped
from the barrel, thudding on the floor and rolling across
the brown braided rug. Grandmother praised the turkey's thighs,
said she was bringing leftovers home to feed her Congo Gray parrot.
I walked with Daddy to the backyard, past the bullet holes
in the door and the pickup truck with the Confederate license plate.
He swiveled the cannon around to face the tombstones
on the other side of the backyard fence. "This way, if I hit anybody,

they're already dead," he declared. He stuffed half a charge
of gunpowder into the cannon and lit the fuse. From the dining
    room,
Mother yelled, *"Daddy, no!"* Then the ground rumbled under my feet.
My head thundered. Smoke drifted over the tombstones.
Daddy laughed. And I thought: When the first drunken Pilgrim
dragged out the cannon at the first Thanksgiving—
that's when the Indians left.

Frank Chin

Pidgin Contest
along I-5

The air war Operation Desert Shield has started. I am in Portland, on the road with my five-year-old son for an adventure during the Chinese New Year's season, when the TV tells me the ground forces of Operation Desert Storm are moving fast. One wants to start the new year right, home with the family. My home is the road. Interstate 5. So, while Mom works teaching school in California, and before Sam himself starts school, I strap our son into the tiny red '77 Honda and get a move on my home again.

The road's changed. America's changed. At first I don't take offense at people sticking their T-shirts in my face when I sit down with Sam after stacking plates at the salad bar at the truck stops. I have gone from truck stop to truck stop for years after discovering that they, of all the roadside cafés, take chicken-fried steak and the salad bar as American art for the stomach. Till this moment I'd found American truck stops to be road-opera idealizations of the naturally democratic old west out of a Sergio Leone spaghetti western. Check your guns, your drugs, your prejudices, and your grudges at the door. All shootouts and fistfights off the premises. No exceptions.

The T-shirt hand-silkscreened on 100-percent cotton with American flag over a map of Saudi Arabia, Iraq, and Kuwait, with the words "THESE COLORS DON'T RUN!" in my face, doesn't bother me. It is the look on the man's face that goes along with the T-shirt that bothers me. I've been the only yellow in roadside restaurants before. I am often the only yellow for miles around. I'm used to it. I'm used to being mistaken for other yellows and other races. It never messes up my enjoyment of the local salad bar and search for the best chicken-fried steak in America.

No one has ever picked a fight with me with a T-shirt before. And all the eyes in the truck stop have never been hard on me, making a big deal of me before. "These colors don't run!" I read aloud. "Amen to that brother. Where can I get one of these righteous T-shirts?"

In a truck stop near Medford, I look up from my salad bar and sirloin into an American flag, red, white, and blue, on a black T-shirt and, in belligerent red across the chest the legend "Try Burning This One, Asshole!"

I have an urge to introduce myself as an Iraqi cabdriver on vacation from New York but chicken out and say, "Boss T-shirt, brah! You think they got T-shirts like that in my son's size? Ooooh, make my boy look sharp!"

We are admiring the hollow bronze man with an umbrella in Pioneer Courthouse Square in Portland. Sam has discovered sculpted animals, beavers, and ducks in the planter boxes. Now he counts the nails in the heel of the bronze man's shoe. I look forward to stopping in the coffee hut on the corner for a cappuccino. Portland is a beautiful little city. Off the road. Out of the World. The kid in a black leather jacket, earrings, and no hair walks by and grumbles something.

"What did he say?" Sam asks.

"I don't know," I say. I have to think. "He said *foreigners*," I say. "Poor kid doesn't know how to cuss." Then I see we are surrounded by these funny-looking white kids who mean, mean, mean to be offensive, don't know how to cuss. As with the college kid who sneered "Literary conservative!" at me for saying texts do not change and the Marxist who'd meant "Cultural nationalist!" to me with contempt, I want to take the fuzz-headed boy aside and teach him how to swear. "You want to rile me, kid, you call me a *Chink!* or you might call me a *Jap!* I'm not a Jap, but I'll know what you mean. But foreigner! Come on! That's too intellectual to really get me on the proper emotional level."

Then I see we are surrounded by the Clairol kids in black leather. I forget about the cappuccino and say, "Let's walk on out of here, Sam."

I see this need to teach our young boy how to properly cuss and offend with the specificity of a smart bomb as the first step toward full literacy and I-5 civility. You read to get the knowledge you need to win a fight, or in this case, pick a fight, and avoid a fight.

On campus I seem to hear something else. I hear white kids on campus bitching about courses that teach nothing but hatred of whites and other kids talking PC, "Political Correctness."

It's a shame white kids are sheltered by lingering white supremacy from the real world till they get to college. Nonwhite kids grow up in America despised by whites from birth, from history, from folklore, from their best friend the TV set. By the time they get to college they've learned to deal with it as a childhood disease. Either that, or it's fried their brains and turned them into gibbering Gunga Dins anxious to bugle the charge of white supremacy to white out their race and culture. Owooooo! Hear that wolf?

A multicultural America, a multicultural I-5, doesn't mean whites have to give up Christianity or hate themselves. It doesn't mean an orgy of mutual hostility either. Nor does it mean racial and cultural exclusivity. One thing it does mean—and I think PC is an attempt toward achieving this—is American standard English, the language all of us have to use to do business with each other, will be the one language reserved for civility, the one language we can speak without provoking each other. The American standard English of the newspapers and TV news, the language of the marketplace, will become more and more a pidgin, like pidgin in Hawai'i.

In pidgin Hawaiians, whites, Christians, pagans, Chinese, Japanese, Portuguese, did business with each other without giving up their identities, or their cultural integrity, or selling their children to monsters.

Political correctness seems to be a too serious and fascist demagogic way of saying *civil language.* Of course, when civility is not our purpose, there are other languages and vocabularies available to us. With the need for a language of civility and doing business with strangers without betraying our secrets or slashing our wrists or starting a car in mind, I suggest PC stand for *pidgin contest.*

Civil language and tolerant behavior can't be imposed from the top without exercising heavy police-state censorship and driving everyone with a discouraging word underground. But in the bustling, competitive, passionate marketplace atmosphere of a port city or corner store, civil language and tolerant behavior are invented, or you go broke, brah.

In *The Movie about Me* there are pidgin contests held to encourage the use of language to trade culture and lit. Pidgin is a live, up-front, face-to-face, present-tense language. The contestants tell heroic classics— *Chusingura, The Oath in the Peach Garden, Robin Hood, The Three Musketeers*— live. They compete with pidgin tellings of the fairy tales, "Jack and the Beanstalk" and "Momotaro, the Peach Boy." On the way back home, driving I-5 South, Sam likes the idea. Yeah, it's better than punching somebody in the mouth and craving a many-fronted race war.

Then we walk back into the real world, a crowded resort restaurant around Lake Mount Shasta in Northern California, to get out of the nasty wind and rain.

"Did you tell them we're closed," a middle-aged, crinkled-up woman bleats to another, taller, less crinkled-up white woman.

"We're closed," the taller woman says. For an instant I don't believe my ears. This has not happened to me since the South in the early sixties. Never in California.

"We're closed," the taller woman says again, and I can see she sees from the look in my eye I don't believe they are closed at all. I am not about to punch either of these old white ladies in the face. I look around for a customer to catch my eye and punch him in the face, and none does. Then I remember Sam, my five-year-old boy about to start school, is with me.

"They're closed, Sam," I say, take his hand, walk out, and wonder what I am teaching my kid letting skinheads and sixties-style white racists in California run us out of town. The winning of the Gulf War seems to have released an ugly brand of American patriotism that expresses itself as righteous white supremacy such as I have never seen before along the road between Seattle and LA I've called home for thirty years. I would have thought a nice cathartic victory would have released more winning sentiments on the road. What has happened to I-5?

Hello America, This Is LA

There are signs the times are freaking out. All over LA wherever I drive, from Echo Park and Silver Lake to Hollywood to downtown and J-Town and Chinatown, I see magpies harassing hawks all over the sky. There are other signs of good times. There is an oriole, bright yellow and stark black on the wings and throat, in our weird tree flowering red fingers the morning of the day my friend the TV goes crazy with bad, bad news.

I pick up Sam from the school bus a little before three. He buckles himself in the back seat, and we're on our way to Chinatown for our usual after-school noodles when the news of the verdict acquitting the cops who'd beaten Rodney King comes between country songs and an appropriately remote broadcast from Hawai'i hyping travel over the LA FM country music station. "It's a bad day to be a cop or black man," I say.

My seven-year-old son knows Rodney King is the black man he'd seen beaten by LA cops on TV last March just after we're back home from a trip up and down I-5 to Seattle, through the Gulf War, and back down a road bristling a new, more blatant white racism. Skinheads in Portland. A resort restaurant in Northern California saying, "We're closed," when they were full of white people stuffing all manner of breakfast in their faces. And home to see Rodney King shot twice with a laser gun and beaten and beaten and beaten.

Between then and now black dislike for Koreans in little mom-and-pop groceries grows. The Korean groceries and liquor stores have all been broken into and/or robbed, and Mom and Pop have the same prejudice about blacks as the white Americans who taught it to them.

It might have helped if the blacks understood Korean manners and Korean culture have been toughened by a long history of being kicked around by the Chinese and the Japanese and a wartime society riddled with vicious spies, where being inquisitive about your neighbors and their personal lives is not necessarily a friendly gesture.

The tension breaks when a Korean grocer shoots a black teenage girl in the back and kills her. The grocer believed this girl was stealing a bottle of orange juice. The store's security camera that recorded the whole event shows the girl approaching the counter with money in her open hand as the grocer rages and screams at her.

The grocer is found guilty of voluntary manslaughter and given a suspended sentence. Blacks are outraged and are even now demanding the recall of the judge who let a Korean woman kill a black teenager without jailtime.

In response to the anger the Korean mom-and-pop grocers stop making change and throwing it at their customers and learn to smile and make Ozzie-and-Harriet Hollywood TV commercial small talk. I find it a little disconcerting. Smiling and small talk as a Korean martial art. The effort the Korean mom-and-pop stores are making to get along with the surrounding community is obvious all over LA. No doubt about it, they're willing to work at getting along. And the standard of getting along is hard-style Disneyland.

After our noodles in Chinatown we drive home past Dodger Stadium, see a hawk flap its wings over a line of palm trees, and see it's being run off by a pair of magpies, see the same thing across the street from our house across our view of the HOLLYWOOD sign, and turn on our friend the TV set and see it is a bad day to be anybody in LA.

Korean mom-and-pops and generic LA minimalls are looter and pyro bait.

On the English-language LA channels some newspeople disconnect major sections of their brains. The pretty faces and trained voices who think they can do the news till the cows come home don't see the cows are home. One reporter has no idea the guns she was describing appearing in the hands of people are real guns, and when the police shove her out of the way she reacts, not to the gunfire, but to the cop's rude shove.

Back in the newsroom a million-dollar anchorman asks a pie-eyed, panic-stricken ninny chattering his teeth in the mike if most of the looters don't look like "illegal aliens."

The pretty face frozen on hold grabs the anchorman's question like a lifesaver and says, "Yes, most of the looters look like illegal aliens." To these fools, I would look like an illegal alien. They're so fried in their insight that if white-haired Barbara Bush, the president's wife, should be pushing a shopping cart she'd look like an illegal alien.

Reporting the looting and burning of Korean stores working into Korea Town proper, the reporters for the English-language news run from pompous to melodramatic to thumb-sucking gibberers. It isn't until the newscopter sees, the wave of looters charge in and out of Fedco, a huge warehouse discount store for government and state employees, that the newsies lose complete control. Mr. Purple Prose of the news-choppers gives up the morally loaded philosophical lingo and says it all in his voice going up and down out of breath as he blurts in amazement and moral outrage, "They're looting Fedco!" as if Fedco is a church or an orphanage.

My neighbors aren't among the looters. College educated. Liberal. Mixed marriages. Middle class. Still they act strange. As the smoke from the fires stuffs the air with the smell of burning rubber and electrical insulation and feathery black leaves of the ash fall on our houses and grass, I see some neighbors come out of their house with a portable TV, turn it on, and get into their outdoor Jacuzzi to what? Work off the tension of the day? Others start barbecuing in their backyard at sunset and invite friends, as if the curfew doesn't include them and the gunfire we hear clearly, a block or a mile away we can't tell, won't come any closer, and the smoke from burning LA won't flavor their meat.

The verdict from Simi Valley tells us all in LA there is no law. The looters don't read the news in the paper. They get it off the TV and the radio, their best friend, their storyteller. The looters are the children of the children who never had a childhood. Kids of kids who grew up alone, who never had a story told them by a live body; who grew up with TV as their storyteller. The black, white, Asian, and Latino kids and families out looting together are just acting like society on their TV acts when there is no law.

Had they a sense of myth that began with a live storyteller telling stories their people have valued through history, and if not those, then stories any people value—Greek myths, Bible stories, Br'er Rabbit, Hans Christian Andersen, the Peach Boy, the Boy born of Lotus—more people might look on themselves as more than the moral equivalent of consumer goods and stay away from the mob.

Then on TV there is a fake Spanish California mission-style minimall with a guard from a private Korean security outfit on the roof with an Uzi, a jumpsuit, a flak jacket, a baseball cap, and dark glasses.

The call had gone out on the channel that airs Korean programming for all good men to come to the aid of their Korea Town at the minimall, and they show up with shotguns, pistols of all kinds, Uzis, and AK-47s. The Alamo in Korea Town is a minimall.

In the race war that's started we're all going to choose up sides and appear at the appropriate minimall to man the barricades? The combined TV of LA with its two Spanish-language channels, and hours of Chinese, Japanese, Korean, Vietnamese, Farsi, and on and on programming, and visions of the action on the streets, is a vision of LA beyond *Bladerunner,* and not real, I think. It's all grotesque exaggeration. And it's impossible to choose up sides. The racially and culturally specific parts of towns, the barrios, the Chinatowns, Li'l Tokyo, Hollywood, Fairfax, blacks, Jews, white Christians, and even the dreamers and movie stars of LA all are too interwoven into each other's business and loyalties to simply drop everything and Alamo up at our minimall behind barricades of rice sacks and shopping carts. We cannot blast and shoot each other into oneness. But we can agree on a common standard and language of civility. For a long time now, people on all sides, high and low, have and have not seemed to have accepted *business* as a synonym for *life.* Now we seem to agree the fire department is a good thing. It's a start. Whole civilizations have been started with less.

No school. Good. Sam's school bus is less than a mile from the downtown collection of courthouses and Parker Center police head-quarters the TV news expects to go up in flames any second now. I take Sam out in the daylight, just down the hill to the Chinese bakery to order a cake for Dana's birthday. We pull open the door and walk in. The bakery is open. Still Mom and Pop the bakers freeze, and their eyes swirl and their breath gets short at the sight of me. "Hi," I say. "We'd like a cake."

They don't understand. They wait for me and my seven-year-old son to stick 'em up, or loot 'em, or trash the joint. "We want to buy a cake," I say.

They don't move.

"We'd like it to say, 'Happy Birthday Mom,' " I say.

Poppa Chinese baker opens his mouth, and nothing comes out.

"Are you open?" I ask.

He nods his head. I start again. They understand.

While Mom and Pop are steaming the medium-sized two-layer cake into being for me, the door opens behind me. I turn and see a young Chinese woman in the doorway. She jumps back. "Are you open?" she asks.

"Yeah, come on in," I say.

"Mom, Dad? You okay?" she asks, and goes behind the counter. She's the daughter. This is her bakery, and she asks me if we're open? Is the young man in the car outside a cop? Welcome to Paranoid City.

We get the cake in a box and take it home.

Then George Bush declares war on LA sounding as frustrated and pained as Alberto Fujimori ruling by mandate in Peru.

Sunday, the family cocooned up snug with our best friend the TV set, I drive to Chinatown along deserted streets in broad daylight. The streets are empty. I take a walk around the places I like to eat and walk into one. Empty. The Mexican kitchen help and the Chinese cooks in their kitchen whites and waiters sit and stand around a table where the owner sits and holds his head in his hands. It's around three in the afternoon. The sun shines outside. In here they don't know if they're opening or closing. Some of the tables are still stacked. Some of the tables on the floor have no tablecloths, no place mats with the lunar zodiac around the edges, no red napkin, fork, spoon, and wrapped chopsticks, no tea cup and water glass. The kitchen is cold. No one notices me.

"Are you open?" I ask.

The owner looks up; everyone looks up. The owner recognizes me as a frequent customer, tries to smile, and looks like he's going to cry. "First the riots. Now the curfew's killing us. We haven't had even one customer in two days till you walked in." Martial law seems to have worked.

On the way back I hear over the radio news of a huge peace rally in Korea Town. People are praying for forgiveness of the looters and peace in LA. Whole families show up. Others stop and join. Estimates range from 30,000 to 100,000. It seems like good news, as I drive past stuff from the looting binge appearing for sale at yard sales. This is the America where reading is only good for reading signs and price tags. There is no story, no myth, no history, no art. Only TV. And now that the U.S. Marines and the army have had a taste of treating American streets like Panama and Grenada, I wonder if they can go home again.

Sam is down to sleep to be up early off to school in the morning tomorrow.

Police State

Every day after school, I pick Sam up at the bus and drive through Elysian Park, past the Dodger Stadium parking lot and Marine Corps and Naval Reserve Training Station, into Chinatown or Little Tokyo for noodles or sushi. Salmon egg sushi was Sam's first solid food. He doesn't like meat. Doesn't like veggies. He likes sushi, rice, and fish. Salmon eggs. Sea eel. Softshell crab. Mackerel pike. Broiled smelt exploding with eggs. I tell Sam of trying to teach his half-sister, Betsy, how to drive in that parking lot and how she managed to drive into the only tree in this huge parking lot. True, it's a pitiful excuse for a tree, next to that pitiful little block house of a ticket office. Sam laughs every time he sees the tree and thinks of Betsy bumping into it.

This is a nice drive between our house and Chinatown and J-Town. We often see hawks perched in the tops of the trees of Elysian Park or cruising over the soft cliffs of Chavez Ravine, across the street from the Dodger Stadium parking lot.

It's a nice time of day. I break from staring at the blank page and screaming screen, do my mailing at the Chinatown or Little Tokyo contract postal station, walk around the town talking about life with Sam, watch the afternoon light reflect off glass walls of one building onto the textured concrete slab of another, snack, and shop for dinner. In Chinatown we walk by the square ponds full of fake rocks painted in fake colors, topped with the statues of Kwan Yin and the gods of wealth, happiness, and long life long ago broken off at the ankles. We look into the waters of one pond for the turtles and usually count more than a dozen basking on rocks and each other, swimming in the shallow water over pennies, and beaking at the puffy body of a dead goldfish. There are feeders grown large on these ponds. One has a golden carp. The other pond has crawdads.

In Little Tokyo there are the big granite boulders in Little Tokyo Village Sam likes to climb. There is the Amerasia Bookstore, where Irene, one of a group of Asian American UCLA students who call themselves Aisarema (Amerasia spelled backwards) and are dedicated to saving the Amerasia Bookstore from closing, stands behind the cash register and folds little origami things for Sam. And all the sushi chefs at Frying Fish know Sam and call his name when we step inside.

One day, walking to sushi, we see National Guard Humvees parked all over the Honda Plaza parking lot. The Humvees are too big to fit in the marked parking spaces. The don't even try. Inside a J-Town fast noodle shop we see the boys of the National Guard in their battle fatigues and flak jackets sitting down working chopsticks and noodles, with their M-16s leaning against the little tables. Sam and I are the only living things on the street. We look on the woman who runs the sushi bar and the chefs who call Sam by name as friends. We all cheer each other up, and I get my appetite back enough to eat.

Chinatown and Little Tokyo are dead. For days, for weeks after the riots, and waiting for the trials of the people arrested in the riots and the trials of the cops who beat up Rodney King to start, Sam and I are the only customers in our favorite J-Town sushi bar. Everyone else who walks in is a cop acting casual. Big guys in suits with guns under their jackets. They crouch over the pictures of the sushi and take a long time reading, looking, and choosing.

One day on our way home on the road past the Marine Corps and Naval Reserve Training Station, we see the cops have set up a satellite dish, telephone lines, a couple of mobile booking stations, a fleet of unmarked pickup trucks in different colors, a fleet of motorcycles, a fleet of black-and-whites, a trailer serving as an on-site office, a phalanx of portable toilets. A command post. A base.

Two, new, washed gray or brown, nondescript four-door American-made Chevies waving several wire antennae like porcupine spines out of the trunks pass us on the inside bumper to bumper doing about sixty. Each car is full of four big men in dark glasses who don't give a thought to the likes of us in this flimsy little toy of a car. They know me before I know they're there. They know my every move before I make it, which is why it's easy for them to sneer their pursuit packages past me. "The Feds, Sam," I say. The two cars race past me bumper to bumper, at the next intersection two more cars swoop in front of the first two, and all continue racing at sixty in a kind of FBI automobile drill team. Sun Tzu the strategist says, Do not fuck with these guys. Even if he didn't say that, he should have, and I treat them like natural wildlife in the park.

For the next several days, we seem to drive home from sushi or noodles just when several pairs of motorcycle cops gurgle their machines toward us through Elysian Park and into the command post and teams of Feds and local cops practice teaming up to trap cars in traffic and shove them over to the curb. Damn, it's a pretty sight. All these big new cars full of big square-jawed, uptight, muscular Americanismo diving and swooping as one out of Dodger Stadium parking lot, past the spiny green baobab trees by Barlow Respiratory Hospital, into shadows of impossibly tall and spindly palm trees in Elysian Park.

Sam enters his softshell crab phase. Every day he orders salmon eggs and a softshell crab appetizer. Miso soup with no tofu, no seaweed, no green onions, just soup. Coke to drink. He also likes the broiled mayonnaise sauce that tops the broiled New Zealand green mussels I order.

I see smoke rising from the corner of the Marine Corps and Naval Reserve Training Station parking lot where the cops have set up a command post. "Oh, no, there's a fire at the command post," I say, and wonder how long ago it started. Is there anything about it on the radio? What happened? Has it started again?

As I roll past I see flames and smoke on the corner and cops in uniform, in their helmets and black leather jackets. They look like the bandits who threaten the village in Kurosawa's *The Seven Samurai,* but with paper plates instead of long weapons in their hands. It's a barbecue, not a bombing.

"It's a barbecue!" I say. "They're having a barbecue. They're roasting steaks and chicken and hotdogs on a barbecue. Whew." I laugh. Sam asks why I'm laughing. "I hope the cops have a fine long evening of barbecue. I never thought I'd ever say that before now." Owooooo!! Hear that wolf?

Aurora Levins Morales

Immigrants

For years after we left Puerto Rico for the last time, I would wake from a dream of something unbearably precious melting away from my memory as I struggled desperately to hold on, or at least to remember that I had forgotten. I am an immigrant, and I forget to feel what it means to have left. What it means to have arrived.

There was hail the day we got to Chicago and we joked that the city was hailing our arrival. The brown brick buildings simmered in the smelly summer, clenched tight all winter against the cold and the sooty sky. It was a place without silence or darkness, huddled against a lake full of dying fish whose corpses floated against the slime-covered rocks of the south shore.

Chicago is the place where the slack ended. Suddenly there was no give. In Indiera there was the farm: the flamboyan tree, the pine woods, the rainforest hillsides covered with *alegría*, the wild joyweed that in English is called impatiens. On the farm there were hideouts, groves of bamboo with the tiny brown hairs that stuck in your skin if you weren't careful. Beds of sweet-smelling fern, drowsy-making under the sun's heat, where the new leaves uncurled from fiddleheads and tendrils climbed and tangled in a spongy mass six feet deep. There were still hillsides, out of range of the house, where I could watch lizards hunt and *reinitas* court, and stalk the wild cuckoos, trying to get up close. There were mysteries and consolations. There was space.

Chicago was a wasteland. Nowhere to walk that was safe. Killers and rapists everywhere. Police sirens. Ugly, angry looks. Bristling hostility. Worst of all, nowhere to walk. Nowhere to go if it was early morning and I had to get out. Nowhere to go in the late afternoon or in the gathering dusk that meant fireflies and moths at home. Nowhere to watch animal life waking into a new day. The animal life was rats and dogs, and they were always awake because it never got dark here: always that sickly purple and orange glow they call sky in this place. No forest to run wild in. Only the lot across 55th Street with huge piles of barren earth, outlines of old cellars, and a few besieged trees in a scraggly row. I named one of them Ceres, after the goddess of earth and plenty who appeared in my high school production of *The Tempest*. Bounteous Ceres, queen of the wasteland. There were no hills to race down, tumbling into heaps of fern, to slide down, on a slippery banana leaf: no place to get muddy. Chicago had grime, but no mud. Slush, but no slippery places of the heart, no genuine moistness. Only damp alleyways, dank brick, and two little humps in the middle of 55th Street over which grass had been made to grow. But no real sliding, no slack.

There are generations of this desolation behind me, desolation, excitement, grief, and longing all mixed in with the dirty air, the noise, seasickness, and the strangeness of wearing a winter coat.

My grandmother Lola was nineteen the day she married my grandfather and sailed away to Nueva York in 1929. She had loved someone else, but his family disapproved and he obeyed their orders to leave for the States. So her family married her to a son of a neighboring family because the family store was doing poorly and they could no longer support so many children. Two months after her first love left, she found herself married and on the boat. She says: "I was a good Catholic girl. I thought it was my duty to marry him, that it was for the good of my family." I have pictures of her, her vibrant beauty wrapped up but not smothered in the winter coats and scarves, in my grandfather's violent possessiveness and jealousy. She is standing in Central Park with her daughters, or with her arms around a friend or cousin. Loving the excitement. Loving the neighbors and the hubbub. In spite of racist landlords. In spite of the girdle factory. In spite of Manolin's temper and the poverty and hunger. Now, retired to Manolin's dream of a little house in Puerto Rico with a yard and many plants to tend, she longs for New York or some other U.S. city where a woman can go out and about on her own, live among many voices speaking different languages, out of the stifling air of that house, that community, that family.

My mother, the child in that Central Park photo, grew up an immigrant child among immigrants. She went to school speaking not a word of English, a small Puerto Rican girl scared out of her wits, and learned fast: learned accentless English in record time, the sweet cadence of her mother's open-voweled words ironed out of her vocabulary, the edges flattened down, made crisp, the curls and flourishes removed. First generation.

The strangeness. The way time worked differently. The way being on time mattered. Four second bells. Four minutes of passing time between classes. A note from home if you were ten minutes late, which you took to the office and traded for a late pass. In Indiera the classroom emptied during coffee season, and they didn't bother to send the inspector up unless we were out for longer than four or five weeks. No one had a clock with a second hand. We had half days of school because there were only four rooms for six grades. Our room was next to the bakery, and the smell of the warm *pan de agua* filled our lungs and stomachs and mouths. Things happened when they were read or "cuando Dios quiere." The público to town, don Paco's bread, the coffee ripening, the rain coming, growing up.

The stiffness. The way clothing mattered with an entirely different kind of intensity. In Indiera, I wore the same wine-colored jumper to school each day with the same white blouse, and only details of the buttons or the quality of the cloth or the presence or absence of earrings, only the shoes gave information about the homes we left at dawn each day, and I was grateful to be able to hide my relative wealth. In Chicago, there were rituals I had never heard of. Kneesocks and plaid skirts and sweaters matching each other according to a secret code I didn't understand. Going steady and wearing name tags. First date, second date, third date, score. The right songs to be listening to. The right dances. The coolness.

In the middle of coolness, of stiffness, of strangeness, my joyful rushing up to say, "I come from Puerto Rico, a nest of beauty on the top of a mountain range." Singing "beauty, beauty, beauty." Trying to get them to see in their minds' eyes the perfect edge of a banana leaf against a tropical blue sky, just wanting to speak of what I longed for. Seeing embarrassed faces turning away, getting the leering voices, singing "Puerto Riiiico, my heart's devotion . . . let it sink into the ocean!" Learning fast not to talk about it, learning excruciatingly slowly how to dress, how to act, what to say, where to hide. The exuberance, the country-born freshness going quietly stale. Made flat. Made palatable. Made unthreatening. Not different, really. Merely "exotic."

I can remember the feelings, but I forget to give them names. In high school we read novels about immigrant families. In college we discussed the problems of other first generations, talked about displacement, talked about families confused and divided, pride and shame. I never once remembered that I was an immigrant, or that both my parents are the first U.S.-born generations of their families.

My father is the First American Boy. His mother, Ruth, was born in Russia. Took the boat with her mother, aunt, and uncle when she was two. My grandfather Reuben was the second son of Lev Levinsky, the first one born in the new country, but born into the ghetto. Lev and the first son, Samuel, were orthodox, old-country Jews, but Reuben and his younger brother Ben went for the new. They worked three or four jobs at once. They ran a deli in shifts and went to law school in their free hours. So Rube grew up and out of the immigrant poverty, still weak and bent from childhood hungers, still small and vulnerable. The sicker he got, the harder he worked to safeguard his wife and sons, adding on yet another job, yet another project until he worked himself to death at the age of forty-six.

My father was the First American Boy: the young genius, the honors student, the PhD scientist. Each milestone recorded in home movies. His letters and report cards hoarded through the decades, still exhibited to strangers. The one who knew what was what. The expert. The one who carried the family spark, the one to boast about. The one with the weight of the family's hope on his shoulders. First generation.

And what am I?

The immigrant child of returned immigrants who repeated the journey in the second generation. Born on the island with firsthand love and the stories of my parents' Old Country—New York; and behind those, the secondhand stories of my mother's father, of the hill town of his long ago childhood, told through my mother's barrio childhood. Layer upon layer of travel and leaving behind, an overlay of landscapes, so that I dream of all the beloved and hated places, and endlessly of trains and paths and roads and ships docking and leaving port and a multitude of borders and officials waiting for my little piece of paper.

I have the passport with which my great-grandmother Leah, traveling as Elisavieta, and her sister Betty (Rivieka) and her brother Samuel and her mother Henke and my grandmother Riva, a round two-year-old to be known all her life as Ruth, and a neighbor who traveled with them as a relative, all came together into New York. I touch the seal of Russia, the brown ink in which their gentile names were recorded, the furriness of the old paper, the place where the date is stamped: June 1906. My great-grandfather Abe had come alone, fleeing the draft, by way of England and Canada, two years earlier.

I don't know what it looked like, the Old Country they left, the little farm in the Ukraine. I will never know. The town of Yaza was utterly destroyed in two gory days in 1942, eight thousand shot and buried in long trenches. My aunt Betty was unable to speak by the time I wanted to ask her: What was it like, a girl of fifteen, to come from that countryside to New York, to suddenly be working ten hours a day in a factory? I have the tiniest fragments, only the dust clinging to their shoes. The dreamy look on my great-grandmother's face one morning when I was ten, watching me play jacks. "There was a game we used to play on the farm, just like that, but with round little stones from the river, tossed from the fronts to the backs of our hands: how many times before they fall?" Pop's, my great-grandfather's painting of the farm he grew up on, and a dozen pages he left in phonetic yiddishy English about the place he grew up in, the horses, the pumpkins, the potatoes, the family decision for him to marry, to flee to New York, where you had to use *tsikolodzi* (psychology) to stay an top.

My grandmother Ruth unexpectedly answering my questions about her earliest memories with a real story, one whole, shining piece of her life: *"Dancing. We were on the boat from Russia. The sun was shining. The place we slept was smelly, stuffy, dark, so all the people were out on the deck as much as possible, sharing food, talking, laughing, playing music. Some of the other passengers were playing accordions and riddles and I began to dance in the middle of the deck. I danced and danced and all the people around me were laughing and clapping and watching me as I spun round and round in my short skirts. It was the happiest moment of my life!"*

My children will be born in California. It's not strange anymore, in this part of the world, in this time, to be born a thousand miles from the birthplace of your mother. My children will hear stories about the *coquis* and coffee flowers, about hurricanes and roosters crowing in the night, and will dig among old photographs to understand the homesick sadness that sometimes swallows me. Living among these dry golden hills, they will hear about rain falling for months, every afternoon at two o'clock, and someday I'll take them there, to the farm on the top of Indiera, redolent of my childhood, where they can play, irreverent, in the ruins of my house. Perhaps they will lie in bed among the sounds of the rainforest, and it will be the smell of eucalyptus that calls to them in their dreams.

Benjamin Alire Sáenz

Exile

That morning—when the day was new, when the sun slowly touched the sky, almost afraid to break it—that morning I looked out my window and stared at the Juárez Mountains. Mexican purples—burning. I had always thought of them as sacraments of belonging. That was the first time it happened. It had happened to others, but it had never happened to me. And when it happened, it started a fire, a fire that will burn for a long time.

As I walked to school, I remember thinking what a perfect place Sunset Heights was: turn-of-the-century houses intact; remodeled houses painted pink and turquoise; old homes tastefully gentrified by the aspiring young; the rundown Sunset Grocery store decorated with the protest art of graffiti on one end and a plastic-signed "Circle K" on the other.

This was the edge of the piece of paper that was America, the border that bordered the University—its buildings, its libraries; the border that bordered the freeway—its cars coming and going, coming and going endlessly; the border that bordered downtown—its banks and businesses and bars; the border that bordered the border between two countries.

The unemployed poor from Juárez knocking on doors and asking for jobs—or money—or food. Small parks filled with people whose English did not exist. The upwardly mobile living next to families whose only concern was getting enough money to pay next month's rent. Some had lived here for generations, would continue living here into the next century; others would live here a few days. All this color, all this color, all this color beneath the shadow of the Juárez Mountains. Sunset Heights: a perfect place with a perfect name, and a perfect view of the river.

After class, I went by my office and drank a cup of coffee, sat and read, and did some writing. It was a quiet day on campus, nothing but me and my work—the kind of day the mind needs to catch up with itself, the kind of uneventful day so necessary for living. I started walking home at about three o'clock, after I had put my things together in my torn backpack. I made a mental note to sew the damn thing. *One day everything's gonna come tumbling out—better sew it.* I'd made that mental note before.

Walking down Prospect, I thought maybe I'd go for a jog. I hoped the spring would not bring too much wind this year. The wind, common desert rain; the wind blew too hard and harsh sometimes; the wind unsettled the desert—upset things, ruined the calmness of the spring. My mind wandered, searched the black asphalt littered with torn papers; the chained dogs in the yards who couldn't hurt me; the even bricks of all the houses I passed. I belonged here, yes. I belonged. Thoughts entered like children running through a park. This year, maybe the winds would not come.

I didn't notice the green car drive up and stop right next to me as I walked. The border patrol interrupted my daydreaming: "Where are you from?"

I didn't answer. I wasn't sure who the agent, a woman, was addressing.

She repeated the question in Spanish, *"¿De dónde eres?"*

Without thinking, I almost answered her question—in Spanish. A reflex. I caught myself in midsentence and stuttered in a nonlanguage.

"*¿Dónde naciste?*" she asked again.

By then my mind had cleared, and quietly I said: "I'm a U.S. citizen."

"Were you born in the United States?"

She was browner than I was. I might have asked her the same question. I looked at her for awhile—searching for something I recognized.

"Yes," I answered.

"Where in the United States were you born?"

"In New Mexico."

"Where in New Mexico?"

"Las Cruces."

"What do you do?"

"I'm a student."

"And are you employed?"

"Sort of."

"Sort of?" She didn't like my answer. Her tone bordered on anger. I looked at her expression and decided it wasn't hurting anyone to answer her questions. It was all very innocent, just a game we were playing.

"I work at the University as a teaching assistant."

She didn't respond. She looked at me as if I were a blank. Her eyes were filling in the empty spaces as she looked at my face. I looked at her for a second and decided she was finished with me. I started walking away. "Are you sure you were born in Las Cruces?" she asked again.

I turned around and smiled, "Yes, I'm sure." She didn't smile back. She and the driver sat there for awhile and watched me as I continued walking. They drove past me slowly and then proceeded down the street.

I didn't much care for the color of their cars.

"Sons of bitches," I whispered, "pretty soon I'll have to carry a passport in my own neighborhood." I said it to be flippant; something in me rebelled against people dressed in uniforms. I wasn't angry—not then, not at first, not really angry. In less than ten minutes I was back in my apartment playing the scene again and again in my mind. It was like a video I played over and over—memorizing the images. Something was wrong. I was embarrassed, ashamed because I'd been so damned compliant like a piece of tin foil in the uniformed woman's hand. Just like a child in the principal's office, in trouble for speaking Spanish. "I should have told that witch exactly what I thought of her and her green car and her green uniform."

I lit a cigarette and told myself I was overreacting. "Breathe in— breathe out—breathe in—breathe out—no big deal—you live on a border. These things happen—just one of those things. Just a game . . ." I changed into my jogging clothes and went for a run. At the top of the hill on Sunbowl Drive, I stopped to stare at the Juárez Mountains. I felt the sweat run down my face. I kept running until I could no longer hear *Are you sure you were born in Las Cruces?* ringing in my ears.

*   *   *

School let out in early May. I spent the last two weeks of that month relaxing and working on some paintings. In June I got back to working on my stories. I had a working title, which I hated, but I hated it less than the actual stories I was writing. It would come to nothing; I knew it would come to nothing.

From my window I could see the freeway. It was then I realized that not a day went by when I didn't see someone running across the freeway or walking down the street looking out for someone. They were people who looked not so different from me—except that they lived their lives looking over their shoulders.

One Thursday, I saw the border patrol throw some men into their van—throw them—as if they were born to be thrown like baseballs, like rings in a carnival ring toss, easy inanimate objects, dead bucks after a deer hunt. The illegals didn't even put up a fight. They were aliens, from somewhere else, somewhere foreign, and it did not matter that the "somewhere else" was as close as an eyelash to an eye. What mattered was that someone had once drawn a line, and once drawn, that line became indelible and hard and could not be crossed.

The men hung their heads so low that they almost scraped the littered asphalt. Whatever they felt, they did not show; whatever burned did not burn for an audience. I sat at my typewriter and tried to pretend I saw nothing. *What do you think happens when you peer out windows? Buy curtains.*

I didn't write the rest of the day. I kept seeing the border patrol woman against a blue sky turning green. I thought of rearranging my desk so I wouldn't be next to the window, but I thought of the mountains. No, I would keep my desk near the window, but I would look only at the mountains.

*   *   *

Two weeks later, I went for a walk. The stories weren't going well that day; my writing was getting worse instead of better; my characters were getting on my nerves—I didn't like them—no one else would like them either. They did not burn with anything. I hadn't showered, hadn't shaved, hadn't combed my hair. I threw some water on my face and walked out the door. It was summer; it was hot; it was afternoon, the time of day when everything felt as if it were on fire. The worst time of the day to take a walk. I wiped the sweat from my eyelids; it instantly reappeared. I wiped it off again, but the sweat came pouring out—a leak in the dam. Let it leak. I laughed. A hundred degrees in the middle of a desert afternoon. Laughter poured out of me as fast as my sweat. I turned the corner and headed back home. I saw the green van. It was parked right ahead of me.

A man about my height got out of the van and approached me. Another man, taller, followed him. *¿Tienes tus papeles?"* he asked. His gringo accent was as thick as the sweat on my skin.

"I can speak English," I said. I started to add: *I can probably speak it better than you,* but I stopped myself. No need to be aggressive, no need to get any hotter.

"Do you live in this neighborhood?"

"Yes."

"Where?"

"Down the street."

"Where down the street?"

"Are you planning on making a social visit?"

He gave me a hard look—cold and blue—then looked at his partner. He didn't like me. I didn't care. I liked that he hated me. It made it easier.

I watched them drive away and felt as hot as the air, felt as hot as the heat that was burning away the blue in the sky.

There were other times when I felt watched. Sometimes, when I jogged, the green vans would slow down, eye me. I felt like prey, like a rabbit who smelled the hunter. I pretended not to notice them. I stopped pretending. I started noting their presence in our neighborhood more and more. I started growing suspicious of my own observations. Of course, they weren't everywhere. But they *were* everywhere. I had just been oblivious to their presence, had been oblivious because they had nothing to do with me; their presence had something to do with some- one else. I was not a part of this. I wanted no part of it. The green cars and the green vans clashed with the purples of the Juárez Mountains. Nothing looked the same. I never talked about their presence to other people. Sometimes the topic of the *Migra* would come up in conversa- tions. I felt the burning; I felt the anger, would control it. I casually referred to them as the Gestapo, the traces of rage carefully hidden from the expression on my face—and everyone would laugh. I hated them.

When school started in the fall, I was stopped again. Again I had been walking home from the University. I heard the familiar question: "Where are you from?"

"Leave me alone."

"Are you a citizen of the United States?"

"Yes."

"Can you prove it?"

"No. No, I can't."

He looked at my clothes: jeans, tennis shoes, and a casual California shirt. He noticed my backpack full of books.

"You a student?"

I nodded and stared at him.

"There isn't any need to be unfriendly—"

"I'd like you to leave me alone."

"Just doing my lob," he laughed. I didn't smile back. *Terrorists. Nazis did their jobs. Death squads in El Salvador and Guatemala did their jobs, too.* An unfair analogy. An unfair analogy? Yes, unfair. I thought it; I felt it; it was no longer my job to excuse—someone else would have to do that, someone else. The Juárez Mountains did not seem purple that fall. They no longer burned with color.

In early January I went with Michael to Juárez. Michael was from New York, and he had come to work in a home for the homeless in South El Paso. We weren't in Juárez very long—just looking around and getting gas. Gas was cheap in Juárez. On the way back, the customs officer asked us to declare our citizenship. "U.S. citizen," I said. "U.S. citizen," Michael followed. The customs officer lowered his head and poked it in the car.

"What are you bringing over?"

"Nothing."

He looked at me. "Where in the United States were you born?"

"In Las Cruces, New Mexico."

He looked at me a while longer. "Go ahead," he signaled.

I noticed that he didn't ask Michael where he was from. But Michael had blue eyes; Michael had white skin. Michael didn't have to tell the man in the uniform where he was from.

*   *   *

That winter, Sunset Heights seemed deserted to me. The streets were empty like the river. One morning, I was driving down Upson Street toward the University, the wind shaking the limbs of the bare trees. Nothing to shield them—unprotected by green leaves. The sun burned a dull yellow. In front of me, I noticed two border patrol officers chasing someone, though that someone was not visible. One of them put his hand out, signaling me to slow down as they ran across the street in front of my car. They were running with their billy clubs in hand. The wind blew at their backs as if to urge them on, as if to carry them.

In late January, Michael and I went to Juárez again. A friend of his was in town, and he wanted to see Juárez. We walked across the bridge, across the river, across the line into another country. It was easy. No one there to stop us. We walked the streets of Juárez, streets that had seen better years, that were tired now from the tired feet that walked them. Michael's friend wanted to know how it was that there were so many beggars. "Were there always so many? Has it always been this way?" I didn't know how it had always been. We sat in the Cathedral and in the old chapel next to it and watched people rubbing the feet of statues; when I touched a statue, it was warmer than my own hand. We walked to the marketplace and inhaled the smells. Grocery stores in the country we knew did not have such smells. On the way back we stopped in a small bar and had a beer. The beer was cold and cheap. Walking back over the bridge, we stopped at the top and looked out at the city of El Paso. "It actually looks pretty from here, doesn't it?" I said. Michael nodded. It did look pretty. We looked off to the side—down the river— and for a long time watched the people trying to get across. Michael's friend said it was like watching the *CBS Evening News.*

As we reached the customs building, we noticed that a border patrol van pulled up behind the building where the other green cars were parked. The officers jumped out of the van and threw a handcuffed man against one of the parked cars. It looked like they were going to beat him. Two more border patrol officers pulled up in a car and jumped out to join them. One of the officers noticed we were watching. They straightened the man out and walked him inside—like gentlemen. They would have beat him. They would have beat him. But we were watching.

My fingers wanted to reach through the wire fence, not to touch it, not to feel it, but to break it down, to melt it down with what I did not understand. The burning was not there to be understood. Something was burning, the side of me that knew I was treated different, would always be treated different because I was born on a particular side of a fence, a fence that separated me from others, that separated me from a past, that separated me from the country of my genesis and glued me to the country I did not love because it demanded something of me I could not give. Something was burning now, and if I could have grasped the source of that rage and held it in my fist, I would have melted that fence. Someone built that fence; someone could tear it down. Maybe I could tear it down; maybe I was the one. Maybe then I would no longer be separated.

*   *   *

The first day in February, I was walking to a downtown Chevron station to pick up my car. On the corner of Prospect and Upson, a green car was parked—just sitting there. A part of my landscape. I was walking on the opposite side of the street. For some reason, I knew they were going to stop me. My heart clenched like a fist; the muscles in my back knotted up. *Maybe they'll leave me alone. I should have taken a shower this morning. I should have worn a nicer sweater. I should have put on a pair of socks, worn a nicer pair of shoes. I should have cut my hair; I should have shaved . . .*

The driver rolled down his window. I saw him from the corner of my eye. He called me over to him—*whistled me over*—much like he'd call a dog. I kept walking. He whistled me over again. *Here, boy.* I stopped for a second. Only a second. I kept walking. The border patrol officer and a policeman rushed out of the car and ran toward me. I was sure they were going to tackle me, drag me to the ground, handcuff me. They stopped in front of me.

"Can I see your driver's license?" the policeman asked.

"Since when do you need a driver's license to walk down the street?" Our eyes met. "Did I do something against the law?"

The policeman was annoyed. He wanted me to be passive, to say: "Yes, sir." He wanted me to approve of his job.

"Don't you know what we do?"

"Yes, I know what you do."

"Don't give me a hard time. I don't want trouble. I just want to see some identification."

I looked at him—looked, and saw what would not go away: neither him, nor his car, nor his job, nor what I knew, nor what I felt. He stared back. He hated me as much as I hated him. He saw the bulge of my cigarettes under my sweater and crumpled them.

I backed away from his touch. "I smoke. It's not good for me, but it's not against the law. Not yet, anyway. Don't touch me. I don't like that. Read me my rights, throw me in the can, or leave me alone." I smiled.

"No one's charging you with anything."

My eyes followed them as they walked back to their car. Now it was war, and *I had won this battle.* Had I won this battle? Had I won?

*   *   *

This spring morning, I sit at my desk, wait for the coffee to brew, and look out my window. This day, like every day, I look out my window. Across the street, a border patrol van stops and an officer gets out. So close I could touch him. On the freeway—this side of the river—a man is running. I put on my glasses. I am afraid he will be run over by the cars. I cheer for him. *Be careful. Don't get run over.* So close to the other side he can touch it. The border patrol officer gets out his walkie-talkie and runs toward the man who has disappeared from my view. I go and get my cup of coffee. I take a drink slowly, it mixes with yesterday's tastes in my mouth. The officer in the green uniform comes back into view. He has the man with him. He puts him in the van. I can't see the color in their eyes. I see only the green. They drive away. There is no trace that says they've been there. The mountains watch the scene and say nothing. The mountains, ablaze in the spring light, have been watching—and guarding—and keeping silent longer than I have been alive. They will continue their vigil long after I am dead.

The green vans. They are taking someone away. They are taking. Green vans. This is my home, I tell myself. But I am not sure if I want this to be my home anymore. The thought crosses my mind to walk out of my apartment without my wallet. The thought crosses my mind that maybe the *Migra* will stop me again. I will let them arrest me. I will let them warehouse me. I will let them push me in front of a judge who will look at me like he has looked at the millions before me. I will be sent back to Mexico. I will let them treat me like I am illegal. But the thoughts pass. I am not brave enough to let them do that to me.

Today, the spring winds blow outside my window. The reflections in the pane, graffiti burning questions into the glass: *Sure you were born . . . Identification . . . Do you live? . . .* The winds will unsettle the desert—cover Sunset Heights with green dust. The vans will stay in my mind forever. I cannot banish them. I cannot banish their questions: *Where are you from?* I no longer know.

This is a true story.

Part III

★　★　★　★　★　★　★

Debates and Contexts

The Legal Mapping
of U.S. Immigration,
1965–1996

by Leti Volpp

To understand why there has been a shift in the population of the United States, such that there are "New Immigrants," requires a look at history. The year 1965 was the watershed of a massive and significant shift that radically transformed the demographics of this country. Before that year, U.S. immigration featured explicit national origins quotas as to who could be admitted to the United States. The 1965 Hart-Celler Immigration Act is often understood as signaling, with the lifting of these quotas, a liberalizing turn from exclusion to inclusion. But understanding this history as a clear narrative of progress would be faulty and inadequate. A cursory examination of immigration law through the 1990s makes apparent the existence of post-1965 regulation and restriction, so that concerns about such issues as foreign policy, capital and labor, race and gender, morality, disease, crime, and culture continue to be expressed through the manipulation of the very bodies of immigrants.

Indeed, for one hundred years immigration law has shaped what we understand as "races" in the United States. While most immigration scholars date the origins of racist exclusion from the United States to the 1882 Chinese Exclusion Act, which prohibited the immigration of Chinese laborers for ten years, an earlier piece of legislation, the 1875 Page Law, almost completely halted the immigration of Chinese women through its focus on purported prostitutes from "Oriental" countries. This was followed by a series of legislative acts that in a piecemeal fashion excluded immigrants from other Asian countries. In 1908, the Gentlemen's Agreement severely restricted Japanese immigration, followed by a 1917 law that prohibited immigration from a "barred zone" that included south Asia through southeast Asia and islands in the Indian and Pacific Oceans. Early nativism was not solely directed against Asian immigrants. It occurred within a broader racial mapping of the United States that featured the conquest and genocide of American Indians, the enslavement and segregation of Blacks, and the territorial dispossession of Mexican Americans.

In addition, early nativism was characterized by both a racial differentiation among white immigrants as well as the consolidation of a white identity. In 1907 Congress formed the Dillingham Commission, which recommended the restriction of the more recent immigrants from southern and eastern Europe who were deemed inferior to earlier immigrants from northern Europe. Legislation in 1921 and 1924 created national origins quotas based upon former census data, in order to re-create the United States in its earlier northern European image. The quotas were allotted to countries in the same proportion that the American people traced their origins to those countries; quota immigrants from southern and eastern Europe were restricted to a ceiling of approximately 150,000 per year, while immigration from northern Europe was unfettered. So the 1924 Immigration Law differentiated Europeans according to nationality and ranked them in a hierarchy of desirability. At the same time, the law also helped construct a white American race, in which persons of European descent shared a common whiteness that distinguished them from those deemed to be nonwhite, who were rendered as unassimilable to the nation (as we see from Mae Ngai's article "The Architecture of Race in American Immigration Law").

In theory, the 1924 act left immigrants from the Western Hemisphere free to immigrate. But, while not subject to numerical quotas or restrictions on naturalization, Mexicans were profoundly affected by other restrictive measures enacted in the 1920s, including deportation policy, the creation of the border patrol, and the criminalization of unlawful entry (aspects also discussed in Ngai's article). The 1924 Act also featured a provision barring admission of any "alien ineligible to citizenship"— which served to effectively end Asian immigration, given that only "whites" or those of "African descent or nativity" were allowed to naturalize as citizens until the 1940s and 50s.

Economic demands, exclusions based on moral and sexual concerns, and politics have defined overlapping and at times competing state policies about immigration. How the U.S. nation has used (and continues to use) immigration to meet capitalist economic demands is painfully apparent in the history of the importation and deportation of workers from Mexico. Because of the labor shortage after World War I, Mexican immigration was encouraged, only to be followed by a mass deportation during the Great Depression, including many who were U.S. citizens. Subsequently, given the great shortage of farm labor during World War II, the Bracero Program was created to import hundreds of thousands of Mexicans without labor protections, followed again, during the recession of the early 1950s, by the deportation of more than one million Mexicans, many without hearings, in a program named "Operation Wetback."

Economics fused with morality in barring from admission those considered least desirable as members of the American nation. Thus, in 1882, "lunatics," "idiots," and any person likely to become a "public charge" were barred from landing. Paupers, polygamists, and those with certain contagious diseases were excluded as of 1891; epileptics, insane persons, and beggars, as of 1903. In 1907 those who were "feebleminded," carriers of tuberculosis, or with some "mental or physical defect" that could affect their ability to earn a living were also prohibited from entry. Alcoholics and "psychotics" were appended to the list in 1917 along with those who were illiterate. 1952 added, drug addicts, and those "afflicted with psychopathic personality, epilepsy, or a mental defect," which was understood to cover those whose sexuality was considered deviant. Congress clarified its intent in 1965 by adding the phrase "or sexual deviation" and deleting epilepsy.

U.S. immigration law has always been used to shape immigrant flows in the service of politics. A 1903 act excluded anarchists or those who sought the overthrow of the U.S. government, or all government. After World War I anarchists were deported and the Palmer Raids rounded up more than 10,000 suspected subversives for deportation in 1919–20. In 1950, Congress made past or present membership in, or an affiliation with, the Communist Party a specific ground for exclusion, and created a broad ground of exclusion for those who sought to engage in activities "prejudicial to the public interest." At the height of the McCarthy Era, the McCarran-Walter Act of 1952, sponsored by a senator who declared that there were in the United States "indigestible blocks" which could not assimilate featured a provision that barred from entry those who had ever written or published or circulated writings advocating certain political views, including communism, anarchy, or overthrowing the U.S. government, or all government. This provision was used at various times to bar such figures as Yasir Arafat, Gabriel García Márquez, Carlos Fuentes, and Graham Greene.

Then came 1965. The act abolished the national origins formula, replacing it with an overall ceiling of approximately 300,000 immigrant visas, which were divided between the Eastern Hemisphere, set at 180,000, with a maximum of 20,000 per country, and 120,000 for the Western Hemisphere. An elaborate system of preferences, first foreshadowed in the McCarran-Walter Act, was developed that is still in operation today, whereby priority was given to reuniting families and to bringing those who had certain desirable or needed skills. The impact of the 1965 act on the racial makeup of the United States can be illustrated through statistics. Overall immigration to the United States has been heavily northern European—49 percent of the worldwide total of lawfully admitted immigrants from 1821 to 1995 were from northern Europe. When northern Europeans and Canadians are combined, the figure rises to 56 percent. But in 1991–95, northern Europeans and Canadians together comprised only 16 percent of the immigrant pool. The countries of birth of the greatest numbers of immigrants in 1995 were, in order, Mexico, then the Philippines, Vietnam, the Dominican Republic, the People's Republic of China, India, Cuba, Ukraine, Jamaica, and Korea.

But it is imperative to note the problems with the 1965 act. While often depicted as liberatory and as heralding a new era of colorblindness, the 1965 act included numerical limits on immigration from the Western Hemisphere for the first time. Legislative history makes clear that this was a concession to increasing racist pressure to restrict immigration from Mexico and countries in the Caribbean, Latin America, and South America. The 1965 act also clarified that persons classified as sexually deviant were to be barred from admission. In a way, the new policies organized around preferences for family-sponsored and employment-based immigration only created new opportunities for regulating immigration admissions (as argued by Lisa Lowe). Political, economic, and moral agendas continued to shape immigration admissions and control post-1965.

The small numerical limits on immigration were increased twenty-five years later in a 1990 act, which lifted the ceiling to a worldwide limit of 700,000 for three years, to drop to 675,000 thereafter. Of these visas, 480,000 were made available for family reunification, 140,000 were set aside for employment-based immigrants, and 55,000 were allotted for a new category called "diversity" immigrants. The employment-based sponsorship category set preferences for highly skilled, professional labor, with, for example, "multinational executives and managers," "outstanding professors and researchers," and those with "extraordinary ability in the sciences, arts, education, business, or athletics" not required to actually prove they have a job offer in hand before receiving a visa. The preferences for highly skilled and professional workers—not to mention temporary visas also issued to such workers—have encouraged what has been criticized as a "brain drain" from other parts of the world.

As it became clear that preference-based immigration from Asia and Latin America was "crowding out" immigration from Europe, especially in the family sponsorship category, Congress began to engage in experiments to "balance" the immigrant pool, in the form of "diversity" visas. During the three years before the permanent program went into effect, 40,000 visas were made available per year primarily to natives of Ireland and Poland. The permanent "diversity" program has largely benefited immigrants from Europe, and secondarily Africa. Many have pointed out that, so far as Europeans go, immigrants from countries who have been "adversely affected" by the 1965 law are from nations that were benefited before 1965, and that the program should in fact be understood as an antidiversity program.

The 1990 act also finally repealed the statutory provision excluding "homosexual aliens." Nonetheless, homophobic discrimination continues in the form of the denial of same-sex marriage as a basis on which to sponsor one's spouse, while heterosexual married couples can bring in their immigrant husbands or wives in this fashion.

The mid 1980s were characterized by two legislative acts concerned with immigrants and illegality. The first was the Immigration Marriage Fraud Act, which was passed in the wake of concerns about an epidemic of fraudulent "green card" marriages. As a result of the act, a new status was created, called "conditional residency," so that recently married immigrant spouses could not become immediately legal permanent residents upon admission, but had to pass through a two-year waiting period. The immigrant spouse had to prove that she had entered into the marriage in "good faith": for the purpose of building a family, and not for immigration benefits. As Anannya Bhattacharjee has argued, this left the motives of the petitioner, often a man, unexamined (for example, his desires for free domestic labor or for a free sex partner). The state, exercising its concerns about which marriages to support and sanction, also deepened the already existing vulnerability of immigrant spouses, by giving batterers new immigration leverage they could use as a threat.

In 1986 Congress also passed the Immigration Reform and Control Act (IRCA), which was conceptualized as a multifaceted attack on undocumented immigration. IRCA included penalties on employers who hired undocumented immigrants (and therefore when we apply for jobs we must now fill out I-9 forms). At the same time, it legalized undocumented individuals who had either resided here for significant periods of time (who, ironically, were now put in the position of having to provide documentation to prove the very presence they had tried to conceal previously) or who had engaged in agricultural labor in the United States. The belief was that by punishing employers who hired immigrants not lawfully able to work, and by legalizing those unlawfully present, illegal immigration to the United States would end. Of course, this approach failed to consider the impetus for illegal (or legal) migration, in the form of continued global injustice and inequities, including disruption brought about by U.S. intervention and imperialism. Importantly, while "illegal immigrants" are most often seen as border-crossing Mexicans, the INS's own statistics reveal that an estimated half of all undocumented immigrants are "visa overstayers": those who lawfully entered on an immigrant visa, and then stayed, once that visa expired.

While the United States was regulating immigration through this series of legislative acts, its demographics were also being shaped by refugees. Americans were largely opposed to the admission of Jewish refugees in the 1930s. Beginning in the 1940s, the United States began to administratively parole European refugees into the country, admitting 250,000 between 1941 and 1945. In 1948, Congress passed the Displaced Persons

Act, allowing for 202,000 war refugees from Europe, which was amended two years later to extend to 415,000 persons. Congress subsequently passed ad hoc legislation to deal with specific refugee crises, notably admitting Hungarians and Cubans. In 1965 Congress created a new immigrant category, for aliens fleeing persecution in a "Communist-dominated" country, or a country "within the general area of the Middle East," or for those "uprooted by catastrophic natural calamity." Those fleeing repressive non-Communist governments outside the Middle East received no protection.

The Refugee Act of 1980, the first piece of comprehensive refugee legislation, failed to eliminate the blatant political bias of earlier refugee admissions. Close to 99 percent of all refugees who settled in the United States between World War II and 1985 were from Communist governments. By 1985, when the United States had admitted 40,000 Hungarians, 750,000 Indochinese and 700,000 Cubans, the government was under increasing fire for its persistent refusal to allocate refugee slots to those fleeing repressive regimes supported by the United States, such as Chileans fleeing Pinochet, as well as Haitians, Salvadorans, and Guatemalans. Haitians began fleeing their country and the regime of Duvalier, propped up by the United States, in significant numbers in the 1970s. They were met by the U.S. Coast Guard by order of the Reagan administration, which intercepted the vessels of the Haitians on the seas, and while mandated to bring anyone legitimately seeking asylum to the United States, returned almost every person to Haiti. This practice of interdiction, in direct violation of international and U.S. law, was upheld as legitimate by the Supreme Court in 1993. Concern about the return of refugees to other U.S. allies, El Salvador and Guatemala, led to the creation of the Sanctuary Movement in the United States, whereby many, often motivated by religious faith, volunteered to shelter refugees from Central America, despite the fact that, if caught, they faced prosecution. Cities such as San Francisco and New York created City of Refuge or

Sanctuary ordinances, whereby refusing to collaborate with the INS in sharing information about refugees residing in their jurisdictions.

Continued anxieties about immigration and immigrants were made boldly manifest in the 1990s. The Commission on Immigration Reform, convened by Congress to study legal immigration, nakedly recommended basing policies solely upon the purported economic gains or burdens of different groups of immigrants. The Commission's 1995 report, while on the one hand lauding the economic benefits associated with certain kinds of skilled legal immigrants—Nobel laureates, for example—at the same time expressed concern about the economic drain of "low-skill" immigrants and elderly immigrants on public services. Apparent in the report is the desire to control immigration to improve U.S. competitiveness in the global marketplace, leading the Commission to recommend seriously reducing family reunification (envisioned as allowing into the country an endless supply of non-European, unskilled immigrants) and to end visas for unskilled labor (as demonstrated by Kunal Parker in his essay "Official Imagination"). The Commission's report fanned the flames of anti-immigrant sentiment, which then coalesced around both legal residents and "illegal aliens."

The Antiterrorism and Effective Death Penalty Act of 1996, passed on the anniversary of the Oklahoma City Bombing, contained myriad anti-immigrant provisions, many of which had nothing to do with either terrorism or crime. The legislation expanded the deportation grounds for immigrants convicted of crimes, and narrowed the provisions for relief which would have otherwise allowed immigrants facing deportation who had strong family ties to stay in the United States.

Against the backdrop of those same elderly immigrants living off the largesse of the U.S. government—as depicted in the Commission's report—Congress then passed the Personal Responsibility and Work Opportunity Reconciliation Act (PRWORA) of 1996, which made even permanent resident aliens ineligible for most federal means-tested benefits, like food stamps and Supplemental Security Income. The law also made it more difficult for prospective immigrants to enter the country, since they had to proffer even greater proof that they would not become a drain on the welfare state, through the form of affidavits from U.S.-based relatives that they would economically support the applicants. An estimated 44 percent of the "savings" created by the act came from slashing benefits to immigrants.

The most severe attack on immigrants came one month later, in the form of the Illegal Immigration Reform and Immigrant Responsibility Act (IIRIRA) of 1996. Most of its provisions focused on increasing the apprehension and speedy removal of undocumented immigrants. But the law also had many other far-reaching effects. The law expanded the grounds on which immigrants could be barred from admission or deported, so that, for example, longtime legal permanent residents who pled guilty to a minor offense for which a sentence of one year or longer could be imposed, were subject to automatic deportation. The law further restricted relief from deportation, instituted mandatory detention for many classes of immigrants, and introduced procedures that would quickly remove immigrants seeking admission—including potential asylum seekers—through "expedited removal" if they had no papers or had papers that seemed fraudulent. In addition, IIRIRA immunized many administrative decisions from review by a federal judge, since immigrants were thought to be clogging the courts with meritless appeals with the collaboration of attorneys and progressive judges.

The anti-immigrant movement was not confined to Congress. Financial anxiety in the state of California fueled by defense cutbacks led to the scapegoating of "illegal immigrants" as a drain upon the state. As a result, the voters in 1994 passed an initiative, Proposition 187, that required health care and social service workers and school teachers to notify the INS of any suspected undocumented clients or students, and to deny them services. The vast majority of the law was immediately enjoined in federal court and never implemented—although its denial of benefits was subsequently enacted by Congress in the PRWORA.

Meanwhile, over twenty states enacted legislation declaring English to be the "official language" and repeated, unsuccessful attempts were made to repeal the provision in the U.S. Constitution guaranteeing citizenship to all born in the United States, regardless of the immigration status of their parents.

These attacks were racialized. A bestselling book published in 1995 by Peter Brimelow (who was asked to testify before Congress), charged that excessive immigration of people of color had changed the ethnic composition of the country, and that the United States should return to its "white ethnic core." The 1990s were very much characterized by a resurgence of racist nationalism aimed at immigrants. The kinds of dynamics at work were illustrated by a 1996 poll of white Americans that indicated that many tend to overestimate the number of people of color in the United States, an overestimation that fueled concerns about people of color "taking over" the country. The poll found that those surveyed thought that 14.7 percent of the U.S. population was Latino, not the actual figure of 9.5 percent, that 23.8 percent of the population was black, not the actual figure of 11.8 percent, and that 10.8 percent of the nation was Asian American, not the actual figure of 3.1 percent. White Americans were underestimated to be only 49.9 percent of the population, not the actual figure of 74 percent.

Racialized attacks of the 1990s largely coalesced around two particular figures—the "illegal alien" and the "criminal alien," amidst a growing differentiation of "good" and "bad" immigrants. Even while the U.S. economy has depended to an enormous extent on labor performed by undocumented workers, the official rhetoric was always one of condemnation of the "illegal." People without lawful immigration status in the United States were constructed as "illegals," so their very essence, their identity in the United States, has been demarcated as breaking the law.

In the context of great public concern about crime, a moral panic about "criminal aliens" simultaneously ensued, whereby immigrants, considered not members of the community, but "guests" who could outwear their welcome, ruptured any right to be here through bad behavior in the form of criminal convictions.

Racialized attacks also took the form of cultural racism, which has positioned the culture of certain communities as either inferior or incompatible with the values of the dominant community. Great attention has been given to the purported cultural oppression of immigrant women, wherein immigrants from certain nations are believed to bring with them to this country a primitive, deviant, and more gender subordinating culture. Thus, the 1990s' attacks on immigrants were also characterized by extensive concern about unassimilable immigrant culture, usually depicted as sexist and backward. While there has been an ostensible celebration of difference in multiethnic America, difference is only valued insofar as it is considered to be palatable and digestible, so that immigrants are considered assimilable to what are purportedly American values.

The narrative that 1965 signifies an exemplary "revolution" in immigration law fragments in this telling of immigration law past and present. While 1965 has indeed signaled a significant demographic shift, celebrating the growth of racial populations fails to address multiple ways in which immigration continues to be restricted (for example, on the basis of class, HIV status, political perspective, U.S. foreign policy), and also ignores the massive regulatory apparatus that has been constructed post-1965 to limit admissions, to expedite deportations, and to restrict the rights of immigrants. The contradictions posed by a more open immigration policy as to national origins with the continued restrictive regime makes manifest both how immigration law services the crass demands of U.S. economic and foreign policies and a real ambivalence about the identity of the United States as a multiethnic nation.

As I write this, we are witnessing the aftermath of September 11,

2001, which threatens to completely transform both immigration law and the experiences of immigrants in this country. Explicit calls for racial profiling, for a moratorium on immigration altogether, for a moratorium on student visas, for complete surveillance of immigrants, are being made. In the USA PATRIOT Act of 2001, legislation has already passed legalizing indefinite detention of immigrants certified as suspected terrorists and creating sweeping new definitions of "terrorists" who will be deported or excluded from the United States. As always, anger and frustration appear to be channeled through the enactment of overbroad legislation targeting immigrants.

©Leti Volpp 2001. Many thanks to Mae Ngai and Nayan Shah for their very helpful comments.

"A Nation of Immigrants"

Select Opinion on Immigration Since 1965

This section—the title is from John F. Kennedy's book of the same name—comprises journalistic writings and editorial cartoons emerging from a few key moments in immigration history since the mid 1960s. Though this slim selection of opinion makes no attempt to be comprehensive, we believe it does convey some sense of the variety of positions and issues debated in public discourse regarding immigration—and also the fire and the fury attending these debates. Along with the other material in this part of the anthology, these examples of editorializing are meant to provide a sense of the context in which the new literature of immigration is produced and disseminated.

The five opinion pieces selected are presented chronologically. The cartoons are interspersed among the essays to illustrate the variety of perspectives and attitudes on this emotionally and politically charged issue. The section is introduced by a photograph of Lyndon B. Johnson signing the Hart-Celler Immigration Act. It represents, as we hope the reader will readily recognize, yet another form of editorializing.

Hart-Celler Immigration Act signed into law by President Lyndon Johnson

A New Day in Immigration

The New York Times Op-ed

September 24, 1965

For the first time in forty years, both houses of Congress have now approved a major revision of the basic immigration law.

Unlike the McCarran-Walter Act of 1952 which in most respects made the law more restrictive, the pending bill is a major reform. To become effective in 1968, it will sweep away the national origins quota system which historically favored immigrants from northwest Europe as against those from eastern and southern Europe.

Citizens of every country will be able to apply for admission to the United States on an equal footing with preferences based on skills and other rational standards rather than race.

The only restrictions will be an overall limitation of 170,000 immigrants a year from outside the Western Hemisphere and a limit of 20,000 for any one country. During the intervening three years, virtually all the existing backlogs of applicants—which have been sizeable in Italy, Greece, and Poland—will be cleared up.

The only important difference between the House and Senate versions which will have to be reconciled in conference is the imposition of a ceiling—for the first time—on immigration from most countries in the Western Hemisphere. The State Department opposes this provision in the Senate bill because it fears an affront to friendly neighbors. But a good case exists for placing immigration from all countries throughout the world on essentially the same basis.

The proposed ceiling for the Western Hemisphere alone is 120,000 persons a year, which is the current level of immigration from the Americas. The effect of the quota and the limit set for the rest of the world would be to keep the number of immigrants entering this country fixed at approximately the same total as has existed in recent years just under 300,000.

Population has been climbing sharply in Latin America. If this resulted in a sudden wave of emigration to the United States that carried the total far above the proposed 120,000 for all the Americas, political pressure for restriction would immediately arise here, as has already occurred in Britain in respect to the nonwhite Commonwealth countries. Rather than invite an ugly situation in the future, it would be an act of prudence and foresight to stabilize hemispheric immigration at its present level on a nondiscriminatory, first-come, first-served basis. The way to do this is to establish the overall limitation of 290,000 broken into 120,000 for the Americas and 170,000 for the rest of the world.

Vietnamese Refugees Caught in Black-White Friction in New Orleans; A Different War

by **Warren Brown**
The Washington Post
July 18, 1978

The Vietnamese refugees who fled here from a falling country three years ago have been caught in the middle of a different war.

The conflict in this semitropical city and its nearby communities is not between communist and noncommunist. It is the long-running battle between black and white Americans; but many of the combatants in both racial camps have come to regard the south Vietnamese as enemies.

It is a peculiar struggle in which groups that should be allies are seemingly cast as opponents, and those that have been historical opponents are seen in many quarters as allies.

For example, there is the Urban League of Greater New Orleans, long the local champion of equal rights. The mostly black league has caused a major controversy here by suggesting that the new minority of south Vietnamese is growing far too rapidly and without due regard to the economic impact it is having on the city's predominantly poor population of blacks.

The immediate target of the league's criticism is the Associated Catholic Charities (ACC), an influential, predominantly white organization dedicated to helping the poor and which directed a portion of the resettlement of Vietnamese refugees in the area. ACC, in the past, has been loyal to the ideals of the Urban League.

Then there is Chalin O. Perez, a powerful white official of nearby Plaquemines Parish (county), the scion of a wealthy family whose opposition to integration and "outsiders" is legend.

Perez, for once, agreed with blacks on something in accusing the federal government and the ACC of "dumping" south Vietnamese refugees into the area, with its French Catholic culture and its fishing heritage.

Perez announced last week that he will take steps that could lead to the departure of Vietnamese fishermen from his parish.

But the conflict swirling around the Vietnamese, about 8,000 of whom are living here and in adjacent towns, involves more than a listing of major players. It is a highly emotional thing, one that is largely a matter of perceptions, of long-held frustrations, and of what local Vietnamese leader Vu Huu Chuong called "dangerous misunderstandings."

Since May 1975, south Vietnamese refugees have flocked to the New Orleans area. An ACC official said his organization was directly responsible for bringing 2,100 refugees and that 5,400 other refugees came to the area on their own.

Many blacks here, like Dyan French Cole, a community activist, complained that the Vietnamese are being used by the whites to frustrate black ambitions for a better place in the local economic and social order.

"Every time you look around, somebody is coming here and being put ahead of the blacks who were born here," Cole said. "We were treated as property from the beginning, never as human beings. Now we are being told to step back and make room for the Vietnamese, just as we were told to step back and make room for the Cubans and everybody else the whites wanted to put ahead of us."

On the other hand, many whites complain that they have already "given in too much" to black demands. It is enough to have one minority group always knocking at your door without having to put up with another—in this case, the south Vietnamese refugees—doing the same thing, disgruntled whites say.

For example, Perez, president of the Plaquemines Parish Commission Council, expressed the feeling of many of his constituents when he said of the refugees: "What we have here is a group of people who have been dumped in our area who are totally unaccustomed to our ways, our manner of living, our mores and our laws."

The Plaquemines leader, who runs the parish from Pointe a la Hache

(Point of the Hatchet), Louisiana, about fifty miles southeast of here, said he is upset by reports that Vietnamese fishermen are violating safety codes, showing up nude in public on their boats, eating the pet cats and dogs of other fishermen, and flouting other social and local fishing industry practices.

He said last week that he will order parish officials to strictly enforce regulations that could drive the Vietnamese fishermen out of the parish by leaving them with no place to dock their boats.

"Just because they are Vietnamese doesn't mean that they are special cause," Perez said in announcing his plans. "It's their business [if they] go some place else to live up to reasonable standards," he said.

The problems here, real and imagined, are plentiful; and they tend to obscure the voices of those people, black and white, who say they welcome the Vietnamese to this area with no strings attached.

New Orleans, for instance, has what urban planners call a "distressed economy." Indeed, New Orleans is said by its mayor, Ernest N. Morial, and other urban planners to have "the most distressed economy of any city its size in the United States."

There are an estimated 586,000 persons residing here, about 51 percent of them black. More than half the blacks, 56 percent, live at or below the poverty level. The city has a 7.6 percent overall unemployment rate. Unemployment in the black community is put at 22 percent for all adults, and at 45 percent for black teenagers.

The two major industries here are the port and tourism. The local, state and federal governments provide about 40 percent of all available jobs in the city. There is a dearth of other gainful employment.

The public school system here, as in other cities, is in disarray. About 85 percent of its estimated 93,000 students are black, and most of them are poor. Housing for the low income is scarce, as evidenced by a public housing waiting list of 10,000 people, most of whom are black.

It is this competition for scarce resources, against a historical background of black-white friction, that is generating much of the discontent about the movement of Vietnamese to this area.

The Rev. Michael Haddad, executive director of the Associated Catholic Charities, which is considered the major force behind the south Vietnamese resettlement program here, said: "The decision to admit more refugees is one that will affect only the poor in this country, and it won't affect the rich or the middle class. I know that's a problem, but the problem was here long before the Vietnamese came.

"The Vietnamese people are not the problem. And you just can't stop them from moving into the area because of all of the other problems that exist."

Clarence Barney, the executive director of the New Orleans Urban League, who has been embarrassingly portrayed in local newspaper editorials and cartoons as being in bed with the arch-conservative Perez, protests that he, too, is against excluding the refugees from this or any other community.

"Our argument is that in a community already troubled by a history of racism, and that has bad housing, bad education, and too-few jobs, it is almost criminal to have a large number of new people come in and enter into unfair competition with the indigenous population that has suffered because of that history," Barney said.

"We ought to assure that the responsibility and obligation for helping the Vietnamese is carried out in such a way so as not to create additional burden and hardships for the people who are already here."

Barney acknowledged that his organization lost much local grace because of his position. But he said that a poll conducted by his group showed that about 92 percent of the community's black leaders agreed with the league's position, and thought that the local media criticism was unjustified.

National Urban League Executive Director Vernon Jordan has publicly adopted a hands-off policy in regard to the New Orleans dispute. But other National Urban League officials say that the organization is concerned about the economic impact of the refugee program on the nation's native poor, and that Barney's position is in accord with that concern.

Mayor Morial was out of town and could not be reached for comment. But other black leaders here say privately that it would be unwise for Morial or any other black politician to intervene in the conflict.

Daniel C. Thompson, a local university vice president and sociologist who also serves as president of the city's Coordinating Council of Black Leadership, explained: "We have never seen blacks in this city so frustrated and mad as they are now about their economic position. There is a kind of reckless anger out there that wasn't there even in the 1960s, when, at least, there was some kind of hope."

Still, Thompson said he believes that much of the confusion and the charges that Vietnamese are displacing blacks and poor whites in jobs and housing could have been avoided.

"The problem is that all of the institutions in this city are either black or white or at least see themselves as either black or white, and there is no single institution around here to facilitate our movement into a desegregating society," he said.

Vu Huu Chuong, who serves as vice chairman of the New Orleans Area Vietnamese Committee, said he agrees with Thompson.

"We hope that the leaders in the black and in the white communities will try to understand the Vietnamese, and try to explain to us clearly what the laws and the customs [are] so that we can make good citizens," he said.

He said that he would like to meet with Barney "and even with Mr. Perez" to discuss the refugees' position. Though his constituents have received considerable harassment from both blacks and whites, according to local officials here, Chuong said the Vietnamese community does not feel unwanted.

"We have many friends here among the blacks and whites. All of this [controversy] has come because of a very dangerous misunderstanding. We hope to resolve that. We will try."

A Troubling Drop in Immigrant "Quality"
by Barry R. Chiswick
The New York Times
December 21, 1986

The debate on the hastily enacted Immigration Reform and Control Act of 1986 has seldom addressed one of the key immigration questions: What is the effect of immigration policy on the job skills of immigrants to the United States? Under our present, nepotistic policy, the workplace "quality" of immigrants is declining steadily, putting strong pressures on our already strained welfare system. Obviously, no one wants to return to the racist policies enacted in the 1920s, and I want to emphasize strongly that talking about quality is not a racist smokescreen. What we need is a policy that encourages admission of immigrants from anywhere in the world who have the skills to prosper in a post-industrial society.

Immigration quality refers to the myriad of skills, entrepreneurship, ambition and motivation embodied in the immigrants. The question of quality is important because immigrants receive wages and salaries in accordance with their productivity. In an earlier era, when there was little government obligation to the poor, there was little concern for skills. Today, with an elaborate income transfer (or welfare) system providing benefits not only for the aged, disabled and single-parent families but also for the "working poor," we cannot be so cavalier about skills.

It is not just that low-skilled immigrants are more likely to need public assistance than are the highly skilled. By adding to the supply of low-skilled workers, wages and job opportunities for all low-skilled members of the labor force are depressed. To the extent that the federal minimum wage or labor-management contracts keep wages up, the downward pressure of an abundant labor supply is expressed as greater unemployment. Lower earnings and a higher unemployment rate for low-skilled workers means not only that more Americans will be eligible for income transfers but that current participants will receive larger benefits.

The 1965 immigration amendments radically altered the way legal immigrant visas are rationed. The act abolished the racist "national origins" quota systems of the 1920s, ending the virtual prohibition of immigration from Asia. It created a rationing system based on nepotism—most non-refugee visas are reserved for the relatives of American citizens or resident aliens. A small number of visas are allocated to professionals and individuals with scarce skills or who would invest in a business.

Immigration from Asia was very small and limited largely to professionals in the two decades prior to the 1965 amendments. The 1965 amendments expanded immigration opportunities, but initially only for highly skilled workers and those who had the capital to establish a business in the United States. These new immigrants then served as sponsors for their less-skilled relatives. As a result, more recent cohorts of Asian immigrants have included a larger number of lesser skilled relatives.

The effects of these policy changes on the source countries and skill levels of immigrants have been dramatic. Immigration and Naturalization Service data show a doubling of the number of legal immigrants from the 1950s to the present. In that time, immigration from Europe and Canada has declined while immigration from Latin America and especially from Asia has increased. Asians composed only 6 percent of immigrants in the 1950s but 36 percent in the 1970s. Overall, the educational level of foreign-born men who came here in the late 1970s is about the same as in the 1950s. But, since schooling levels in the United States and in the countries of origin have risen over this period, this represents a relative decline in educational levels.

Educational levels of the growing, legal immigration from the Western Hemisphere has been decreasing. This is partly due to deteriorating economic and political conditions in the countries of origin and declining costs of transportation and communication. It also arises from the greater ease of obtaining a visa based on kinship rather than one's own skills.

The trend to poorer quality immigrants is likely to be exacerbated by the 1986 act, which granted amnesty to aliens in the country illegally. In general, illegal aliens are low-skilled workers—with amnesty, they are more likely to become a permanent feature of the labor market. The legislation may also increase incentives for illegal entry. During the amnesty application period (starting in the spring and lasting for one year), there will be a strong incentive for illegal entry. Furthermore, the newly legalized aliens can serve as sponsors for relatives not already in the United States.

The national origins quota system, in force from the 1920s to the 1960s, focused on the question, "Where do you come from?" Current policy focuses on the question, "To whom are you related?" An alternative approach for nonrefugee visas is to focus on the question, "How productive will you be?" Rationing visas on the basis of the applicants' skills or likely productivity would require a point system, in which applicants would receive points for schooling, work experience, occupational skills and other characteristics that would enhance their productivity. Married couples could receive additional points on the basis of a spouse's skills. Individuals or families with more than a threshold number of points would be granted a visa, without regard to the country of origin. The successful applicant's spouse and minor children would also receive visas. The threshold could be raised or lowered to control the number of immigrants.

This policy need not ignore kinship. For humanitarian reasons, the spouse and minor children of U.S. citizens could still be granted visas. And for other applicants a small number of points could be awarded if a citizen or resident alien agrees to serve as a sponsor.

An emphasis on skills is absolutely not a backdoor return to the racist, national origins quota system. The small number of immigrants admitted on the basis of their skills or investor status during the past two decades have been disproportionately from third world countries. This pattern is likely to continue under the proposed immigration policy.

An immigration policy that favors productive applicants would have many beneficial effects. It would ease competition in the labor market between low-skilled natives and low-skilled immigrants, calming social tensions and lowering the proportion of the population below the poverty line. And a policy based on the applicant's own characteristics is closer to the American ideal.

Barry R. Chiswick, visiting professor at the University of Chicago's Center for the Study of the Economy and the State, is coauthor of "The Dilemma of American Immigration."

Immigration's Whistling Kettle

by **Daniel James**
The Washington Times
December 4, 1994

Both sides in the debate over California's Proposition 187, which denies certain public benefits to immigrants who enter that state illegally, ignore the basic facts that make immigration a major national and even foreign issue. It is primarily Mexico's failed economy that motivates the uncontrolled inflow of illegal and legal immigrants northward—the "push" factor. The "pull" factor—the lure of jobs in America—is secondary.

The cruel truth is that Mexico, notwithstanding its laudable economic reforms, suffers from massive unemployment—underemployment estimated at 40 percent to 50 percent of its work force. Each year, 1 million youths come of working age, reports the Mexican government, but at best perhaps only half of them find jobs.

That leaves an estimated 500,000 or more idle Mexican youngsters to worry about annually. Should Uncle Sam feel obligated to receive such huge numbers year after year without any foreseeable letup?

The North American Free Trade Agreement is supposed to create jobs on both sides of the border. But experts agree that no appreciable number will materialize for ten to fifteen years. With 300,000 illegals entering the United States annually, the Immigration and Naturalization Service estimates conservatively, between now and 2008 we can expect 3 million to 4.5 million new illegals. The actual total is likely to be much higher, if current immigration policies remain unchanged.

It is time to face up honestly to the much bigger and more frightening problem: legal immigration. Approximately 1 million persons reach the United States each year, legally, and their number keeps rising. Thus 10 million to 15 million documented persons are projected to arrive by 2008. Together with illegals, the grand total of all immigrants should range between 13 million and 19.5 million—up to half the projected population of Central America.

The bottom line is that these numbers have a mounting price tag. The $3 billion that California Governor Pete Wilson estimates the state's illegal immigrants to cost pales before the total national cost of all immigration in this decade: $670 billion.

That is the staggering amount arrived at in a study on "The Costs of Immigration" by Donald Huddle, economics professor emeritus at Rice University, Houston. Dr. Huddle studied twenty-two major local, state and federal public assistance programs that benefit the projected total stock of 29.4 million legal and illegal newcomers between 1970 and 2002, and found they will cost taxpayers $668.5 billion net during the decade ending in 2002. Included in the total cost, though impossible to quantify in human terms, are benefits paid to 2.07 million U.S. citizens displaced in 1992 by immigrants. Analysis shows blacks are disproportionately displaced by immigrants, in housing as well as employment. South Central Los Angeles, scene of the 1992 Rodney King riots, is typical. No wonder so many California blacks voted for Proposition 187.

If Newt Gingrich, Bob Dole and the new Republican congressional majority are really sincere about cutting expenses and balancing the budget, they will find some specific places in the Huddle study. But they must also face squarely the principal source of the immigration problem: Mexico.

For years, Mexico has pursued an unwritten policy of regarding us as the "safety valve" for its expanding population, which approaches 100 million—nearly equal to that of Britain and France combined—and is increasing exponentially. It claims that closing the border would provoke a "social explosion" at home. So Washington has obliged by leaving it porous, enabling our neighbor to export its potential social upheaval to California.

The fear that Proposition 187 might undermine Mexico's "right" to do so is what motivated Mexican officials, from outgoing President Carlos Salinas de Gortari on down, to stage an unprecedented protest against it. The protest was sparked by the Ministry of Foreign Relations, a no-torious leftist stronghold. A similar display of egregious meddling by Americans in Mexican legislation would have provoked an uproar, and it probably would not have been purely vocal.

It is to be hoped the GOP-dominated Senate Foreign Relations Com-mittee will deal frankly with Mexico's spurious "safety valve" policy. Perhaps Bill Clinton can be persuaded, as well, to discuss it with the new Mexican president, Ernesto Zedillo, at the Americas summit in Mi-ami this week. Proposition 187 is wrong in seeking to spur the depor-tation of a substantial portion of California's 1.6 million illegals. That's obviously impossible, and inhumane. But it does send a signal to Mexico that we can no longer afford them. Neither can we any longer afford uncontrolled millions of legal immigrants. Clearly, there is a real need to reform our entire immigration policy—which Republicans might make the eleventh point in their "Contract with America."

On the other hand, the Jack Kemps and Bill Bennetts are romantic reactionaries when they reach back more than a century to justify their opposition to Proposition 187 and other immigration-reform measures. Times have changed radically since then. As elder statesman George Kennan points out, we are "very much a polyglot country," so the issue is not racism, as Messrs. Kemp and Bennett charged intemperately. "What I have in mind here," continues Mr. Kennan, "are the sheer numbers. There is such a thing as overcrowding. . . . There are limits to what the environment can stand."

Perhaps the shrill voices serving the open-border lobbies can descend enough decibels to permit a calm, reasoned national debate on what is surely the overriding question facing America: What kind of nation do we want to be?

Daniel James is the author of "Illegal Immigration—an Unfolding Crisis" (1991), and co-chairman of the new American National Council on Immigration Reform (ANCIR).

$4,000: The Price of a Mexican

by Patrisia Gonzales and Roberto Rodriguez
Column of the Americas
from Universal Press Syndicate
August 31, 2001

A friend of ours over for breakfast started sobbing when we told her that a south Texas rancher who shot an unarmed Mexican from behind was fined $4,000, put on probation and set free. *"No valemos nadaaaaa,"* she said. Her tearful words need no translation.

Her reaction moved us. Actually, it shook us. We stopped to say a prayer for the slain Eusebio de Haro and his family. It was no hyperbole when we recently wrote that in the United States, a dog's life is worth more than that of a Mexican.

The Sam Blackwood trial in Brackettville, along with the countless murders and needless deaths that have been occurring all along the U.S./ Mexico border (since before we were born) illustrates this. The only difference is that nowadays, they're also occurring elsewhere in the southern United States—where 3 million Mexicans/Central Americans live—a place not normally associated with anti-Mexicanism.

It's a wonder that this May 2000 murder and recent outrageous court decision is even news. It's right out of a 50s' western in which the gunslinger brags about the number of cowboys he's killed—"not counting Mexicans." The fact is, for killing a Mexican, Blackwood was convicted simply of a misdemeanor "dangerous conduct" charge.

The context no doubt will help explain this travesty. As reported in the *San Antonio Express-News,* a rancher friend of Blackwood, testifying about encounters other ranchers have with migrants, said: "We usually tell each other about our woes, about our wetback problems."

One can sincerely empathize with these woeful ranchers: $4,000 is a hefty sum to be paying for helping to exterminate wetbacks. That's the message many of us, including ranchers, hear daily, don't we?—from billboards to talk-radio hosts; from draconian propositions to vigilantism. After years and years of dehumanizing Mexicans, of a vicious anti-immigrant campaign by people in and out of government, we see the result. This killing came at the same time that Arizona ranchers were recruiting vigilantes nationwide to help do the work of the *"migra,"* or U.S. border patrol.

Despite the completely unprovoked nature of the shooting, Blackwood didn't even stand trial for murder. According to testimony by de Haro's friend, Javier Sanchez, they had stopped at Blackwood's ranch for a drink of water. The rancher refused; then after they left, he tracked them down and shot de Haro from behind. De Haro, bleeding to death, asked the rancher: "Why did you do that? I didn't do nothing."

The dehumanization of Mexicans is so ingrained here that when migrants are killed or found dead—which is often—they are rarely referred to as Mexicans. They are called illegal aliens, or illegals or even wetbacks. (If they're wearing suits, regardless of nationality, they're often upgraded to Hispanics.) Usually, they aren't named. And when it involves an unjustified killing, especially by a law enforcement officer, forget about it. If it's vigilantes, it's usually "self-defense," and aggravated assault is about the most serious charge one can expect. Often, they're cheered on by like-minded demagogues.

Bob Rivard, editor of the *Express-News,* pondered in a column recently about what would have happened if de Haro had killed Blackwood? That's a rhetorical question in Texas, the death penalty capital of the world.

That's why the dog reference. Just recently, in a road-rage incident, a northern California man was appropriately given a three-year sentence for killing a dog. But for rage against a Mexican? Less than the price of a used car.

For those who often ask why we use the word "dehumanization," rather than "racism," this case provides the answer. To dehumanize (including, but not limited to, reasons of race) is to degrade, stereotype, caricaturize, trivialize, devalue, humiliate, invisibilize, alienize, scapegoat, criminalize and demonize. In effect, it's to make one less than human, not simply in society and the media, but also inside of a courtroom.

That's why Blackwood isn't the sole culprit. Like a "Los Tigres Del Norte" song, which proclaims that migrants die twice unless buried in their homeland, de Haro was killed twice. The second time was when the grand jury charged Blackwood with a misdemeanor.

Adding insult, the jury could have given the rancher a year. But apparently he was needed in the free world.

To Blackman, we ask: Why did you kill him? He didn't do nothin' but walk through "your" land. To the jury: Why did you even bother fining him? He was just taking care of our wetback problem. To the Justice Department: Any chance of prosecuting Blackwood on federal civil rights violations?

Gonzales and Rodriguez write a syndicated column for Universal Press Syndicate. Gonzales is the author of the forthcoming *The Mud People: Anonymous Heroes of Mexico* and co-author of *Gonzales/ Rodriguez: Uncut & Uncensored*. Rodriguez is the author of *Justice: A Question of Race*.

AMERICAN CITIZEN: "What weight can my vote have against this flood of ignorance, stupidity and fraud?"
(from the *Ram's Horn*, 31 October 1896)

Between Necessity and Freedom

A Roundtable Discussion on
Recent Immigration Issues

The following roundtable was held on November 29, 2001, at the Downtown Campus of the University of Texas at San Antonio. The roundtable was meant to generate some of the context for the new literature of immigration gathered in this anthology—to thrash out some of the central issues in the contemporary debates about immigration, to get activists and scholars from the immigrant communities talking about the nature of contemporary immigration as they see it. The questions and answers that follow are clearly marked by place and date—proximity in space to the Mexico/Texas border and in time to the catastrophe of 9/11. Some of the discussion focuses on the nature and history of immigration across that specific border and on the challenges issuing from that specific event. Nevertheless, the effect of the roundtable is to highlight the enduring themes of immigration in general, to show how immigration is often enough driven by the twin engines of necessity and freedom—flight from a life reduced to scraping together the bare, necessary minimum and quest for a life capable of delivering some freedoms. It is here—between necessity and freedom—that immigrant hopes are born either to flourish or to die.

The roundtable was moderated by Anannya Bhattacharjee.

I would like to welcome María Jiménez, who has been an activist for close to thirty years. Currently she is the director of the Immigration Law Enforcement Monitoring Project (ILEMP) at the American Friends Service Committee office in Houston, Texas.

I would also like to welcome Jerome Ceille. He is the secretary-treasurer of FLOC, the Farm Labor Organizing Committee. It is a union that is affiliated with the AFL-CIO and is based in Toledo, Ohio. FLOC has been organizing farmworkers for the last few decades. Before FLOC, Jerome was the lead organizer with Toledoans United for Social Action, a citywide community organization. And he was a member of Direct Action Research and Training Network (DART) in Miami, Florida. He is married with one child.

Also joining us is Grace Chang, from Washington state. She has recently published a book called *Disposable Domestics: Immigrant Women Workers in the Global Economy.* She got her Ph.D. in ethnic studies from U.C. Berkeley. And she is an activist originally from Oakland. Now she teaches ethnic studies and women's studies at Evergreen State College in Washington state. She teaches courses in social protest movements, women and globalization, and women and violence.

And finally I would like to introduce Raquel Marquez, an assistant professor at U.T. San Antonio. She is a scholar on border issues and teaches courses on race relations and Latina studies. She has conducted binational research on women's migration from Mexico to the United States focusing especially on the border.

AB: María, it is hard to begin without talking about 9/11 first. Many say that the terrorist attacks on New York and Washington on September 11 this year have radically changed the context of social justice work.

MJ: After 9/11, the issues for the immigrant rights movement have become more accentuated when it comes to the issue of police relations—not only the border patrol and local police, but at all levels. But fundamentally the issues are still the same. Since they arise from the same needs, the same campaigns are still there to be fought.

What is different is that the immediate impact of the 11th was to demobilize the immigrant community. Many of us worked for many years to organize immigrants, whether they were documented or not, to assert their needs before institutions. In the particular work that we do, we take delegations of immigrants to Austin, to Congress, to lobby. That mobilizing is really difficult to do now, mainly because multi-agency enforcement is now in all the airports. For instance, in Houston we now have about six border patrol agents physically in the airport. And so literal mobility in the social movement was drastically curtailed.

But at the same time people did not disband. I think that people started to understand how to deal with the context we are in. Immediately organizing began to emphasize local work and to redefine a strong coordination at the national level so that the movement will continue. That is what I think is the most dramatic thing that we saw happen after 9/11. The work at the agenda and policy levels was, as someone put it, a train that was delayed but not derailed. And so now, as we are beginning to see how policy makers at different levels begin to articulate the issues, we need to get back to the immigrants' agenda—particularly the issue of the new amnesty, that is, legalization of undocumented immigrants. As far as other local work like access to medical care, ability to obtain a driver's license, etc., most or all of that work will continue.

But again, the immediate impact was to demobilize the communities. And that could be seen as a setback, but at the same time it is also an opportunity because it will force us to reorganize, so that in the long run we will be more effective.

AB: I have heard you say before that the policies that get put in place on the Mexico/U.S. border provide us with a preview of the policies that would get implemented in the interior of the United States. So looking back over your work, do you still feel the same way?

MJ: Well, on the Mexico/U.S. border, for decades now, but particularly in the 90s, there have been operations by several agencies simultaneously. Take for instance the use of the military. The border patrol would call the military and they would conduct operations with the local police and sometimes they would call on the District Attorney and U.S. Customs. And so multi-agency operations were fairly common on the U.S./Mexico border, including the presence of the National Guard. What we see after the 9/11 is that this same concept, the multi-agency cooperation, has been transferred to the airports. And probably we will be seeing it slowly along the Canadian border. And so in that sense it is the transfer of the same type of operation. And this is nothing new because there was already talk by the government regarding this in 1996. At least two years ago the issue of border security was defined as a primary issue.

And the same type of operations and focus as that of U.S. immigration law enforcement on the Mexican border has begun to be talked about and applied to borders across the continent from Panama to Canada. We see that Mexico now has its own border patrols along the southern Mexican border and even along the northern Mexican border for the first time. This past July there was a multinational operation intercepting the flow of undocumented persons throughout this region. And then the United States started an operation called Operation Disrupt. This particular operation has the effect of advancing economic integration in the Americas so that it will accelerate. The whole issue of border security and the control of workers has become accelerated and the models of border patrol and population control and so forth produced along the U.S./Mexico border are being applied elsewhere in the United States and also throughout the continent.

AB: I want to turn to you now, Jerome. U.S. immigration policies directly affect the rights of workers in this country and your organization has been organizing farmworkers who are largely immigrants for close to thirty years. Farmworkers also have to deal with different immigration programs, which have been known by various names: Bracero, guest worker, H2A. Can you walk us through some of these programs and tell us a little about the kind of policies FLOC would consider humane and just for the workers that you are organizing?

JC: Many of the seven thousand members of FLOC, which is a union and part of the AFL-CIO, come traditionally from Texas into the midwest or come from Florida. And now a huge number of immigrants come from various parts of Mexico. The Bracero Program and the H2A Program were both started about the same time during World War II to bring workers into the United States. I think the H2A Program started with sugarcane workers in Florida being brought in from Caribbean countries. The difference between the Bracero Program and the H2A Program—or one of the differences—is that H2A workers were given nonimmigrant temporary visas. The Bracero Program was between the government of Mexico and the government of the United States. Thank God that the Bracero Program is gone. We are now involved in trying to eliminate the H2A Program.

The H2A Program is a program of the Department of Labor, which is driven by the need for cheap labor in certain industries. The H2A happens to be for agriculture and there are other sections of the same program for other industries. FLOC is concerned with the H2A because of the great number of H2A workers recruited to North Carolina, for instance, on contracts that include three crops of cucumbers, sweet potatoes, and tobacco. The workers are recruited from Mexico for those seasons—there are two harvests of pickles during the summer and sweet potatoes and tobacco. We are also starting to see a lot of H2A workers in the mid-west. Some are even in Michigan during this season cutting

Christmas trees. And of course picking vegetables and fruits in Michigan and Ohio and Indiana. The need for a new policy is pretty evident because the H2A Program is driven by the needs of a corporate industry that wants cheap labor. And so this type of industry brings the workers in. There are protections written in the law but of course they are not enforced. So the worker under the H2A Program is basically enslaved by the process. And the hope of many of the workers is to make enough money to take back or to send back to their families at the end of the season.

Baldemar Velasquez, the president of FLOC, and a delegation mainly of young people recently visited the widow of a worker who died in North Carolina. The worker died probably of pesticide poisoning and his bones were actually only found under a pecan tree several months later. And they were able to identify him only by the region that he worked in, the clothing, the shoes, and sandals, and so forth. So we were visiting the widow of Reymundo Hernández in Cintlalli, deep in Mexico, to show her the relationships he had, and to show her some of the donations that people had given to her family through our work. But also to demonstrate the connection that exists between the lack of work in Mexico and the worker who is being driven into the United States. And to give people a sense of what the effect is on the family in Mexico and a sense of the impact of U.S. policies on workers in Mexico. The bottom line is that we have to change the program so the workers come here with travel rights and with labor rights—the right to organize, the right to change employers. Under the H2A Program they are prohibited from changing employers. If they find the situation desperate, they can't change their work. So those are some of the changes needed. For us it's not a matter of tinkering with the H2A Program, but really of drawing up new policies—new border policies and new immigrant worker policies—for the agricultural workers and all immigrant workers.

AB: It is challenging to organize workers. It is even more challenging to organize workers who are moving back and forth across the border.

Also, often the companies pass their responsibilities towards workers to subcontractors and so on. Can you give us some examples of the strategies that FLOC has used to rise up to those challenges?

JC: Some of you may remember the boycott of Campbell's products some fifteen years or so ago because of the treatment of the migrant farmworkers in northwest Ohio. That was FLOC's boycott, which ended with a march from Toledo to Camden, New Jersey, the headquarters of Campbell's Food. It was a boycott that lasted some nine to ten years, but which finally brought about three-party contracts amongst farmers, workers and processing companies in our area. And that is really our goal. Because for a while FLOC was fighting with farmers to raise the wages and conditions. And obviously farmers do not set the price of tomatoes and pickles. They are set by the corporation that processes them. And so our thought was to bring them to the table. And that was what was done.

What we are trying to do is to have the same multi-party contract in North Carolina for the workers. And the company there is Del Monte Pickle Company. So we are trying to push the company, like we did with Campbell's, to sit down and negotiate a three-party contract. Because that is the only way to the pockets—the deep pockets of the industry are with the corporations, not the farmers. And we are at a point in Ohio where the relations with the farmers have turned around. And some are advocating with us for better housing and other changes in the industry.

AB: And what about the movement of the workers back and forth across the border? How do you all deal with that?

JC: Well, a certain amount of cross-border organizing has to take place. What we are doing is setting up hiring halls so that workers in Mexico, for instance, can come to a FLOC hiring hall and get related to work in North Carolina, Ohio, and Michigan. And so that is going to be our answer for the movement of workers. That they will be coming *through* the union into their work. And in that sense they will have the protections of the union grievance processes and so forth.

AB: I also wanted to hear from you about the important move that the AFL-CIO made last year, and renewed in 2001 again, supporting the cause for amnesty of undocumented workers. What is going to happen to that? How has that played out in the struggle around legalization and amnesty and in your work?

JC: I think that the organizing that María was talking about actually was part of the pressure that moved the AFL-CIO—the organizing of the workers themselves, because the union is finding that is one of the newest groups that can be organized. And that is the future of some of the unions. I mean if you look at some of the unions' memberships now they are growing in the Hispanic population. And so, I think the AFL-CIO is responding to that, responding to the pressure of the organizing. Really they have not done much since the forums that were held in 2000, I'm sorry to say.

AB: Grace, in your book *Disposable Domestics* that came out earlier this year you made some interesting links between low-wage immigrant workers and welfare workers (those who receive welfare payments on the condition of welfare work). Can you tell us more about these links between the immigrant communities and communities of color?

GC: If I can go back a little bit to one of María's comments about the new multi-agency collaborations—what we see and have seen more and more in the last three or four years, is this phenomenon of the INS collaborating with the Department of Human Services, the welfare departments.

And this is the most common scenario: The INS will come and raid a workplace and take out a large group of immigrant workers, whether they are documented or not, and put them through deportation proceedings. And then they often turn around to the local Department of Human Services and say: "Look we now have X-number of jobs that are available at this workplace. So would you like to bring in your welfare workers to fill these jobs?" And of course this not only pits various communities of color against one another, but particularly low-wage immigrant workers against no-wage or welfare workers.

There was a very interesting comment that was made by a white worker at one of the sites where this happened. It was a construction site. He said: "What are we going to have to do, go through thirty men before we can find one who wants to work? It's just a waste of time. Who wants to train somebody that isn't going to work? He'll say, 'I can collect welfare, I do not need to work.'" And the white worker said, "I'd rather have a Latino worker." This is disturbing because it reflects how this type of program really reinforces all the racist stereotypes against people of color. If you are Latino, you are seen as an ideal worker, super exploitable. Meanwhile, blacks are seen as lazy, shiftless, not wanting to get off welfare. So this kind of program pits people against one another quite literally, on a pragmatic level, but also ideologically. And of course the main problem with these programs is that you are displacing one group of people—immigrant workers—through terrorizing INS raids in order to create not jobs, but job vacancies, which were already filled by workers who were being exploited. And this is touted as creating new jobs.

AB: It seems that at different times the types of threats that the immigrants are thought to pose are interpreted differently. There was a time when immigrants were seen as taking away everybody's jobs. Then immigrants became portrayed as a drain on national resources. Then immigrants were blamed for traffic jams. Can you tell us a little bit about such changing perceptions of threats?

GC: Essentially I think what we see here is very well-crafted rationalizations for imposing more and more brutal policies on immigrants. What we see is that more women and whole families are migrating as opposed to the past when just the male migrants came without their families. And when you have greater settlement you also have this perception that immigrants are coming in and literally eating up all the resources around. Women are perceived as the leaders and the breeders of the families, right? As the reproducers of the consumers.

And I think that is why we see this shift in the rhetoric. Certainly there is still rhetoric around jobs, but more rhetoric came into play around Proposition 187 in California in 1994 focused on immigrants as resource drains and welfare abusers. We saw it in the media, on the news, on *48 Hours,* showing some of these women coming across the border and sitting in public hospitals waiting to give birth. And the implication was that hospitals and the local towns were overwhelmed by children using everything from health care to public schooling. It's very serious imagery and I think it had just exactly the effect that it was intended to have: that there was this huge immigrant menace. And that that menace was a population of new consumers, of people with needs for basics like food and health care and schooling. This has very much influenced the American public to look at immigrants not just as a threat in the job market, but as a threat to public resources, to their very land and air.

AB: Are these fears valid?

GC: All the research on undocumented immigrants points to the reality that immigrants, in fact, underutilize social services and public services exactly because of the discourse around their alleged use of welfare and public resources. Even when there are programs that they are eligible for, or that their children who are U.S. citizens would be eligible for, they are still avoiding the use of these various forms of assistance. Often because of the fear that it would jeopardize their immigration status or the ability to get permanent residency eventually. And this was already true before Proposition 187 and it was true before the 1996 immigration act. But this underutilization was particularly dramatic following all the hysteria around Proposition 187. There was a great fear that we saw reflected in calls to hotlines after Proposition 187. It wasn't only that people were now experiencing more hardships, but they were very reluctant to claim the services they needed, especially medical care.

AB: Raquel, maybe you can expand on something Grace mentioned earlier. Is it true that more women are crossing borders, immigrating, and doing low-wage immigrant work? If it is true, how does it change the way we look at immigration?

RM: First, let me answer, yes. More women are immigrating from places like Mexico, where my expertise lies, and they're working in low-wage jobs. Let me give a little bit of background on women's participation in the labor market. You have to start with looking at Mexican migration to the United States. It is a direct result of binational agreements between Mexico and the United States made in the early 50s in response to growers and their demands for workers to harvest their crops. And not just workers, but cheap workers. As a result we had the Bracero Program. And it was through the Bracero Program and subsequent binational agreements that Mexican workers began this migration process back and forth between Mexico and the United States. Then in the early 60s, when the Bracero Program ended, there was a mad rush to create something that would provide work for the displaced migrant workers. So you had the rise of the *maquiladora* industry, which was put in place on the Mexican side of the border to provide work for this returning male migrant population. Therefore, initially the idea was to provide jobs for the returning men. By the 70s and the 80s what we see happening is that the *maquiladora* industry began to have this shift to a preference for female workers. And in the last twenty to twenty-five years more women have migrated internally from Mexico to the border areas.

So to return to the initial question as to why women are immigrating from Mexico and why they work in low wage jobs . . . If you look at Mexico first, on the Mexican side the jobs in the *maquiladora* industry provide somewhat decent wages by Mexican standards for young, unskilled, and inexperienced workers. But these are also jobs that have very few benefits. There is a high turnover. The working conditions are poor. And if you go to certain states like Tamaulipas where workers have very few rights, then women are routinely given six-month contracts, which give them even fewer benefits or no benefits. And in addition to that you have to keep in mind that women are fired when they get pregnant and as they get older. All you have to do is to look at the *maquiladora* labor force. In the last forty to forty-five years it has not aged. The *maquiladora* labor force is still between sixteen years and thirty years old and it has never aged.

If you cross over to the U.S. side of the border, industrial growth in Texas border cities has basically remained stagnant, with the exception of Laredo with its recent boom. And unemployment is high. Many women find that they cross over to the U.S. side in response to the fact that the Mexican labor market does not offer lifetime work opportunities; as they get older, their response is to take the migration process one step further and cross into the United States. But when they get to the United States the jobs or the skills that they may have gained in the *maquiladora* labor force don't necessarily transfer. So they find themselves in difficult or worse conditions.

AB: You have done a lot of work documenting life histories of women who are moving from the interior of Mexico to the border and then into the United States. Can you tell us a little bit about how migration experiences are distinct for women as opposed to men who are doing the same thing?

RM: You always have to go back to the fact that migration is an economic decision. On an individual level both men and women migrate due to the basic need to work. They need to work and they need to be able to feed their families. At the nation-state level countries open and close their doors based on their companies' needs for labor. So the bottom line is that it is an economic decision either way.

Women or Mexican women's experiences are distinct from men for two basic reasons. One is that the women come with different skills and fewer skills than men do. And so their work options are limited, more limited than men's. Men may have skills in carpentry or masonry, so they are able to find other work opportunities outside of the *maquiladoras*. And the second reason is because women are the primary caretakers of their families. It doesn't matter what side of the border you are on, women are still the primary caretakers of the family. And this has a tremendous impact on women. We have seen that typically men will send remittances back to Mexico for a period of time until they start their own family here in the United States. And maybe they will continue to send money for a short period of time after that. But the money flow begins to get smaller. Women, on the other hand, continue to send money, and there is evidence that women continue to send money for as long as ten years. And their goal is always ultimately to bring their children, to get reunited with their families. It is important to understand this properly. Women are the ones who eventually negotiate the settlement process. They are the ones that enroll the children in school. They are the ones that set up the contracts when they buy a car, or when they buy a home. They are the ones that run the finances for the family. So policy makers need to take all this into account and ensure that women have the necessary skills to make these decisions.

AB: María, since we are talking so much about crossing borders, I would like to ask you a tough question: Just what exactly would a just border policy look like? There doesn't seem to be a consensus that we should have an open border even among social justice people. Can you tell us a little bit more about these debates, what you think, and what the American Friends Service Committee thinks?

MJ: First of all, the AFSC does not support open borders because we feel the issue is very complex. There are populations that we have worked with for many years that want borders defined. The native peoples of the United States, for instance. Or for many years AFSC worked with the Palestinians in the Gaza Strip for the definition of the Palestinian state. So the issue of borders is very complex. And so we have framed our position on borders simply as one in favor of the human right of mobility. And this works because, as native people always say, since time immemorial human beings have moved for a better life. Or in order to escape oppression.

There have always been restrictions on mobility throughout history. Currently, it is the nation-state that is basically outlawing the movement of people across international borders. In the current context we feel that the human right of mobility is an unrecognized right. And so for us border policy has to be defined in terms of the people that we work with—giving them equal conditions of mobility across international borders. And eventually moving towards a recognition of this as a right. What do I mean by this?

Well, when we analyzed border policies all over the world, we found they don't vary whether it is South Africa, Mexico, or the United States. In this time of globalization and economic restructuring, if you look at immigration and border policies anywhere they are very much the same. International law basically states that the nation has the right over the individuals to decide who enters, how, what conditions they enter under, what rights they have, when and if they stay, and they have the right to define how a person becomes a complete member of that nation state, which is citizenship. And so when we look at border policies what we see is that the human right to mobility in the current global economic structure is guaranteed for the very powerful economic, political, and social elites—that is, a CEO of a transnational corporation, for example, has no problems crossing borders safely and legally. Political representatives, presidents, secretaries of states, prime ministers have no problems crossing borders legally and safely. And even wealthy refugees such as the Marcoses, when they ran from the Philippines, had no problems. I often point out that Carlos Salinas de Gortari is the only Mexican that I know who had no problems getting a visa to cross the border. The very highest level of the economic, political, and social elites has no problems crossing borders legally and safely.

The border patrols, militarized borders, the walls and the barriers— these are for the international working and displaced poor. And in that sense border policy works to reinforce social, economic, and political inequalities on a global scale. And because of that it is like any other issue. If you work on education issues, you work on how to give maximum opportunity and equal conditions for people to be able to receive the best education possible. From our perspective, the fight to reform immigration law is to make it easier to cross the border legally. Whether it is through amnesty or temporary residency, and so on, the fight is to try to equalize the conditions that allow people to move across international borders. It is unfair, from our perspective, that if you are poor the choice you have is to risk your life and maybe die simply because you have to earn a living. And if you are very wealthy, you have other choices. This is how our current immigration law is. For instance, an investor under our current immigration law does not come into the United States illegally. Do you know of any illegal investors? They are afforded temporary residency at the border and they come into the United States with the condition that they invest a million dollars for two years and set up a business with eight workers. And if at the end of that two-year period you meet that condition, then you get your green card. That is something that is not afforded to a farmworker, or a domestic worker, or a hotel and restaurant worker. So for us that is very unfair. For us the small "r," the small reform or revolution, is to work for making legal crossing a possibility for the international working poor and the international people who are displaced. That is one way. But we realize that we are also part of the forces that want to reconstruct society and create a society that is just and at peace. And where we have true democracy. As for the big "R," the Revolution, it would require global economic restructuring.

For instance, Grace mentioned the raids. After surveying for many years the border patrol and the INS and its police forces, one of the things that struck us as interesting was the following question: Why is it that the only area of labor/management relations that is enforced with an armed group is in the area of the relation between employer and the unauthorized international laborer, the undocumented immigrant? Why? We don't see, for instance, armed police come into a work site and try to enforce minimum wage laws. We don't see an armed force come to enforce safety and occupational laws. We don't see them even come to try to enforce tax laws. So why, we asked ourselves, why is this the only area of management and labor relations that is enforced on a group and is reflected in our border policy?

Our answer was to look at the history of the United States and other societies, particularly in the era of slavery in the United States. The slave patrols were the first police forces that were funded by government in the history of the United States. The role of the slave patrols was to restrict the mobility of the enslaved population in order to reproduce the existing strategy of economic development and their economic, political, and social relations. That made economic development possible. These police forces restricted the movements of the enslaved populations. Even to move between plantations you had to have documents. And even freed slaves had to have documents to show that they were free. We feel that in the current period the issue of the restriction of the mobility of the international working poor is key in sustaining the strategy of development created by the global elites. And that is the strategy of profits and low wages.

If you fortify borders you force the labor to stay in countries where the labor-intensive production units are placed. And if they happen to cross the border, then this illegal population is inserted into the dynamic sectors of the economy and is highly fireable and able to be exploited. What the current period illustrates for us is that under the scheme of border security the only other way to control labor is to actually develop special guest worker programs like the H2A Program. That is legalization as defined by the bosses. Not legalization or amnesty as defined by the workers, which is a big difference.

AB: I think what we should do now is give our speakers a minute or two for some closing thoughts. And I was hoping that during those closing thoughts Jerome and María could give us a sense of some opportunities for the future to end on a positive note, and whatever else you want to include.

JC: Well, one of the opportunities in organizing that came to my mind as María talked about the slave patrols is some of the work that we are doing in North Carolina. We are trying to form alliances with the African American community. Obviously the migrant workers are considered the new slaves of the south. To have a dialogue between the African American community and the Latino community is exciting, especially as workers dialoguing with one another. It's an opportunity to learn about each other, to learn each other's history and culture. It is difficult at times because of barriers of language, but it's a chance to create alliances. And these alliances can become active alliances of people working together. For instance, this past summer we had a Juneteenth celebration in Raleigh, North Carolina, that was sponsored by African American unions and FLOC, where the Latino and African American communities came together.

I think that's one opportunity. The other opportunity is to work globally. Companies like Campbell's and Heinz are already buying pickles from outside the United States, and when we try to challenge their labor policies in North Carolina, they'll say, "Look, if you're going to keep pressuring us in this state to raise wages, we'll just buy our pickles from India." So even with added transportation costs it is more profitable for them to import from some other place where they can exploit workers. When we improve conditions for immigrant workers here we need to work to improve conditions for workers in Mexico and in India and around the world because capital moves wherever it can find cheap labor.

MJ: We're still doing the same thing we've always been doing but now from a different perspective. We see this as an opportunity for base building—the fact that we now have to concentrate locally. For us it's always been very important that immigrants, documented or not, are the engineers of social change. That requires base building. We do a lot of training work—how to organize, how to document violations of human rights. And we work directly with immigrants. We are training for civic participation. So that work is being sustained.

In addition to intensified base building, a second strategy is alliance building. The current world situation has created new areas for organizing and networking. Right now many people are interested in civil liberties. We have seen that immigrant workers are also worried about the issue of peace and the restrictions on civil liberties. Finally, I agree we have to insert the international because we are dealing with an international phenomenon. In Houston there are several international networks throughout the region working on this issue. There is a new term that has been coined, "glocal," the global and the local together, that is very useful. That is the approach we think is necessary. But the priority has to be base building.

GC: If I can build on what María is saying... If you look at the antiglobalization movement, many of us are very dissatisfied with the way it is predominantly white. This is an issue for migrant workers and for the large percentage of people of color, as one critic put it, who live globalization even though they may not use the term globalization. One of the questions I often get is: If people are not migrating in order to steal jobs or social services, then why are they migrating? I think people tend to be more aware of the role of military interventions in the Third World as a factor that forces people to migrate. But they are less aware that there are also important economic interventions—such as policies by the International Monetary Fund—which force people to migrate.

RM: I was trying to think of how to end on a positive note. I hope one of the things that academics and activists can do is hold more forums like this so that we have opportunities for public debate and public discussion about immigration issues. Immigration flows are not going to stop unless at some point we eliminate inequality, which is quite unlikely to happen. So what we need to focus on is addressing the need for workers' rights not just here in this country but throughout the world. As academics and activists we should foster public discussion on these issues because they are important issues, and they concern people who are basically trying to feed their families. We need to ensure that these discussions take place in a decent and respectful way.

The New Immigration and the Literature of Asian America

by Seung Hye Suh and
Robert Ji-Song Ku

For the first time in U.S. history, the Immigration Act of 1965 made it possible for significant numbers of immigrants from Asia to enter the country. This was to change profoundly the face of America, as millions of Asians, along with Africans, Latin Americans, and Caribbean islanders, among others, crossed U.S. borders and staked their claims *as* Americans. Asian American literature, post-1965, testifies to the vast diversity of human experiences arising from and intersecting with these immigrant experiences. Yet, the very notion of a post-1965 Asian American literature—that is, a body of American literature by writers of Asian descent within a period inaugurated by the 1965 immigration laws—challenges us to come to terms with a number of creative tensions, if not contradictions, that lie at the heart of what it means to be an Asian in America and produce the literature that might be called Asian American. This essay discusses some of these issues in an attempt to contribute to ongoing interpretations of a body of literature that is still very much in the making.

Prior to 1965, Asian American writings that seemed to command the most interest from American publishers and readers were texts that could be read as ethnographic accounts of the writer's community. This ethnographic bent in Asian American literature most often manifested itself in literary autobiographies: Lee Yan Phou's *When I Was a Boy in China* (1887), Etsu Sugimoto's *Daughter of the Samurai* (1925), New Il-Han's *When I Was a Boy in Korea* (1928), Younghill Kang's *The Grass Roof* (1931), Carlos Bulosan's *America Is in the Heart* (1943), Jade Snow Wong's *Fifth Chinese Daughter* (1945), Monica Sone's *Nisei Daughter* (1953), to name just a few. Texts such as these tended to be evaluated less as literary works and more in terms of their relationship to anthropological truth. Such readings reinforced notions of Asian American writers not as literary artists but as naive translators of the exotic within the American metropole.

Autobiographies were by no means the only Asian American literary works published prior to 1965; yet such work as the poetry and short fiction of Carlos Bulosan, Toshio Mori's *Yokohama, California* (1949), the short stories of Hisaye Yamamoto, and John Okada's *No-No Boy* (1957), despite their literary excellence and their incorporation of vital social commentary, were in their time neither as well known nor as well appreciated by American audiences as the autobiographies. Moreover, the year 1965 did not mark the end of the Asian American "autoethnography," as Françoise Lionnet has termed the ethnographic autobiography. In fact, this literary legacy continued and continues on, as evidenced by the critical approaches to and commercial successes of post-1965 works ranging from Maxine Hong Kingston's *The Woman Warrior* (1975) to David Mura's *Turning Japanese* (1991).

Yet 1965 does signal a number of departures from the autoethnographic tradition in Asian American literature. We have witnessed the blossoming of Asian American literary writing in every genre, style, and theme, displacing the autobiography as the central mode of Asian American literary discourse. In companion to the works cited above, consider this small sampling of the diversity of post-1965 Asian American literature: Jeanne and James Houston's *Farewell to Manzanar* (1973), Alan Chong Lau's *Songs for Jadina* (1980), Maxine Hong Kingston's *China Men* (1980), Theresa Hak Kyung Cha's *DICTEE* (1982), Wendy Law-Yone's *The Coffin Tree* (1983), Marilyn Chin's *Dwarf Bamboo* (1987), Frank Chin's *The Chinaman Pacific and the Frisco R.R. Co.* (1988), David Henry Hwang's *M. Butterfly* (1988), John Yau's *Radiant Silhouettes* (1989), Eric Chock's *Last Days Here* (1990), Jessica Hagedorn's *Dogeaters* (1990), Peter Bacho's *Cebu* (1991), Karen Tei-Yamashita's *Brazil-Maru* (1992), Fae Myenne Ng's *Bone* (1993), Chitra Divakaruni's *Arranged Marriage* (1995), Chang-rae Lee's *Native Speaker* (1995), R. Zamora Linmark's *Rolling the R's* (1995), Meena Alexander's *Manhattan Music* (1997), Li-Young Lee's *Winged Seed* (1999), and David Wong Louie's *The Barbarians Are Coming* (2000).

In the context of this much-expanded field of literary endeavor, we may note a number of shifts in Asian American literature. First, the demographic and social changes within Asian communities in the United States—changes such as the shift from mainly American-born to mainly foreign-born communities that have taken place partly as a result of these very immigration laws—demand that we question the meaning and relevance of the *pan-Asian* category itself. In addition, the past several decades have witnessed an unprecedented globalization in migration, technologies of communication, cultures, and capital; in post-1965 Asian American literature, we see more engagement with the realities of this multiracial, globalized, and many-voiced America. One of the most interesting features of contemporary Asian American literature is the tension between the literary depictions of recent Asian immigrants and the more assimilated sensibilities that often characterize the narrative voice through which Asian immigrants' lives are inscribed into American culture. This disjuncture is at times subtle and at others quite explicit, distinguishing the sensibilities of the text from the lives and subjectivities of the recent immigrants depicted in the text. The tension is linked to but not reducible to the relatively higher degree of assimilation of the

Asian American or Asian immigrant author to dominant American perspectives. Although certainly we find traces of these questions in Asian American literature prior to 1965, they were not fundamental, whereas in the current period these issues have come to the fore.

I

Prior to World War II, a major shift took place within the Asian population in the United States. For the first time in the history of Asians in America, the majority of the Asian American population was U.S. born. These generations, born in the United States prior to 1965 when the immigration laws reversed this trend, came of age in the socially turbulent years of the 1960s and 70s, were influenced by the civil rights, Black Power, and women's movements, and became a visible part of the anti-Vietnam War, Asian, and other third world liberation movements. Perceived and dismissed as perpetual foreigners and outsiders to American culture and society, this group had, by the mid 1970s, begun widely using the term "Asian American" to describe themselves, emphasizing that they were Americans, first and foremost.

It was at this time that literature written by people of Asian descent in the United States became known as "Asian American literature," rapidly ushering in the increasing significance of Asian American pan-ethnicity. Writers of Asian descent who published prior to the 1970s were now all placed under the Asian American banner, which reached back to draw in such figures from earlier decades of the twentieth century as Sui Sin Far, Younghill Kang, the poets of Angel Island, Carlos Bulosan, Hisaye Yamamoto, Toshio Mori, Louis Chu, among others, none of whom were described as "Asian American" prior to the 1970s. This group, newly constituted and canonized as Asian American, could now retroactively join forces with Asian American writers just coming of age in the 1970s and 1980s: Maxine Hong Kingston, Frank Chin, Jeffery Paul Chan, Janice Mirikitani, Jessica Hagedorn, Lawson Fusao Inada,

Merle Woo, Russell Leong, Vince Gotera, Cathy Song, Kimiko Hahn, Shawn Wong, Garrett Hongo, Alan Chong Lau, Wing Tek Lum, Nellie Wong, Amy Uyematsu, Faye Chiang, Genny Lim, Al Robles, and Kitty Tsui, to just scratch the surface.

Most vociferous in leading this charge were Jeffrey Paul Chan, Frank Chin, Lawson Fusao Inada, and Shawn Wong, the editors of *Aiiieeeee!: An Anthology of Asian-American Writers* (1974), four of the most provocative and macho writers ever to emerge out of Asian America. Their important collection joined a generation of such other landmark and similarly "Asian-and-proud" anthologies as the student-published *Roots* and *Asian Women*, as well as *Yellow Pearl*. It was followed by *Breaking Silence* and *Making Waves*, both key collections of Asian American women's writings. Though quite different in their emphases, all these anthologies grounded themselves in an Asian American paradigm that gained its currency in the wake of the social and political kinesis of the 1960s and 70s. A shared Asian American social and political identity provided the rationale for such texts even when they embodied challenges to this identity from feminist and other perspectives within the Asian American community, indeed even through these challenges. Asian American feminist contestations, for instance, of the gender biases and sexist assumptions of Asian American cultural nationalism, while construed by some as undermining pan-Asian unity, can, on the other hand, be appreciated as an attempt to forge an ultimately more inclusive and representative Asian American identity.

However, since 1965, the viability of the term "Asian American" has been called into question. Among reasons for this shift: Asian immigrants who have recently come to the United States share little with those from other Asian ethnic groups or nations. They speak different languages, practice different religions, ground themselves in different cultural traditions, and sometimes hold historical enmities rooted in their histories in Asia. And so critics such as Lisa Lowe, while still embracing the pan-ethnic paradigm, strongly emphasize the heterogeneity within Asian America.

Furthermore, dominant discourses, partly as a response to challenges from colonized nations for independence and from social, political, and economic groups marginalized within the nation for inclusion, equity, or radical change, shifted to the work of undermining the basis for the formation of such blocs, a development that achieved its apex in the decades immediately following 1965. For example, we can observe that while during this time such developments in literary and cultural theory as post-modernity, post-structuralism, the critique of essentialism, and critical analyses of the construction of nationalisms undoubtedly brought crucial insights to our understanding of literature and society, they have also functioned to destabilize through their radical skepticism the very foundations for any easy assumption of "the Asian American voice," signaling the declining significance of Asian American pan-ethnicity as a social and political identity. If the three major anthologies of the 1990s (*The Open Boat, Charlie Chan Is Dead,* and *Premonitions*) are premonitory, they indicate a radical shift toward the brandishing of *differences* amongst Asian American writings—and, by extension, the differences amongst the Asian American ethnic groups—by all but vilifying the commonalities that were once considered so pithy and true. The most important connection was, of course, the idea of a shared legacy of oppression common to Americans of Asian descent and a will to overcome this legacy through pan-Asian unity.

Finally, some within Asian communities have turned away from the Asian American category because, as important and progressive as it may have been in the 1970s, the term "Asian American" in its usage and functions today is more problematic. Rather than demonstrate the Americanness of the Asian population, the term disguises the continued economic, legal, and cultural marginalization of Asian communities in the United States, communities that are now again majority immigrant, non-native

English-speaking, and who, unlike their predecessors, are able to maintain ties to their culture and countries of origin to an unprecedented degree through the technologies of the telephone, internet, and mass media, as well as the relatively greater ease of long-distance travel. The term also often serves to mask inequities and disparities under the pan-ethnic umbrella, favoring primarily east Asian communities over south, southeast, and west Asian communities, and those with greater economic means over those Asian communities living in poverty. The status of Pacific islanders and their literature, sometimes understood to fall within the Asian American rubric, is generally further marginalized within the Asian American category.

In short, the formation of Asian American pan-ethnic unity in the years immediately following 1965 was in fact an outcome of social, historical, and political developments in America preceding this time, whereas changes set in motion in and around 1965 gave rise in subsequent decades to conditions that would destabilize the foundation of this unity. As we will see in the following sections, these shifts can be read in the literature that treats the experiences of recent Asian immigrants to America.

II

Post-1965, we witness a gradual departure from the expectation that a writer of color in America must write about his or her own specific community and that the primary theme will be the process of assimilating into a white American society. Again, this is not to state that all Asian American writers prior to 1965 treated this theme, but rather that those texts that did consistently emerged as the most read and best known. An illustration of this shift: Vijay Seshadri's "Made in the Tropics." In the poem by this poet of south Asian descent, a Jamaican community in the Bronx, New York City, gathers for a concert. Such a representational backdrop boldly refuses the autoethnographic frame within which

Asian American literature is often uncritically expected to emerge. The representation of this gathering furthermore emphasizes the connection between the concertgoers and their native country. The reggae that connects the Jamaican coastal town of Savanna-La-Mar to the Gun Hill Road neighborhood of the Bronx is amplified through the highly ambivalent metaphor of a chain linking Jamaican people at the concert in the Bronx to each other *and also* to Jamaica.

Contrast this "chain" to the way in which, over seventy years earlier in the same city, Jamaican-born poet Claude McKay evokes his homeland. In "The Tropics in New York" (1922), nostalgic memories of home triggered by the sight of tropical fruit in a New York City shop window evoke for the poetic voice a painful and isolated sense of yearning, dislocation, and distance, in the absence of any trace of a Jamaican community. In Seshadri's poem, whatever value we accord to the chain, the metaphor operates to further solidify a direct connection to the Jamaican nation already made explicit by the occasion: an exuberant celebration of Jamaican independence. The attendees are a few of the numbers of Jamaicans in contemporary, post-1965 New York, whose migration, the poem suggests, tilts the earth toward the sun, literally reducing the distance from the tropics by bringing tropical weather closer to New York. Seshadri's poem appears in a post-1965 context in which there are much higher levels of migration. Once here, furthermore, immigrants' ties to their home countries are strengthened by technological advances in communication and the greater ease and relatively lower cost of international travel. The physical presence in the United States of increasing numbers of immigrants in both relative and absolute terms, immigrants who have greater access to their home countries and cultures, reinforces cultural and national identity through the establishment of types of communities that were unimaginable just a few decades before.

The poem includes a small but significant detail: the linkage of the concertgoers in the Bronx to the Jamaican nation is enabled by the vehicles that transport the featured performers to the concert site, motorcycles identified as Japan-made, that is, "steeled [...] art" embraced by the reggae stars. This detail, the only reference to anything Asian in the poem, calls to mind the Asian American poet's own role in bringing about this literary scene in which Asians are made conspicuous by their absence. However, the Japanese motorcycles also remind us that even such cyclical evocations of nationhood as Jamaica's annual Independence Day take place within multinational and multiracial cultural contexts. A south Asian American poet's description of a Jamaican concert edged with reference to Japanese bikes is not simply a testament to multicultural America but a rendering of specific and differentiated cultural, national, and economic relationships. Asian American literature bears the traces of global capitalism, technology, migration from south to north, new possibilities for national identity in immigrant communities, the reshaping of American culture, and the unifying power of music.

III

Post-1965, we see a widening schism between the "Asian American" narrative or poetic voice and the immigrant experiences represented in the literature. Asian American writers often pen literary characters who, though sharing the ethnic or racial identities of the writers, reside none-theless in worlds that are culturally, epistemologically, linguistically, and often also economically distant and separate. The Asian American literary texts that most often find their way to publication and widespread ac-claim are, not surprisingly, those that adopt perspectives with which the mainstream of American readers can readily identify, perspectives that are often at some distance in terms of knowledge and understanding from that of the recently arrived post-1965 immigrants who populate many of the texts. This phenomenon may be tied to the material histories of individual writers, many of whom are not themselves immigrants, or have immigrated at an age young enough to attain relative comfort in

American culture and command proficiency—even perhaps virtuosity—in the English language, or hail from relatively elite backgrounds in their home countries where they already entered into western or American modes of thought; in any case, the writer often occupies a tenuous position with regard to recent low-income Asian immigrants who lack the command of English that the writers possess. Regardless of the reasons for it, we can observe that much Asian American literature produced since 1965 ironically runs the risk of "orientalizing" Asian immigrant lives.

In addition, Maxine Hong Kingston, Amy Tan, Chang-rae Lee, Chitra Divakaruni, Nora Okja Keller, M. Evelina Galang, David Henry Hwang, Gish Jen, David Mura, Garrett Hongo, Li-Young Lee, Kimiko Hahn, and many others often construct literary characters, both male and female, who enter into what Trinh T. Minh-ha, in *Woman Native Other* (1989), calls a "sense of specialness":

It is not unusual to encounter cases where the sense of specialness, which comes here with being the "first" or the "only" woman, is confused with the consciousness of difference. One cannot help feeling "special" when one figures among the rare few to emerge above the anonymous crowd and enjoys the privilege of preparing the way for one's more "unfortunate" sisters. Based on what other women are not (capable of) doing, such a reward easily creates a distance—if not a division—between I-who-have-made-it and You-who-cannot-make-it. Thus despite my rhetoric of solidarity, I inwardly resist your entrance into the field, for it means competition, rivalry, and sooner or later, the end of my specialness. I shall, therefore, play a double game: on the one hand, I shall loudly assert my right, as a woman, and an exemplary one, to have access to equal opportunity; on the other hand, I shall quietly maintain my privilege by helping the master perpetuate his cycle of oppression.

A case in point: Bharati Mukherjee's *Jasmine* (1991):

Jasmine, a young woman originally from a poverty-stricken rural village in India, arrives in Flushing, Queens, after phantoming her way across three continents, passing through "wars, through plagues." She travels the "zigzag route," with forged travel documents and "aerogram promising a job or space to sleep." Mukherjee situates Jasmine amongst the "outcasts and deportees, strange pilgrims visiting outlandish shrines." They are Filipinas, Muslims, Sri Lankan Tamils, Bahrainis, Ugandans, Surinamese Indians, Arabs, and Africans. Jasmine, we are to believe, *is one of them.*

In Flushing, she finds that the English she previously learned is deserting her. She is, after all, living amongst *them,* in a "cocoon" she needs to "hatch out of." Because Flushing is populated by hordes of others like her, south Asian immigrants recently arrived, Jasmine is overwhelmed—if not disgusted: the Pakistani shops, Indian restaurants, Urdu and Hindi films, Punjabi newspapers, Sikh families, saris, salwar-kameez outfits, and other South Asian clothing—all remind her of her Indianness. She disdainfully describes the apartment in which she finds herself living as a place of "artificially maintained Indianness," and expresses pity toward those *other* Indians, especially women, her doppelgangers, her competitors, who are incapable of transcending their mundane, peasant desires to merely recreate an Indian ghetto in a land so vast, wondrous, and full of promise as America. "Flushing, with all its immigrant services at hand, frightened me," says Jasmine, herself an Indian immigrant.

On more than one occasion, Jasmine is described in the novel as "special": prettier than the "others," the other Indian girls and women, that is—smarter, more adventurous, much braver. This perhaps explains why she is afraid of Flushing, a place that could just as easily be depicted by Mukherjee as dynamic, heterogeneous, and multitudinous. This sort of fear of immigrants, of course, is not unique to Mukherjee's *Jasmine.* American literature, past and present, bursts at the seams with it. What is perhaps surprising is the manifestation of it in post-1965 Asian American literature. We see various representations of Asian Americans fearing Asian immigrants by Maxine Hong Kingston in her memoir *The Woman Warrior*, by Amy Tan (through the four Chinese American daughters) in *The Joy Luck Club*, and by Chang-rae Lee (through Henry Park) in *Native Speaker*. These writers create central characters who are "special" in the way that Jasmine is special, characters who, while appearing to be *amongst* the post-1965 immigrant Asian American population demographically, anthropologically, or sociologically, are distinguished within the texts as possessing a sophistication or a sensibility that sets them apart and renders them much more "American."

So where does Jasmine eventually find the version of America she was desperately seeking? "I became an American in an apartment on Claremont Avenue across the street from a Barnard College dormitory," she says. She becomes an American, or so the novel posits, when she falls in love with a handsome, dashing, college professor—her white employer. He and his wife have hired her as a live-in nanny—an undocumented domestic worker—for his daughter, whom Jasmine affectionately calls "my child." It is noteworthy that not once in Flushing does she come across an Indian American child she can call her own.

In representing the immigrant experience for an American readership, while desperately dodging the status of the representative for it, the "Asian American" writer reveals much more ambivalence than meets the eye. The writer is sometimes able to point out the way to transcend typically orientalist thinking. Yet ultimately, taken not as a series of individual works but as a body, we find again and again in Asian American literature the distancing of immigrant identities, the repeated evocation but inevitable marginalization of the "non-special" Asian immigrant voice.

Maxine Hong Kingston's poem "Absorption of Rock" illustrates this situation. The "we" repeatedly invoked establishes itself as a sensibility firmly grounded in American culture and social norms. To this collective subjectivity, Laotian embroidery is a "mystery," evoking typically orientalist vocabulary about Asians; however, the phrase that makes the Asian look foreign is undone in the very next one by the comparison of this mystery to that of face cards, objects seen in everyday American life. Yet in the end, the Laotian refugees, the blond-bearded Vietnam vet, and the Vietnamese and H'mong who are afraid of the Lao, all in different ways surviving the impact of the war, are *all* distanced from the poetic voice. The trauma of the war in an Asian homeland, the belief in a Laotian man's ability to cause rocks to appear in one's stomach, the experience of migration as refugees—these are produced by the Asian American literary sensibility as distant, unknowable, inaccessible realities.

*   *   *

At the beginning of the twenty-first century, we stand before an open door. Still within the post-1965 period, we can already attest to changes that will once again renew questions about Asian American literature. While new immigrants from Asia and other parts of the world continue to join us, the children of post-1965 immigrants are also coming of age. We can expect to see Asian American literary texts with a renewed grounding in American culture, but one that is quite different from the America of the 1960s and 70s. It is an America where even as we witness the destruction of local cultures by global capital we can find a moment to ask what it means when a Chinese American student in Durham, North Carolina, who speaks only English, has her sartorial, musical, and aesthetic sensibilities shaped by hip-hop videos produced in Seoul by bilingual Korean youth who lived in Los Angeles and moved back; an America where the son of a restaurant worker from Dhaka living in New York City's Lower East Side has mostly Latino friends, goes to the mosque each week with his father, and while everyone else sleeps tonight will be writing Bangla poetry into Asian American literature; an America where Asian American literature will continue to transform itself as it transforms its readers.

Amor de lejos:
Latino (Im)migration
Literatures

by B. V. Olguín

When the protagonist in Daniel Venegas's 1928 neopicaresque novella *The Adventures of Don Chipote, or When Parrots Breast-Feed,* decides to emigrate from Mexico to the United States to "bring back all the gold that there is over there," the results are humorously disastrous. Having fled the economic and political turmoil that followed the 1910 Mexican Revolution, Don Chipote (modeled on Miguel de Cervantes's witless innocent, Don Quixote), experiences a series of beatings, incarcerations, and other misadventures. In the end, he can only find work as a dishwasher and laborer in El Paso and Los Angeles. Don Chipote remains hopeful, however, that his nascent bilingual skills will enable upward class mobility despite the fact that his vocabulary consists of no more than several horribly butchered English words and phrases such as *dones* ("donuts"), *jamaneg* ("ham and eggs"), *toquinglis* ("talk English"), and *guasumara* ("what's the matter"). Ironically, Don Chipote's linguistic claim to inclusion as an American simultaneously demarcates the limits to his immigrant desire to assimilate and accumulate wealth: he is no closer to becoming a full-fledged American citizen than the Chicanos he ridicules for losing their Mexican cultural heritage and alternately emulates for their ability to acculturate. Indeed, the subjunctive subtitle of Venegas's original Spanish-language text (*Cuando los péricos mamen*) suggests that Mexicans will become full-fledged Americans only when parakeets, which have no lips, can suckle; that is, never.

Yet while *The Adventures of Don Chipote* explores the ambiguous political and cultural status of the Mexican immigrant in the United States, it is also the first ever literary work to mention the term "Chicano," thereby recognizing that even as the Mexican-cum-Mexican American is always seen as different from other residents of the United States, he or she is by now unique and established enough to have a separate name. Significantly, Venegas's tale is located in the American southwest and not only involves Mexican immigrants but Mexican Americans who never immigrated to the United States. Rather, they became citizens after the end of the U.S.-Mexican War in 1848, when the United States annexed over one-half of Mexican national territory and subsequently absorbed and "naturalized" the remaining residents. Many of these new *Mexican* American citizens were dispossessed and transformed into landless migrants. *The Adventures of Don Chipote,* like the various types of immigration stories and poems produced by other Latin American and U.S.-based Latina/o authors in recent decades, thus calls attention to the complex ways in which the historical experiences of international immigration, transnational migration, colonization, and exile can intersect with one another. More important, Venegas's text illustrates how these intersecting experiences relate to the evolution of contemporary U.S. Latina/o identities.

Any exploration of contemporary U.S. Latina/o identities in modern narratives of (im)migration—the parenthesis draws attention to the vexed problem of labeling experiences referred to above—must first account for the different and overlapping histories of the various U.S. Latina/o subgroups: Mexican American (or Chicana/o), Puerto Rican (and Nuyorican), Cuban American, Dominican American, and Colombian American, as well as other South and Central American populations in the United States. While many Mexicans like Don Chipote immigrate to the United States (sometimes permanently), others like the Chicanos he encounters became American residents and citizens through imperialist wars of conquest and colonization. Puerto Ricans, who have had a large presence in the United States since the eighteenth century, also were colonized by the United States after the Spanish American War ended in 1898, when the United States invaded and occupied the island of Puerto Rico along with Cuba, the Philippines, and several other former Spanish colonies. Puerto Ricans became U.S. citizens in 1917 with the passage of the infamous Jones Act that enabled them to be drafted for military service yet still denied them the right to vote in federal elections. Puerto Rican history and national identity appears even more complicated today given that many (though not all) Puerto Ricans frequently cross-migrate between the U.S. eastern seaboard, where they are concentrated, and the island nation. In fact, more than half of Puerto Ricans live on the U.S. mainland! Transmigration also is common among Dominican Americans. The fastest growing U.S.-based Latina/o group, Dominican Americans have radically transformed the character of established areas in the United States such as the Washington Heights neighborhood in Manhattan, which is now populated almost entirely by Dominican Americans. Washington Heights is such an established part of the Dominican American diaspora that many prominent citizens of the Dominican Republic are born there.

Cuban Americans, on the other hand, have a unique unidirectional immigration history that arises from the impasse between the United States and Cuba following the Cuban Revolution in 1959. There are several major waves of Cuban immigration to the United States: the first occurred from 1959–62, when the largely creole elite and middle-class professionals fled the nation after the new revolutionary administration nationalized industry and private property; the second was in 1973, which also involved educated, primarily white, immigrants from a variety of occupational backgrounds; and the third was the Mariel boat-lift in the

1980s, which involved a variety of Cuban citizens from all generations, and included a large number of mestizos, mulattos, and blacks of very limited economic means. Cuban immigration to the United States also includes a steady stream of illegal Cuban immigrants who brave the dangerous Florida Straits on makeshift rafts or clandestine ferries. Salvadoran and other Central American immigration patterns to the United States similarly are influenced by political conflicts and warfare, especially the Marxist and nationalist insurgencies in the 1960s, 70s, and 80s. U.S. attempts to undermine these social movements through covert and overt interventions subsequently generated lethal waves of death squad activities, which increased emigration out of the country. The increasing economic and political instabilities in South American countries such as Colombia also have led to tremendous growths in immigration to the United States. Due in large part to the increasing militarization of the crisis in Colombia, Colombian Americans have become a rapidly growing presence in various regions throughout the United States, but especially in southern cities such as Miami, renowned as the informal capital-in-exile of Latin America.

While there are many reasons for Latin American immigration to the United States, warfare continues to be a major catalyst. Paradoxically, U.S. military intervention into Latin America has brought Latin Americans and U.S. Latina/os of various backgrounds into contact in increasingly complicated ways: some are American GIs participating in U.S. military campaigns; others are internationalist insurgents fighting against the U.S. military and its allies; and yet others are antiwar activists and artists. Like the multinational and multiracial subjects of the former British empire, whose descendants eventually returned to the seat of colonial power in London and other major British cities, these new U.S. Latina/os are both the product of and a threat to U.S. imperialism—that is, their hybrid cultures, which are becoming more and more mainstream, potentially disrupt xenophobic notions of American national identity. Indeed, in the last three decades immigration from and cross-migration between former third world colonies and first world empires have led to an explosion of provocative literary expressions of a radical new paradigm of identity: the hybrid transnational citizen.

Like recent south Asian authors of the British Commonwealth, Latina/o authors based in the United States are renowned for exploring the complex aspects of modern national identity through aesthetically innovative forms. Significantly, these U.S.-based Latina/o writers have achieved growing success apart from the literary histories of their ancestral lands in Latin America. While many early Latina/o narratives were written in Spanish, today there are many English-language collections of U.S. Latina/o literatures, which in part indicates the mainstreaming of Latina/o culture in the United States. Even the venerable Norton, Prentice-Hall, and Oxford University presses have published or have forthcoming major anthologies of U.S. Latina/o literatures. Indeed, there has been a veritable explosion of Latina/o literature anthologies, from general collections to more focused texts on specific U.S. Latina/o subgroups such as *Growing Up Chicana/o, Aztlán and Viet Nam: Chicano and Chicana Experiences of the War, Puerto Ricans Writers at Home in the U.S.A., Nuyorican Literature,* and *Growing Up Puerto Rican.* There are also anthologies dedicated to special themes relevant to all of these groups such as *Growing Up Latino: Memoirs and Stories, ¡Floricanto Si!: A Collection of Latina Poetry, Compañeras: Latina Lesbians, Hispanic American Literature, Barrios and Borderlands: Cultures of Latinos and Latinas in the United States,* and *Aloud!: Voices from the Nuyorican Poet's Cafe.* Aside from being frequently taught in universities throughout the world, many U.S.-based Latina/o authors such as Puerto Rican Nicholasa Mohr, Dominican American Julia Alvarez, and Cuban American Cristina Garcia have made their way into secondary curricula. Some, like Chicana Sandra Cisneros, are even used for standardized tests. This canonization also includes U.S. Latina/o authors such as newcomer Junot Díaz and veteran author and television commentator Richard Rodriguez, whose works are frequently published in national magazines such as *The New Yorker* and *Harpers.*

The growing institutional success of U.S. Latina/o authors from all these different subgroups, however, has been accompanied by a problematic standardization of the aesthetic and historical nuances of the literature of each subgroup. (Related to this is the use of the term "Hispanic" to create, at least rhetorically, the image of a unified power bloc in electoral politics, which purportedly enables the individual groups to have more electoral clout.) Even more troubling is the effacement of the differences between U.S. Latina/os and Latin Americans. For instance, the planned *Norton Anthology of Latino Literature,* which is edited by Mexican national Ilan Stavans, conflates Latin American and U.S. Latina/o authors under the overarching and profoundly ambiguous rubric of "Latino" even though Norton Press would never publish an anthology that conflated American and British literatures as one literary tradition. However, this is not to say that the term is not useful. The term "Latino," as used in this anthology, refers less to a population and more to a social phenomenon by which U.S.-born or raised people of Latin American descent distinguish themselves from their Latin American ancestors. In fact, an anthology devoted in part to the literatures of Latina/o immigration is not only unique, but timely and significant because it illuminates the complex negotiations of power and national identity within the ambiguous transitional space where Latin Americans become U.S. Latinas and Latinos. Latina/o (im)migration literatures, that is, permit us to map out the similarities and differences of various Latin American-cum-U.S. Latina/o populations by calling our attention to how the different histories of each population interact with U.S. history and culture to enable the creation of new identities in the United States.

The Theme of Displacement

(Im)migration is a common theme in writings by Latin Americans like Daniel Venegas as well as actual immigrants such as nineteenth-century writers like Mexican Josephina Niggli and Puerto Rican Jesús Colón. This theme has also remained a constant feature in the literature by U.S.-born and raised authors from various Latina/o family histories. Despite the divergent backgrounds of many of these authors, and the equally diverse treatments of the topic of Latina/o (im)migration, their texts all symbolically exploit the experience of movement. As in the Medieval picaresque genre that serves as a model for Venegas's short novel, movement in contemporary Latina/o immigration literatures is both real and metaphorical. The diverse protagonists in these works engage in lateral movement across geographic space—from nation to nation as well as travel within a nation. They also experience vertical movement, such as a transformation of their class status, moral standing, or political ideology. However, unlike the ideologically conservative Medieval picaresque tales, which originally were written by Catholic priests as moral allegories designed to warn against deviation from church doctrine, modern picaresque-influenced Latina/o immigration narratives and poems from the 1960s to the present express a wide range of ideologies about the relationship between the individual and society at large.

Beyond simple celebrations of new cultures and identities, Latina/o (im)migration narratives and poems often illustrate the traumatic aspects of displacement by focusing in part on how immigration, migration, exile, and colonization place people in a state of national limbo. Indeed, displacement is the precondition for the (im)migration saga and, along with the related theme of relocation, helps frame the fundamental features of the new U.S. Latina/o. Even before Venegas, nineteenth-century Latina/o authors such as Cuban exile José Martí and Mexican national Amparo Ruiz de Burton, for instance, explored the traumas of exile and colonization in their verse and prose. Martí, who spent many years in exile in the United States before he died in combat fighting against the Spanish colonial power in Cuba, wrote polemical essays against Spanish colonialism and U.S. imperialism in his 1892 treatise *Our America*. He also wrote poignantly of his experiences as an exile in the United States in his 1881 essay "Two Views of Coney Island." In her 1885 semi-autobiographical romance novel, *The Squatter and the Don,* Ruiz de Burton similarly explores the traumatic realities of her life as a Mexican woman who marries a U.S. Army officer who participated in the U.S.-Mexican War that ultimately resulted in Ruiz de Burton's loss of her vast land holdings. As Américo Paredes would later express in his collection of poetry *Between Two Worlds,* published in 1991 but consisting of poems mostly written fifty years earlier, Ruiz de Burton's autobiographical character finds herself caught between two worlds: her old Mexican past in which she enjoyed a life of affluence, and the new Mexican American present in which she has been dispossessed and transformed into a colonial subject. As such, these authors anticipate the (im)migration, colonization, and exile sagas of contemporary Latin American and U.S. Latina/o narratives and poems by writers such as Luis Alberto Urrea, Sandra Cisneros, and Judith Ortiz Cofer.

While Martí, Ruiz de Burton, and Paredes express the angst associated with life in a new land (or an old land under a new colonial government), Urrea explores the theme of displacement through graphic descriptions of the horribly grotesque living conditions that befall Latin American migrants who were not able to cross over to the other side. Urrea begins the journalistic vignettes that comprise his 1993 *Across the Wire: Life and Hard Times on the Mexican Border,* with a shocking reexamination of the myth of the American El Dorado. Through vivid descriptions of people living in infernolike dumps where they both defecate and find their meals, Urrea grounds the Latina/o immigration experience in the traumatic material realities of these makeshift way stations that, inevitably, have become established squatter communities. Too many people who left their lands with illusions of "bringing back all the gold that there is over there" are caught in a desperate subhuman existence and nationless space: they are on the margins of their own nations and not yet part of the new intended destination of high-rise buildings, factories, and middle-class homes that beckon—and sometimes mock—from across the wire fence that separates Mexico from the United States. A similarly bleak portrait of immigration, migration, and exile is presented in Helena Viramontes's short story "Cariboo Cafe" and Ramón "Tianguís" Pérez's memoir, *Diary of an Undocumented Immigrant.*

On the other hand, Sandra Cisneros examines the tragic consequences for the immigrants who actually succeed in making it to the other side of national demarcation zones. In her story "Geraldo No Last Name," she writes about a Latin American immigrant male who befriends Marin, a young Mexican American woman at a dance. When Geraldo unexpectedly is killed in a hit-and-run accident later that night, Marin, who was his occasional dance partner earlier that evening, does not know what to say to the hospital workers and police except that his name was Geraldo. This is all she knows about him. Traumatized, Marin tries to convince herself that the tragedy has not affected her. The narrator notes:

What difference does it make? He wasn't anything to her. He wasn't her boyfriend or anything like that.

Illustrating the wide cultural gap between Latin American immigrants and U.S.-born or raised Latina/os, the narrator adds in Marin's voice:

Just another *brazer* who didn't speak English. Just another wetback. You know the kind. The ones who always look ashamed.

Thus, the narrator in Cisneros's story juxtaposes Geraldo's untimely and tragic death to the dejected countenance of the immigrant males who still live. Instead of gathering gold, they are forced to live in squalid cramped conditions, endure back-breaking menial labor, and suffer various types of exploitation at the hands of unscrupulous employers and even governments through worker-exchange programs such as the infamous Bracero Program. ("Brazer" is a denigrating term for "braceros," which literally means "men with arms.") Like most Latina/o immigration tales, Cisneros's story does not offer a happy ending, but rather refers to Geraldo's family members across the border who slowly but steadily forget about the young man who went north to find his fortune. Thus, this story of hope and ignoble, anonymous death alludes to the countless immigrants who drown in the Rio Grande, are killed by border bandits and border patrol vigilantes, or perish in the unforgiving sun of the Arizona desert on their quest for a new beginning. Cisneros's depiction of the tragic reality awaiting so many who make it across the wire shows it to be a cruel complement to Urrea's exploration of the Latin American immigrant's "middle passage."

In *The Latin Deli,* Judith Ortiz Cofer's 1995 collection of stories and poetry, the Manhattan-based Puerto Rican author in another vein explores the sense of personal and cultural loss that some Latin American immigrants experience through their displacement. The title poem is exemplary. Set in a small rural town in the southern state of Georgia, which continues to attract many Latin American immigrants and U.S. Latina/o migrants because of its growing economy, the poem begins by recounting how a series of characters from different Latin American backgrounds all attempt to satiate their profound sense of loss and longing. They do so through the food they purchase at a local mom-and-pop deli:

... they walk down the narrow aisle of her store
reading the labels of packages aloud, as if
they were the names of lost lovers: *Suspiros,*
Merengues, the stale candy of everyone's childhood.

The seemingly insignificant foodstuffs gain a metaphorical significance that enables the immigrant and exile shoppers to unite symbolically with their lost lands. But as the poem continues, these hopes are revealed to be illusions: despite their well-intentioned plans for a "glorious return" home with the money they hope to make in "El Norte," the fact is that the countries they left many years ago have drastically changed, so much so that they may even have become as foreign as their new "home." In the end, whether they realize it or not, or whether they can accept it or not, these Latin Americans have become members of a new community of exiles and immigrants in the United States. Or, as Cofer notes in her poem "Exile," they are "neither here nor there." Indeed, this sense of being "in-between and nowhere at once" is a theme that occupies a prominent place in the literature of other Puerto Rican writers such as Abraham Rodriguez, Ed Vega, and Julio Marzán.

Latina/o Relocations

Latin American and U.S. Latina/o literatures intersect at the place where immigrants simultaneously lament the loss associated with their flight from the ancestral land and acknowledge the new realities and possibilities that confront them. Dominican American Julia Alvarez, the author of the bestselling autobiographical novel *How the Garcia Girls Lost Their Accents,* explores some of the difficulties and potential opportunities that modern immigration presents for Latin Americans and U.S. Latina/os. Her novel is written as a series of vignettes that trace the lives of the four Garcia sisters as they grow from young girls in the Dominican Republic to mature women in the United States. Significantly, the lives of these sisters, who were members of an influential Dominican family in Santo Domingo before the dictatorship of General Rafael Trujillo, is transformed after the family is forced to flee the island due to political turmoil that included an invasion by the U.S. Marines. For the Garcia sisters, the United States becomes a liberating space where they are able to break free of the patriarchal constraints that ruled their lives on the island. However, despite this newfound freedom, the family's immigration has resulted in their father's loss of prestige and economic power. They are forced to live in a humble tenement building in New York City. Moreover, the girls experience other difficulties such as eating disorders as well as economic and cultural prejudice as they pursue the American Dream that, sadly, privileges outward beauty, cultural homogeneity, and material wealth. Alvarez also indirectly introduces the theme of in-group racism in a scene where one of the sisters relishes her whiteness. Even at an early age, this Garcia sister knows that if she succeeds in losing her accent, her white skin will enable her to assimilate. The unspoken fact is that others with darker skin cannot.

Like Alvarez, other Latina/o authors examine the issues of racism, cultural alienation, and identity formation through the theme of the quest, which is common in (im)migration and exile narratives. The tense balance between the old and the new is perhaps best expressed in Junot Díaz's story "Fiesta, 1980," which takes place in the primarily Latina/o area of the Bronx borough of New York City. This story is told from the point of view of a young Dominican American boy, Yunior, who observes the various rituals of the adults and adolescents at a family party in a relative's home. The mood is festive and some characters even cross sexual and cultural taboos, an important component of Latina/o and immigrant coming-of-age stories. On the surface, the party seems to suggest a success story where immigrants toast to their fortune. However, during the ride home to New Jersey from the party, the young narrator of the story gets carsick and ruins the family's new Volkswagen van. While the resultant stench is not nearly as unbearable as Urrea's city dump, the awful smell nonetheless spoils the family's symbol of their newfound wealth. In this way Díaz subtly suggests that the immigrant quest is not always completely satisfying for all the immigrants and their descendants, a topic whose complexity is further explored in Benjamin Sáenz's work "Exile," as well as Teresa Palomo Acosta's poem "Crossing a 'piece of earth,'" both of which are included in this anthology.

Other authors such as Cuban American Gustavo Pérez-Firmat, Chicana Gloria Anzaldúa, and Puerto Rican Aurora Levins Morales focus on the hybrid cultures of these newly relocated Latin American immigrants and exiles as well as their U.S. Latina/o offspring. In his 1994 multigenre memoir *Life on the Hyphen: The Cuban-American Way,* Gustavo Pérez-Firmat departs from the conventional Cuban American theme of political exile that historian Maria Cristina Garcia claims has become more a myth than a reality, and instead focuses on the difficulties and possibilities of a bilingual and bicultural identity.

Chicana author Gloria Anzaldúa, for instance, similarly explores the growing ambiguities about Latina/o identity in particular and American national identity in general through her metaphor of the borderlands. In her 1987 mixed-genre memoir *Borderlands/La Frontera: The New Mestiza,* Anzaldúa grounds her discussion of Mexican American history in the brutal realities of warfare, political repression, and dispossession that accompanied the U.S. annexation of Mexican national territory. But she also transforms the troubling and violent U.S./Mexico border into a metaphor for identity in the United States and even the world at large. Anzaldúa relishes her complicated hybrid identity in the Southwest and the United States as a whole by proclaiming:

> To live in the Borderlands means to
> put chile in the borscht,
> eat whole wheat tortillas,
> speak Tex-Mex with a Brooklyn accent.

This notion of a borderlands identity has become increasingly prominent in scholarly and popular discussions of identity, especially as the U.S. demographic profile is steadily transformed into a minority-majority population. Indeed, whites already are a minority in states such as California. Latina/o (im)migration tales, Anzaldúa reveals, have enabled us to rethink the mainstream.

Aurora Levins Morales, a Latina who shares a Puerto Rican and a Jewish heritage, further elaborates this notion of a borderlands identity by introducing the idea of transmigration. That is, her recovery of American immigration history along with her constant transit from one national and cultural context to another enables Levins Morales to continually augment her cultural repertoire without completely sacrificing her individual identity as a Latina. In her poem, "Child of the Americas," she expresses this new transnational Latina identity:

I am not African. Africa is in me, but I cannot return.
I am not Taína. Taína is in me, but there is no way back.
I am not European. Europe lives in me, but I have no home there . . .

I am a child of the Americas,
a light-skinned mestiza of the Caribbean,
a child of many diaspora, born into this continent at a crossroads.

Levins Morales reminds her reader that America was transformed by many waves of immigration from Europe, Africa, and in more modern times, Latin America. Moreover, even as she recognizes her African, European, Native American, and Latin American heritages, she also refuses the fatalist attitude that posits Latina/os as trapped between worlds. Significantly, Levins Morales does not relish the past or lament its loss, but rather celebrates her new reality as a transnational citizen who exists at the intersection of many national cultures and histories even as she is a Latina firmly grounded in the United States. Precisely because of her transmigrations, Levins Morales is, as she proclaims, "whole."

The theme of transmigration is directly related to the transnational imagination expressed by Levins Morales and serves as the basis for Latina/o reverse migration narratives by authors such as Salvadoran/ Mexican American Rubén Martínez and Chicana Ana Castillo. In his 1992 multimedia testimonio, *The Other Side,* Martinez explores the differences between himself and his conservative middle-class family members in San Salvador, El Salvador. During a much-anticipated family visit to the country during the bloody civil war in the 1980s, Martínez realizes that he has less in common with his Salvadoran blood relatives and more in common with the Los Angeles Chicano barrio youth culture he covered as a journalist for the *L.A. Weekly* newspaper. Ana Castillo writes about a similar epiphany in her semi-autobiographical novel *The Mixquiahuala Letters.* In this 1986 experimental novel, which is made up of a series of letters that can be read in three possible sequences, Castillo's alter-ego protagonist, Teresa, is confronted by brutally oppressive sexism on a visit to Mexico, where Mexican men view her and her female companion Alicia as "hot blooded" Latinas or worse, just as white men do in the United States. Without stereotyping all Latin American males as "macho"—after all, these Chicanas are objectified by sexist men of all races—Castillo uses this novel to meditate on Chicana sisterhood. While past experiences of racial discrimination prevent Castillo's characters from conceptualizing the United States as the type of liberating space that Alvarez's characters relish, they still must confront their reality as Mexican Americans—that is, as U.S. Latinas—and the fact that they are seen as "different" both in the United States and in Latin America.

On the other hand, a defiant theme of reconciliation with the United States and reconstruction of new identities here is also to be found in the Latina/o literatures of (im)migration. Examples of works not yet mentioned with such a theme are Achy Obejas's 1994 testimonial *We Came All the Way from Cuba So You Could Dress Like This?,* Richard Rodriguez's 1992 *Days of Obligation,* and Miguél Piñero's 1980 poem "A Lower East Side Poem." As the title indicates, Obejas' parents experience culture shock at the sight of their daughter's appearance, lifestyle, and identity as an out Latina lesbian. They are simply unable to recognize the new culture of their young U.S. Latina offspring. But as Obejas's work stresses, this new culture is partially unrecognizable precisely because it is new and different: it is both Latin American and American, or at the intersection of the two; that is, U.S. Latina/o. At the other end of the ideological spectrum, Richard Rodriguez, who is infamous for his political diatribes against affirmative action and his even more outrageous attempts to scrape off his brown skin in his 1982 memoir *Hunger of Memory,* rejects the very idea of a border as a meaningful symbolic space in his 1992 collection of essays, *Days of Obligation.* In this collection, he attempts to revisit his Mexicanness in order to further repudiate it. For him, the Mexican youth he sees in Tijuana are Mexican, and he too is not a Mexican American but an American. For Rodriguez, there is no middle ground and no ambiguity. Ironically, his recent collection of essays is titled *Brown,* and focuses on the "browning" of America, thereby offering him the opportunity to simultaneously reject and embrace his racial identity without hyphenating it. He is Mexican and American without necessarily being a Mexican American.

Miguél Piñero more overtly attempts to resolve U.S. Latina/o anxieties about their relation to América Latina and the United States of America in his renowned "A Lower East Side Poem." Rather than lament his loss of his Latin American culture, he illustrates how this culture has now become an integral part of the United States. He proudly demands to be buried in the working-class Lower East Side of Manhattan, which at the time was primarily populated by Puerto Ricans and other ethnic and racial minorities. Significantly, he does not want to return to Puerto Rico; rather, he wishes for his remains to become part of the cityscape of his home in the Lower East Side. Unlike Venegas's characters, who are represented as being damned if they stay in the United States of America, U.S. Latina/o authors such as Rodriguez, Obejas, and Piñero defiantly proclaim their different identities as U.S. Latina/os as totally coherent. This is where they belong, in life and in death, forever hereafter. That is, they belong to the United States and the United States belongs to them.

List of Contributors

ABOUT THE EDITORS

Louis Mendoza is an associate professor of English and Mexican American studies at the University of Texas at San Antonio. His areas of expertise are Chicana/o literature, cultural studies, and prison literatures. His volume of literary criticism, *Historia: The Literary Making of Chicana and Chicano History,* was published by Texas A&M Press. He is the associate dean of the College of Liberal and Fine Arts for UTSA-Downtown.

S. Shankar is the author of the novel *A Map of Where I Live,* the volume of criticism *Textual Traffic: Colonialism, Modernity, and the Economy of the Text,* and translator of Komal Swaminathan's seminal Tamil play *Thaneer, Thaneer.* He teaches in the department of English at the University of Hawaii at Manoa.

ABOUT THE CONTRIBUTORS

Teresa Palomo Acosta is from McGregor, a central Texas town. She is the author of *Passing Time, Nile Notebooks,* and *Nile and Other Poems.* She currently lives in Austin, Texas, where she is completing a co-authored book with Ruthe Weingarten on Texas Mexican women entitled *Empowering Women: A Tejana History, 1700–2000.* She has been published in numerous anthologies, including the foundational *Festival de Flor y Canto, An Anthology of Chicano Literature.*

Agha Shahid Ali was born in New Delhi on February 4, 1949. He earned a Ph.D. in English from Pennsylvania State University in 1984, and an M.F.A. from the University of Arizona in 1985. His volumes of poetry include *Rooms Are Never Finished, The Country Without a Post Office, The Beloved Witness: Selected Poems, A Nostalgist's Map of America, A Walk Through the Yellow Pages, The Half-Inch Himalayas, In Memory of Begum Akhtar and Other Poems,* and *Bone Sculpture.* Agha Shahid Ali died on December 8, 2001.

Julia Alvarez is author of three bestselling novels, *How the García Girls Lost Their Accents, In the Time of Butterflies,* and *¡Yo!.* She is also an essayist and a prizewinning poet. Originally from the Dominican Republic, she currently lives in Vermont where she is a professor of English at Middlebury College.

Tara Bahrampour is Iranian American. She lives in New York City. As a graduate of the Columbia University School of Journalism, she has written for The *New York Times Magazine, The Wall Street Journal, The New Republic,* and *Travel and Leisure.*

Frank Chin is a critically acclaimed playwright, novelist, essayist, and political activist living in Los Angeles. In addition to his collection of essays, *The Bulletproof Buddhist*, his works include the stage plays *The Year of the Dragon* and *The Chickencoop Chinaman*, the novels *Donald Duk* and *Gunga Din Highway*, a volume of short stories entitled *The Chinaman Pacific and the Frisco R.R. Co.* He was a co-editor of the anthologies *Aiiieeee!* and *The Big Aiiieeee!*

Sandra Cisneros is a Chicago-born American novelist, short-story writer, essayist, and poet currently living in San Antonio, TX. Cisneros's works include *Caramelo, The House on Mango Street, Woman Hollering Creek and Other Stories*, and the poetry collections *Bad Boys, Loose Woman, and My Wicked, Wicked Ways*. She has also written a book for juveniles, *Pelitos*. Cisneros has also contributed to numerous periodicals, including *Imagine, Contact II, Glamour, The New York Times, The Los Angeles Times,* and *The Village Voice*.

Andrei Codrescu was born in Sibiu, Romania. He emigrated to the United States in 1966 and became a U.S. citizen in 1981. He is a poet, novelist, essayist, screenwriter, a columnist on National Public Radio, and editor of Exquisite Corpse, an online literary journal. Codrescu is the MacCurdy Distinguished Professor of English at Louisiana State University in Baton Rouge.

Judith Ortiz Cofer is the author of *Woman in Front of the Sun: On Becoming a Writer*, a collection of essays; a novel, *The Line of the Sun; Silent Dancing*, a collection of essays and poetry; two books of poetry, *Terms of Survival* and *Reaching for the Mainland;* and *The Latin Deli: Prose and Poetry*. Her work has appeared in *The Georgia Review, Kenyon Review, Southern Review, Glamour,* and other journals. She is the Franklin Professor of English and the director of the creative writing program at the University of Georgia. She is a native of Hormigueros, Puerto Rico.

Martín Espada, poet and educator, was born in Brooklyn, New York. Espada's books of poetry include *A Mayan Astronomer in Hell's Kitchen:*

Poems, Imagine the Angels of Bread, City of Coughing and Dead Radiators, Rebellion Is the Circle of a Lover's Hands, and *Trumpets from the Islands of Their Eviction.* He has edited several anthologies including, *El Coro: A Chorus of Latino and Latina Poets* and *Poetry Like Bread: Poets of the Political Imagination from Curbstone Press.* His prose collection, *Zapata's Disciple: Essays,* was published in 1998. Espada lives in Amherst, Massachusetts, where he is an associate professor of English at the University of Massachusetts-Amherst.

Jessica Hagedorn was born in the Philippines. She lives in New York City. Her first novel, *Dogeaters,* was nominated for the National Book Award in 1990. She is a performance artist and poet and is also the author of *Danger and Beauty: Poetry and Prose,* as well as *The Gangster of Love.*

Robert Ji-Song Ku is acting director of the Asian American studies program and assistant professor of English at Hunter College. His essays, fiction, poetry, and reviews appear in a variety of publications, including *Amerasia Journal, The Journal of American Drama and Theatre,* and the anthologies *Teaching Asian America, Asian American Literature,* and *The Language Reader.* His scholarly interests include twentieth-century American literature, Asian American studies, pidgin and creole English literatures, and the study of ethnographic displays. He currently serves on the board of directors for Asian Pacific Americans in Higher Education.

Nola Kambanda was born in Burundi to Rwandese parents. She emigrated to the United States to pursue a B.S. in electrical engineering at California State University, Los Angeles. She lives in southern California.

Jamaica Kincaid is a novelist and poet. She is the author of *Lucy, At the Bottom of the River, Annie John,* and *A Small Place.* She was born in Antigua and lives in Vermont.

Maxine Hong Kingston was born in Stockton, California. She was the first of six American-born children. Her work includes: *The Woman Warrior: Memoirs of a Girlhood Among Ghosts, China Men, Hawaii One Summer,* and *Tripmaster Monkey: His Fake Book.* She teaches in the department of English at UC-Berkeley.

Tato Laviera was born in Puerto Rico in 1951 and has lived in New York City since 1960. He is the author of the award-winning books, *La Carreta Made a U-Turn, Enclave, Mainstream Ethics,* and *AmeRícan.* He is the bestselling Hispanic poet of the United States.

Chang-rae Lee is a second-generation Korean American who immigrated to the United States with his family at the age of three. He was raised in Westchester, New York, and graduated from Yale University with a degree in English and from the University of Oregon with a MFA in writing. His first novel, *Native Speaker* (1995), won the PEN/Hemingway Award and the American Book Award. His second novel is *A Gesture Life.* He is the director of the MFA program at Hunter College in New York City.

Li-Young Lee was born in Jakarta, Indonesia, and moved to America with his family to escape political repression. Educated at the University of Pittsburgh, the University of Arizona, and the State University of New York, Lee has published two books of poems, *Rose* and *The City in Which I Love You,* as well as a prose memoir, *The Winged Seed: A Remembrance.*

Frank McCourt was born in 1931 in Brooklyn, New York, to Irish immigrant parents. He moved to Ireland at age four with his parents and brothers, where he grew up in Limerick, Ireland, and returned to America in 1949. For thirty years he taught in various New York City high schools, including Stuyvesant, and in city colleges. He is the author of the critically acclaimed and award-winning *Angela's Ashes* and *'Tis*. He lives in New York City and Connecticut.

Aurora Levins Morales is an award-winning writer, essayist, and historian of Puerto Rican and Jewish descent. She writes and speaks about multicultural histories of resistance, feminism, the uses of history, cultural activism, and the ways that racism, anti-Semitism, sexism, class, and other systems of oppression interlock. Her most recent works are *Medicine Stories*, a collection of essays on culture and politics, *Remedios: Stories of Earth*, and *Iron from the History of Puertoriqueñas*. She is co-author with her mother of *Getting Home Alive*, a dialogue in prose and poetry about identity, family, and the immigrant experience.

Rob Nixon grew up in South Africa near the Karoo. He emigrated to the United States in protest against apartheid. He is professor of English at the University of Wisconsin. He work has appeared in *The New Yorker, The Atlantic Monthly, The Village Voice,* and *Outside Magazine*.

Achy Obejas is a widely published and award-winning poet, fiction writer, and journalist. Born in Chicago, she is the author of *We Came All the Way from Cuba so You Could Dress Like This?* and *Memory Mambo*. Her poetry has been featured in *Conditions, Revista Chicano-Riquena,* and *Beloit Poetry Journal*. Her short stories have been published in magazines such as *Antigonish Review, Phoebe,* and *Third Woman,* and in numerous anthologies, including *Discontents, West Side Stories,* and *Girlfriend Number One*. She writes a weekly column for the *Chicago Tribune* and is a regular contributor to numerous other Chicago-area publications.

B. V. Olguín is an assistant professor of English at the University of Texas at San Antonio. He has previously taught at the University of Texas at Austin and Cornell University. He has published articles in U.S.

Latina/o, Latin American, and American literary and cultural studies in journals such as *Cultural Critique, Frontiers,* and *American Literary History.* His book, *La Pinta: History, Culture, and Identity in Chicana and Chicano Convict Discourses,* is forthcoming from the University of Texas Press.

Gary Pak lives in Kaneʻohe, Hawaiʻi. He is the author of a novel, *A Ricepaper Airplane,* and a collection of short stories, *The Watcher of Waipuna,* which won the Association for Asian American Studies 1993 National Book Award for Literature. A children's play, *Beyond the Falls,* was produced in 2001. Pak teaches at the University of Hawaiʻi at Manoa.

Ramón "Tianguis" Pérez is originally from San Pablo Macuiltianguis, a village in Oaxaca, Mexico. He currently lives in the state of Veracruz in Mexico, where he works as a photographer. In addition to *Diary of an Undocumented Immigrant,* he is also the author of *Diary of a Guerrilla: A True Story from an Ongoing Struggle.*

Richard Rodriguez is an editor at Pacific News Service, and a contributing editor for *Harper's Magazine, U.S. News & World Report,* and the Sunday "Opinion" section of the *Los Angeles Times.* In addition to his three books, *Hunger of Memory, Days of Obligation: An Argument with My Mexican Father,* and *Brown,* as well as two BBC documentaries, Rodriguez has published numerous articles in *The New York Times, The Wall Street Journal, The American Scholar, Time, Mother Jones,* and *The New Republic,* as well as other publications.

Benjamin Alire Sáenz's first book of poems, *Calendar of Dust,* was awarded an American Book Award in 1991; his second collection of poems, *Dark and Perfect Angels,* won a Southwest Book Award. In 1992, he was awarded a Lannan Literary Fellowship. His third book of poems, *Elegies in Blue* is forthcoming in 2002. He has also published a collection of short stories, *Flowers for the Broken,* and two novels, *Carry Me Like Water* and *The House of Forgetting* as well as two bilingual children's books, *A Gift from Papa Diego* and *Grandma Fina's Wonderful Umbrella,* named the Best Children's Book in 1999 by the Texas Institute of Letters. His third children's book, *The Dog Who Loved Tortilla,* is due out in 2002. He teaches creative writing at the University of Texas in El Paso, where he lives.

Vijay Seshadri was born in India and came to the United States in 1959, at the age of five. He grew up in Columbus, Ohio, and has lived in many parts of the country, including the northwest, where he spent five years working in the fishing industry, and on New York City's Upper West Side, where he was a sometime graduate student in Columbia's Ph.D. program in Middle Eastern Languages and Literature. His poems, essays, and reviews have appeared in *AGNI, Antaeus, Boulevard, The Nation, The New Yorker, The Paris Review, Shenandoah, The Southwest Review, The Threepenny Review, Verse,* and *Western Humanities Review.* A collection of his poetry, *Wild Kingdom,* was published in 1996 by Graywolf Press. He currently makes his home in Brooklyn with his wife and son.

Seung Hye Suh teaches at Scripps College. She has also taught in Asian American studies at Hunter College, CUNY, New York University, Barnard College, Duke University, and Columbia University, where she received her doctorate in English in 2001. She has published in *States of Confinement: Policing, Detention and Prisons, BLU, Sarami Saramehgeh* [People to People], and in *ColorLines.* She is a founding member of Nodutdol for Korean Community Development.

Helena María Viramontes teaches creative writing and literature at Cornell University. Originally from Los Angeles, she is the author of *The Moths and Other Stories, Under the Feet of Jesus, Paris Rats in East L.A.,* and *Their Dogs Came with Them.* She is also the co-editor of *Chicana Creativity* *and Criticism: Creative Frontiers in American Literature* and *Chicana Writers: On Word and Film.*

Leti Volpp is an associate professor at American University Law School. Before entering law teaching, she worked as a public-interest attorney defending the rights of immigrants. She is the author of several articles examining questions of immigration, culture, gender, and race.

A Select Bibliography
of the New Immigration
Literature, Scholarship,
and Resources

Acosta, Teresa Palomo. *Nile and Other Poems*. Austin: Red Salmon Press, 1999.

Aleinikoff, Thomas Alex, David Martin, and Hiroshi Motomura. *Immigration and Citizenship: Process and Policy*. Eagan, MN: West Wadsworth, 1998.

Alexander, Meena. *Manhattan Music*. San Francisco: Mercury House, 1997.

Algarín, Miguel, and Bob Holman. *Aloud!: Voices from the Nuyorican Poet's Café*. New York: Holt, 1994.

Algarín, Miguel, Miguél Piñero, and Richard August, eds. *Nuyorican Poetry: An Anthology of Puerto Rican Words and Feelings*. New York: William Morrow, 1975.

Alvarez, Julia. *How the Garcia Girls Lost Their Accents*. Chapel Hill: Algonquin, 1991.

Anzaldúa, Gloria. *Borderlands/La Frontera: The New Mestiza*. San Francisco: Aunt Lute, 1999.

Ashabranner, Brent K. *Still a Nation of Immigrants*. New York: Cobblehill, 1993.

Augenbraum, Harold, and Ilan Stavans. *Growing Up Latino: Memoirs and Stories*. Boston: Houghton Mifflin, 1993.

Bacho, Peter. *Cebu*. Seattle: University of Washington Press, 1991.

Bhattacharjee, Anannya. "The Public/Private Mirage: Mapping Homes and Un-domesticating Violence Work in the South Asian Immigrant Community," in *Feminist Genealogies, Colonial Legacies, Democratic Futures*. Ed. M. Jacqui Alexander and Chandra Talpade Mohanty. New York: Routledge, 1997.

Brimelow, Peter. *Alien Nation: Common Sense About America's Immigration Disaster*. New York: HarperPerennial, 1996.

Bruchac, Joseph, ed. *Breaking Silence: An Anthology of Contemporary Asian-American Poets*. Greenfield Center, NY: Greenfield Review Press, 1983.

Buchanan, Pat. *The Death of the West: How Dying Populations and Immigrant Invasions Imperil Our Country and Civilization*. New York: Dunne Books, 2001.

Castillo, Ana. *The Mixquiahuala Letters*. New York: Anchor, 1992.

Cha, Theresa Hak Kyung. *DICTEE*. Berkeley: University of California Press, 2001.

Chan, Jeffrey Paul, et al. *Aiiieeeee!: An Anthology of Asian-American Writers*. New York: Meridian Books, 1974.

Chin, Frank. *The Chinaman Pacific and the Frisco R.R. Co*. Minneapolis: Coffeehouse Press, 1988.

Chin, Marilyn. *Dwarf Bamboo*. Greenfield Center, NY: Greenfield Review Press, 1987.

Chock, Eric. *Last Days Here*. Honolulu: Bamboo Ridge Press, 1990.

Chong Lau, Alan. *Songs for Jadina*. Greenfield Center, NY: Greenfield Review Press, 1980.

Cisneros, Sandra. "Geraldo No Last Name," in *The House on Mango Street*. New York: Vintage, 1991.

Cofer, Judith Ortiz. *The Latin Deli: Prose and Poetry*. Athens: University of Georgia Press, 1993.

Colón, Jesús. *The Way It Was, And Other Writings*. Houston: Arte Público Press, 1993.

Del Rio, Eduardo. *The Prentice Hall Anthology of Latino Literature*. Upper Saddle River, NJ: Prentice Hall, 2002.

De Jesús, Joy L., ed. *Growing Up Puerto Rican*. New York: William Morrow, 1997.

Díaz, Junot. *Drown*. New York: Riverhead, 1996.

Divakaruni, Chitra. *Arranged Marriage: Stories.* New York: Anchor, 1995.

D'Souza, Dinesh. *The End of Racism: Principles for a Multiracial Society.* New York: Free Press, 1996.

Ferraro, Thomas. *Ethnic Passages.* Chicago: University of Chicago Press, 1993.

Foner, Nancy. *From Ellis Island to JFK: New York's Two Great Waves of Immigration.* New Haven: Yale University Press, 2000.

Foner, Nancy, Ruben Rumbaut, and Steve J. Gold, eds. *Immigration Research for a New Century: Multidisciplinary Perspectives.* New York: Russell Sage Foundation, 2000.

Garcia, Cristina. *Dreaming in Cuban.* New York: Ballantine, 1993.

Hagedorn, Jessica, ed. *Charlie Chan Is Dead: An Anthology of Contemporary Asian American Fiction.* New York: Penguin, 1993.

Heyck, Denis Lynn Daly, ed. *Barrios and Borderlands: Cultures of Latinos and Latinas in the United States.* New York: Routledge, 1994.

Hongo, Garrett, ed. *The Open Boat: Poems from Asian America.* New York: Anchor, 1993.

Houston, Jeanne and James. *Farewell to Manzanar: A True Story of Japanese American Experience During and After the World War II Internment.* New York: Bantam, 1973.

Kanellos, Nicolás, ed. *Herencia: The Anthology of Hispanic Literature in the United States.* Oxford: Oxford University Press, 2002.

———. *Hispanic American Literature: A Brief Introduction.* New York: HarperCollins, 1995.

Kennedy, John F. *A Nation of Immigrants.* New York: HarperCollins, 1986.

Kim, Elaine H., and Lilia V. Villanueva. *Making More Waves: New Writing by Asian American Women.* New York: Beacon, 1997.

Knippling, Alpana Sharma. *New Immigrant Literatures in the United States: A Sourcebook to Our Multicultural Heritage.* Westport, CT: Greenwood Press, 1996.

Law-Yone, Wendy. *The Coffin Tree.* New York: Knopf, 1983.

Legomsky, Stephen H. *Immigration and Refugee Law and Policy.* New York: Foundation Press, 1997.

Levins Morales, Aurora. "Child of the Americas," in *Barrios and Borderlands: Cultures of Latinos and Latinas in the United States.* Ed. Denis Lynn Daly Heyck. New York: Routledge, 1994.

Lew, Walter K. *Premonitions: The Kaya Anthology of New Asian North American Poetry.* New York: Kaya Press, 1995.

Lim, Shirley Geok-Lin, ed. *Reading the Literatures of Asian America.* Philadelphia: Temple University Press, 1992.

Linmark, R. Zamora. *Rolling the R's.* New York: Distributed Art Publishers, 1995.

López, Tiffany Ana. *Growing Up Chicana/o.* New York: Avon, 1993.

Louie, David Wong. *The Barbarians Are Coming.* Berkeley: Berkeley Publishing Group, 2000.

Lowe, Lisa. *Immigrant Acts: On Asian American Cultural Politics.* Durham, NC: Duke University Press, 1996.

Mariscal, George. *Aztlán and Viet Nam: Chicano and Chicana Experiences of the War.* Berkeley: University of California Press, 2000.

Martí, José. "Our America" (1892). *Herencia: The Anthology of Hispanic Literature in the United States.* Ed. Nicolás Kanellos. Oxford: Oxford University Press, 2002.

———. "Two Views of Coney Island" (1881). *Herencia: The Anthology of Hispanic Literature in the United States.* Ed. Nicolás Kanellos. Oxford: Oxford University Press, 2002.

Martínez, Rubén. *The Other Side: Fault Lines, Guerilla Saints, and the True Heart of Rock 'N' Roll.* London: Verso, 1992.

Marzán, Julio. "The Ingredient," in *Growing Up Puerto Rican.* Ed. Joy L. De Jesús. New York: William Morrow, 1997.

Medina, Rubén. *Amor de lejos/Fools Love.* Trans. Jennifer Sternback and Robert Jones. Houston: Arte Público Press, 1986.

Milligan, Bryce, Mary Guerrero Milligan, and Angela De Hoyos, eds. *¡Floricanto Sí!: A Collection of U.S. Latina Poetry.* New York: Penguin, 1998.

Mohr, Nicholasa. *In Nueva York.* Houston: Arte Público Press, 1993.

Mukherjee, Bharati. *Jasmine.* New York: Grove Press, 1991.

Muller, Gilbert. *New Strangers in Paradise: The Immigrant Experience and Contemporary American Fiction.* Louisville: University of Kentucky Press, 1999.

Mura, David. *Turning Japanese: Memoirs of a Sansei.* New York: Anchor, 1992.

Ng, Fae Myenne. *Bone.* New York: HarperPerennial, 1994.

Ngai, Mae. "The Architecture of Race in American Immigration Law: A Reexamination of the Immigration Act of 1924." *Journal of American History,* 86, no. 1 (1999): 67–92.

Nigli, Josefina. *Mexican Village.* Albuquerque: University of New Mexico Press, 1994.

Obejas, Achy. *We Came All the Way from Cuba So You Could Dress Like This?: Stories.* Pittsburgh: Cleis Press, 1994.

Paredes, Américo. *Between Two Worlds.* Houston: Arte Público Press, 1991.

Parker, Kunal. "Official Imaginations: Globalization, Difference, and State-Sponsored Immigration Discourses." *Oregon Law Review,* 76 (1997): 691–730.

Payant, Katherine, and Toby Rose. *The Immigrant Experience in North American Literature: Carving Out a Niche.* Westport, CT: Greenwood Publishing Group, 1999.

Pérez, Ramón "Tianguis." *Diary of an Undocumented Immigrant.* Houston: Arte Público Press, 1991.

Pérez-Firmat, Gustavo. *Life on the Hyphen: The Cuban-American Way.* Austin: University of Texas Press, 1994.

Piñero, Miguél. "A Lower East Side Poem," in *La Bodega Sold Dreams.* Houston: Arte Público Press, 1980.

Portes, Alejandro, and Ruben G. Rumbaut. *Legacies: The Story of the Immigrant Second Generation.* Berkeley: University of California Press, 2001.

———. *Ethnicities: Children of Immigrants in America.* Berkeley: University of California Press, 2001.

Ramos, Juanita. *Compañeras: Latina Lesbians: An Anthology.* New York: Routledge, 1994.

Rodriguez, Abraham. *The Boy Without a Flag.* New York: Milkweed Editions, 1992.

Rodriguez, Richard. *Days of Obligation: An Argument with my Mexican Father.* New York: Penguin, 1992.

———. *Hunger of Memory: The Education of Richard Rodriguez.* Boston: D. R. Godine, 1982.

————. *Brown: The Last Discovery of America*. New York: Penguin, 2002.

Ruiz de Burton, Amparo. *The Squatter and the Don*. Houston: Arte Público Press, 1992.

Sáenz, Benjamin Alire. "Exile," in *Flowers for the Broken: Stories*. Seattle: Broken Moon Press, 1992.

Simone, Roberta. *The Immigrant Experience in American Fiction*. Lanham, MD: Scarecrow Press, 1995.

Skrentny, John David. *Color Lines: Affirmative Action, Immigration, and Civil Rights Options for America*. Chicago: University of Chicago Press, 2001.

Sowell, Thomas. *Barbarians Inside the Gates: And Other Controversial Essays*. Hoover Institution Press Publication, No. 450, 1999.

Stavans, Ilan, ed. *The Norton Anthology of Latino Literature*. New York: Norton, 2003.

Takaki, Ronald. *Strangers from a Different Shore: A History of Asian Americans*. New York: Little, Brown, 1998.

————. *A Different Mirror: A History of Multicultural America*. New York: Little, Brown, 1994.

Tei Yamashita, Karen. *Brazil-Maru*. Minneapolis: Coffeehouse Press, 1992.

Turner, Faythe, ed. *Puerto Rican Writers at Home in the U.S.A.: An Anthology*. Seattle: Open Hand Publishing, 1991.

Urrea, Luís Alberto. *Across the Wire: Life and Hard Times on the Mexican Border*. New York: Anchor, 1993.

Vega, Ed. "Spanish Roulette," in *Casualty Report*. Houston: Arte Público Press, 1991.

Venegas, Daniel. *Las Aventuras de Don Chipote: o, cuando los péricos mamen*. México, D.F.: secretaría de Educación Pública, 1984.

————. *The Adventures of Don Chipote: Or, When Parrots Breast-Feed*. Trans. Ethriam Cash Brammer. Houston: Arte Público Press, 2000.

Viramontes, Helena. "The Cariboo Cafe," in *The Moths and Other Stories*. Houston: Arte Público Press, 1995.

Volpp, Leti. "Talking 'Culture': Gender, Race, Nation and the Politics of Multiculturalism." *Columbia Law Review*, 96, no. 6 (1996): 1573–1617.

Wong, Cynthia Sau-Ling. *Reading Asian American Literature*. Princeton: Princeton University Press 1993.

Yau, John. *Radiant Silhouettes: New and Selected Work, 1974–1988*. Santa Rosa, CA: Black Sparrow, 1989.

Websites

Center for Immigration Studies, *http://www.cis.org/topics/history.html*

Immigration History Research Center, *http://www1.umn.edu/ihrc/*

The Lesbian and Gay Immigration Rights Taskforce, *http://www.lgirtf.org*

U.S. Immigration History Resources, *http://www.snowcrest.net/jmike/immigration.html*

"The Best Sites for Immigration Editorials," *<http://www.pageseeker.com/results. htm?ppsid=ezcyber/0001/0001/1&search=Immigration+editorials>*

Permissions

Newspaper articles

Images

Photograph of Lyndon Baines Johnson courtesy of Corbis.

"It's time to reclaim America from illegal immigrants!"—"I'll help you pack." By Steve Kelley. Copyright © 1994, Copley News Service. Reprinted with permission.

"Chinese Migrants Pretend to Be Cuban Six Year Olds," by Malcolm Mayes. Copyright © Malcolm Mayes/Artizans.com. Reprinted with permisison of Artizans Syndicate.

"I was born in Mexico..." by David Horsey, 2001. © Tribune Media Services, Inc. All Rights Reserved. Reprinted with permission.

"Let me guess... you're all Mexican?"—"Sí." By Steve Breen. Copyright © 2001, Copley News Service. Reprinted with permission.